FTCE Prekindergarten / Primary PK-3

Teacher Certification Exam

By: Sharon Wynne, M.S.
Southern Connecticut State University

"And, while there's no reason yet to panic, I think it's only prudent that we make preparations to panic."

XAMonline, INC.
Boston

Copyright © 2009 XAMonline, Inc.

All rights reserved. No part of the material protected by this copyright notice may be reproduced or utilized in any form or by any means, electronic or mechanical, including photocopying, recording or by any information storage and retrievable system, without written permission from the copyright holder.

To obtain permission(s) to use the material from this work for any purpose including workshops or seminars, please submit a written request to:

XAMonline, Inc.
21 Orient Ave.
Melrose, MA 02176
Toll Free 1-800-509-4128
Email: info@xamonline.com
Web www.xamonline.com
Fax: 1-781-662-9268

Library of Congress Cataloging-in-Publication Data

Wynne, Sharon A.
    Prekindergarten/Primary PK-3: Teacher Certification / Sharon A. Wynne. -2nd ed. ISBN 978-1-60787-012-8
    1. Prekindergarten/Primary PK-3.   2. Study Guides.   3. FTCE
    4. Teachers' Certification & Licensure.   5. Careers

Disclaimer:
The opinions expressed in this publication are the sole works of XAMonline and were created independently from the National Education Association, Educational Testing Service, or any State Department of Education, National Evaluation Systems or other testing affiliates.

Between the time of publication and printing, state specific standards as well as testing formats and website information may change and will not be included in part or in whole within this product. Sample test questions are developed by XAMonline and reflect similar content as on real tests; however, they are not former tests. XAMonline assembles content that aligns with state standards but makes no claims nor guarantees teacher candidates a passing score. Numerical scores are determined by testing companies such as NES or ETS and then are compared with individual state standards. A passing score varies from state to state.

Printed in the United States of America   œ-1

FTCE: Prekindergarten/Primary PK-3
ISBN: 978-1-60787-012-8

Project Manager:	Sharon Wynne, MS
Project Coordinator:	Victoria Anderson, MS
Content Coordinators/Authors:	Fran Stanford, MS
	Victoria Anderson, MS
	Christina Godard, BS
	Kimberly Putney, BS
	Vickie Pittard, MS
	Deborah Suber. BS
	Kelley Eldredge, MS
Sample test:	Shelley Wake, MS
	Deborah Harbin, MS
	Christina Godard, BS
	Kim Putney, BS
	Carol Moore, BS
	Vickie Pittard, MS
Editors: Proof reader	Janis Mercer, MS
Copy editor	Janis Mercer, MS
Sample test	Shelley Wake, MS
Production	David Aronson
Graphic Artist	Jenna Hamilton

Table of Contents

Great Study and Testing Tips!

What to study in order to prepare for the subject assessments is the focus of this study guide, but equally important is *how* you study.

You can increase your chances of truly mastering the information by taking some simple, but effective, steps.

Study Tips:

1.   Some foods aid the learning process. Foods such as milk, nuts, seeds, rice, and oats help your study efforts by releasing natural memory enhancers called CCKs (*cholecystokinin*) composed of *tryptophan*, *choline*, and *phenylalanine*. All of these chemicals enhance the neurotransmitters associated with memory. Before studying, try a light, protein-rich meal of eggs, turkey, and fish. All of these foods release the memory enhancing chemicals. The better the connections, the more you comprehend.

Likewise, before you take a test, stick to a light snack of energy boosting and relaxing foods. A glass of milk, a piece of fruit, or some peanuts will release various memory-boosting chemicals and help you relax and focus on the subject at hand.

2.   Learn to take great notes. A by-product of our modern culture is that we have grown accustomed to getting our information in short doses (e.g., TV news sound bites or USA Today style newspaper articles).

Consequently, we've subconsciously trained ourselves to assimilate information better in neat little packages. If your notes are scrawled all over the paper, the flow of the information is fragmented. Strive for clarity. Newspapers use a standard format to achieve clarity. Your notes can be much clearer through use of proper formatting. A very effective format is called the *Cornell Method.*

Take a sheet of loose-leaf, lined notebook paper and draw a line all the way down the paper about 1-2" from the left-hand edge.

Draw another line across the width of the paper about 1-2" up from the bottom. Repeat this process on the reverse side of the page.

Look at the highly effective result. You have ample room for notes, a left hand margin for special emphasis items or inserting supplementary data from the textbook, a large area at the bottom for a brief summary, and a little rectangular space for just about anything you want.

3. <u>**Get the concept then the details**</u>. Too often we focus on the details and don't gather an understanding of the concept. However, if you simply memorize only dates, places, or names, you may well miss the whole point of the subject.

A key way to understand information is to put it in your own words. If you are working from a textbook, automatically summarize each paragraph in your mind. If you are outlining text, don't simply copy the author's words.

Rephrase them in your own words. You remember your own thoughts and words much better than someone else's and subconsciously tend to associate the important details to the core concepts.

4. <u>**Ask Why?**</u> Pull apart written material paragraph by paragraph and don't forget the captions under the illustrations.

Example: If the heading is "Stream Erosion," flip it around to read "Why do streams erode?" Then answer the questions.

If you train your mind to think in a series of questions and answers, you will not only learn more but also lessen test anxiety because you are used to answering questions.

5. <u>**Read for reinforcement and future needs**</u>. Even if you only have 10 minutes, put your notes or a book in your hand. Your mind is similar to a computer; you have to input data in order to process it. *By reading, you are creating the neural connections for future retrieval.* The more times you read something, the more you reinforce the learning of ideas.

Even if you don't fully understand something on the first pass, *your mind stores much of the material for later recall.*

6. <u>**Relax to learn, so go into exile**</u>. Our bodies respond to an inner clock called biorhythms. Burning the midnight oil works well for some people, but not everyone.

If possible, set aside a particular place to study that is free of distractions. Shut off the television, cell phone, and pager and exile your friends and family during your study period.

If you really are bothered by silence, try background music. Light classical music at a low volume has been shown to aid in concentration over other types. Music without lyrics that evokes pleasant emotions is highly suggested. Try just about anything by Mozart. It relaxes you.

7. <u>**Use arrows not highlighters**</u>. At best, it's difficult to read a page full of yellow, pink, blue, and green streaks. Try staring at a neon sign for a while and you'll soon see that the horde of colors obscures the message.

A quick note, a brief dash of color, an underline, and an arrow pointing to a particular passage is much clearer than a horde of highlighted words.

8. <u>**Budget your study time**</u>. Although you shouldn't ignore any of the material, *allocate your available study time in the same ratio that topics may appear on the test.*

Testing Tips:

1. Get smart; play dumb. Don't read anything into the question. Don't make an assumption that the test writer is looking for something else than what is asked. Stick to the question as written and don't read extra things into it.

2. Read the question and all the choices *twice* before answering the question. You may miss something by not reading carefully and then re-reading both the question and the answers.

If you really don't have a clue as to the right answer, leave the question blank on the first time through. Go on to the other questions; they may provide a clue as to how to answer the skipped questions.

If later on, you still can't answer the skipped ones . . . *Guess.* The only penalty for guessing is that you *might* get it wrong. Only one thing is certain; if you don't put anything down, you will get it wrong!

3. Turn the question into a statement. Look at the way the questions are worded. The syntax of the question usually provides a clue. Does it seem more familiar as a statement rather than as a question? Does it sound strange?

By turning a question into a statement, you may be able to spot if an answer sounds right, and it may also trigger memories of material you have read.

4. Look for hidden clues. It's actually very difficult to compose multiple-foil (choice) questions without giving away part of the answer in the options presented.

In most multiple-choice questions you can often readily eliminate one or two of the potential answers. Therefore, you have only two real possibilities and automatically your odds go to Fifty-Fifty for very little work.

5. Trust your instincts. For every fact that you have read, you subconsciously retain something of that knowledge. On questions that you aren't really certain about, go with your basic instincts. **Your first impression on how to answer a question is usually correct.**

6. Mark your answers directly on the test booklet. Don't bother trying to fill in the optical scan sheet on the first pass through the test.

Just be very careful not to miss-mark your answers when you eventually transcribe them to the scan sheet.

7. Watch the clock! You have a set amount of time to answer the questions. Don't get bogged down trying to answer a single question at the expense of 10 questions you can more readily answer.

THIS PAGE BLANK

COMPETENCY 1.0 KNOWLEDGE OF CHILD GROWTH AND DEVELOPMENT

Skill 1.1 Identify the major effects of genetics, health, nutrition, public policy, environment, and economics on child development

In today's push toward academic achievement and standards, we often forget the importance of a child's emotional and physical growth and health. New teachers may be tempted to teach more or harder for fear that, if they don't, their students will not learn. Yet, both new and veteran teachers must remember that child development plays a critical role in the academic success of individuals.

While all children develop at different rates and every child has unique attributes, teachers have some responsibility for raising concerns about the emotional or physical states of their students. In the presence of abuse, this responsibility is a legal one, but other concerns may also merit discussion with counselors or administrators.

Genetics

Genetics plays an important role in a child's development, affecting many attributes to their ability to learn. Genetics accounts for many factors of a student's learning including IQ level, which methods of learning (for example, visual, auditory, kinesthetic, etc) work best for individual children, and learning exceptionalities and disorders. How much genetics affects student learning varies, and research is continually being completed to uncover how strongly genetics affects a student's intelligence and predisposition to certain conditions.
[V1]

Intelligence Quotient

One's Intelligence Quotient, or IQ, is a score that comes from one of several standardized tests designed to measure intelligence. These tests are used as predictors of educational achievement and children with low scores are often placed in special needs classes or receive help from paraprofessionals both inside and outside the school. Although there are factors that affect one's IQ, such as the family and maternal environment, disease, and injury, there is overwhelming proof from the research that genetics plays a large part in determining a child's IQ. Researchers originally thought that IQ would improve as the child got older, but the results show that the IQ actually lessens with age.

Neurotic Disorders[jmm2]

[v3]Emotional disorders can seriously hamper a child's normal development. When a child is experiencing trauma or emotional stress of some kind, this causes the child to become nervous and afraid of the simplest things. Thus the child will shy away from some experiences that could be very educational and necessary for social, emotional and moral development.

Sometimes emotional disorders escalate so quickly and become so severe that the child's well-being is threatened. Teachers and parents must recognize the signs of severe emotional stress that may be detrimental to the child. Various forms of emotional disorders, including neurosis, are potentially dangerous. Neuroses are the second most common group of psychiatric disturbances of childhood, and symptoms include extreme anxiety related to over dependence, social isolation, sleep problems, unwarranted nausea, abdominal pain, diarrhea, and headaches.

Some children exhibit irrational fears of particular objects or situations; others become consumed with obsessions, thoughts, or ideas. Depression is one of the most serious neuroses. The child is sad, cries, shows little or no interest in people or activities, has eating and sleeping problems, and sometimes talks about wanting to be dead. Teachers must listen to what the child is saying and take these verbal expressions very seriously. Perhaps what happened at Columbine, Colorado; Jonesboro, Arkansas; and Lake Worth, Florida could have been prevented if adults had recognized the signs.

For more information on neurotic disorders in childhood: http://www.depression-guide.com/child-psychiatry/childhood-disorder.htm

Psychotic Disorders

Psychosis, which is characterized by a loss of contact with reality, is an even more serious emotional disorder. Psychosis is rare in childhood, but when it does occur, it is often difficult to diagnose. One fairly constant sign is the child's failure to make normal emotional contact with other people. The most common psychosis of childhood is schizophrenia, which is a deliberate escape from reality and a withdrawal from relationships with others. When this syndrome occurs in childhood, children continue to have some contact with people; however, a curtain exists between them and the rest of the world. Schizophrenia is more common in boys than in girls. A habitually flat or agitated facial expression is one of the major signs of this disorder. Children suffering from schizophrenia are occasionally mute, but at times they talk incessantly and use bizarre words in ways that make no sense. Their incoherent speech often contributes to their frustration and compounds their fears and preoccupations and is the most significant sign of this very serious disturbance.

> **Read more about psychotic disorders:**
>
> http://www.webmd.com/schizophrenia/guid e/mental-health-psychotic-disorders

Early Infantile Autism

Unlike genetic disorders, research has not supported hereditary links to having this disorder. Early infantile autism may occur as early as the fourth month of life. Suddenly the infant lies apathetic and oblivious in the crib. In other cases, the baby seems perfectly normal throughout infancy, and the symptoms appear without warning at about eighteen months of age. Because of the nature of the symptoms, autistic children are often misdiagnosed as mentally retarded, deaf-mute, or organically brain-damaged. Boys are twice as likely to be autistic as girls.

According to many psychologists who treat autistic children, these children seem to have built a wall between themselves and everyone else, including their families and even their parents. They do not make eye contact with others and do not appear to hear those who speak to them. They cannot empathize with others and cannot appreciate humor.

Autistic children usually have language disturbances. One third of them never develop speech at all but may grunt or whine. Others may repeat the same word or phrase over and over or parrot what someone else has said. They often lack inner language as well and cannot play by themselves above a primitive, sensory-motor level.

Frequently, autistic children appear to fill the void left by the absence of interpersonal relationships with a preoccupation with things. They become compulsive about the arrangements of objects and often engage in simple, repetitive physical activities with objects for long periods of time. If these activities are interrupted, they may react with fear or rage. Others remain motionless for hours sometimes moving only their eyes or hands.

On intelligence tests, autistic children score from severely subnormal to high average. Some, while functioning poorly in general, exhibit astonishing ability in isolated skill areas. They may be able to memorize volumes of material, sing beautifully, or perform complicated mathematical problems.

The cause of early infantile autism is unknown. Years ago some psychiatrists speculated that these children did not develop normally because of a lack of parental warmth. Since the incidence of autism in families is usually limited to one child, experts now think this cause is unlikely. Other theories include metabolic or chromosomal defects as causes; however, no evidence substantiates these theories.

The prognosis for autistic children is discouraging. Only about five percent of autistic children become socially well adjusted in adulthood. Another twenty percent make fair social adjustments. The remaining seventy-five percent are socially incapacitated and must be supervised for the duration of their lives. Treatment may include outpatient psychotherapy, drugs, or long-term treatment in a residential center, but neither the form of treatment nor the lack of treatment seems to make a difference in the long run.

Find out more about autism:

http://en.wikipedia.org/wiki/Early_infantile _autism

Factors of a Student's **Environment**

Generally, teachers and parents should know what specific attributes develop over time in children. There is usually no cause for alarm, as many children do develop later in childhood (and certain domains may develop later than others). Concern regarding intervention might arise when teachers notice that certain functions or attributes seem abnormally absent. In such a case, certain tasks may be very difficult for a child. Later in childhood, a large concern of teasing and bullying may arise, and the teacher may want to ensure that the child is fully protected.

When in doubt, though, the teacher should privately discuss the concern with a special education teacher or school psychologist first. That professional may be able to assist the teacher in determining whether it would be important to evaluate the child, or whether it would be important to contact the parent to ask questions, seek clarification, or point out a potential delay.

Very often, though, parents will be aware of the delay, and the child will be able to receive special accomodations in the classroom. Teachers should be forewarned about this by the special education personnel prior to the beginning of the schoolyear.

For further reading on how environment affects child development:

http://www.schoolfile.com/cap_start/childde velop.htm

Emotional Factors

In early elementary school, children are particularly affected by emotional upsets in family structure, and they are particularly susceptible to emotional harm when they are not cared for in an appropriate manner at home.

While it would be too easy to say that teachers should look out for children who show signs of emotional abuse or emotional neglect, whenever a teacher does notice something unusual in a child's behavior, it might be a good idea to look into it. A note of caution, though: teachers should remember that a student's privacy is extremely important.

Furthermore, teachers should remember that all schools, districts, and states have very specific procedures and laws about the reporting of concerns. Yet, it goes without saying that teachers who see problems should figure out procedures for dealing with them.

When children are emotionally neglected or have recently endured family upsets, what sorts of things would this impact in a child? Well, first, the level of attention toward school will be greatly reduced. While children may actually think about these things, they may also show signs of jealousy of other children, or they may feel a sense of anger toward other children, the teacher, or their parents.

Aggression is a very common behavior of emotionally-neglected children. When a child has had little verbal interaction, the symptoms can be rather similar to the symptoms of abuse or neglect. The child might have a "deer in the headlights" look and maintain a very socially awkward set of behaviors. In general, such a child will have a drastically reduced ability to express him or herself in words, and often, aggression can be a better tool for the child to get his or her thoughts across.

Behavioral Factors

The home environment and even the neighborhood can have an affect on the development of children and cause them to come to school with behavior problems. Recent studies indicate that children from neighborhoods where there are few affluent families tend to exhibit more behavioral issues in school than those who do, such as not paying attention, fighting and in general causing disturbances in the class.

There are also issues that do cause children to have behavior problems, such as the mother consuming alcohol while pregnant and an exposure to violence in the home. The teacher has to be very observant of how children behave towards one another in the classroom to rule out any possibilities that some children may be bringing their frustrations with the home environment into the school setting.

Environmental Factors

Environmental factors that can cause delays in the development of some children could include:

- Lead poisoning
- Exposure to contaminants in water, food and air

Because children are exposure to contaminants can be more harmful for them that it is for adults. The body's systems and organs are still developing and due to the fact that children often out foreign objects in their mouths only adds to the amount of exposure for them.

Sadly, not every student comes from a stable home environment. Legally, teachers and school administrators are required to report abuse. When you suspect abuse, the best action is to contact a superior immediately. However, while the symptoms of abuse are thought to be physical (and therefore visible), mental and emotional abuse is also possible. The impact of abuse on a child's development is often extensive. Abused children can be socially withdrawn, and, as one might suspect, their minds are not always on their schoolwork. Significant emotional damage does occur, and teachers may notice very awkward social behavior around other children and adults.

Familial Factors

The student's capacity and potential for academic success within the overall educational experience are products of her or his total environment: classroom and school system; home and family; neighborhood and community in general. All of these segments are interrelated and can be supportive, one of the other, or divisive, one against the other.

As a matter of course, the teacher will become familiar with all aspects of the system, the school and the classroom pertinent to the students' educational experience. This would include not only process and protocols but also the availability of resources provided to meet the academic, health and welfare needs of students. But it is incumbent upon the teacher to look beyond the boundaries of the school system to identify additional resources as well as issues and situations that will affect (directly or indirectly) a student's ability to succeed in the classroom.

Families with higher incomes are able to provide increased opportunities for students. Students from lower income families will need to depend on the resources available from the school system and the community. The classroom teacher should orchestrate this in cooperation with school administrators and educational advocates in the community.

Family members with higher levels of education often serve as models for students, and have high expectations for academic success. Families with specific aspirations for children (often, regardless of their own educational background) encourage students to achieve academic success, and are most often active participants in the process.

A family in crisis (caused by economic difficulties, divorce, substance abuse, physical abuse, etc.) creates a negative environment, which may profoundly impact all aspects of a student's life, and particularly the ability to function academically. The situation may require professional intervention. It is often the classroom teacher who recognizes a family in crisis situation and instigates an intervention by reporting on this to school or civil authorities.

Regardless of the positive or negative impacts on the students' education from outside sources, it is the teacher's responsibility to ensure that all students in the classroom have an equal opportunity for academic success. This begins with the teacher's statement of high expectations for every student, and develops through planning, delivery and evaluation of instruction, which provides for inclusion and ensures that all students have equal access to the resources necessary for successful acquisition of the academic skills being taught and measured in the classroom.

Linguistic Factors

Early theories of language development were formulated from learning theory research. The assumption was that language development evolved from learning the rules of language structures and applying them through imitation and reinforcement. This approach also assumed that language, cognitive, and social developments were independent of each other. Thus, children were expected to learn language from patterning after adults who spoke and wrote Standard English. No allowance was made for communication through child jargon, idiomatic expressions, or grammatical and mechanical errors resulting from too strict adherence to the rules of inflection (childs instead of children) or conjugation (runned instead of ran). No association was made between physical and operational development and language mastery.

In the linguistic approach, studies spearheaded by Noam Chomsky in the 1950s formulated the theory that language ability is innate and develops through natural human maturation as environmental stimuli trigger acquisition of syntactical structures appropriate to each exposure level. The assumption of a hierarchy of syntax downplayed the significance of semantics. Because of the complexity of syntax and the relative speed with which children acquire language, linguists attributed language development to biological rather than cognitive or social influences.

Socio-Cognitive Approach

Under the socio-cognitive approach, theorists in the 1970s proposed that language development results from sociolinguistic competence. Language, cognitive, and social knowledge are interactive elements of total human development. Emphasis on verbal communication as the medium for language expression resulted in the inclusion of speech activities in most language arts curricula.

Unlike other approaches, the socio-cognitive allowed that determining the appropriateness of language in given situations for specific listeners is as important as understanding semantic and syntactic structures. By engaging in conversation, children at all stages of development have opportunities to test their language skills, receive feedback, and make modifications. As a social activity, conversation is as structured by social order as grammar is structured by the rules of syntax. Conversation satisfies the learner's need to be heard and understood and to influence others. Thus, the choices of vocabulary, tone, and content are dictated by the ability to assess the language knowledge of the listeners. The learner is constantly applying cognitive skills to using language in a social interaction. If the capacity to acquire language is inborn, without an environment in which to practice language, a child would not pass beyond grunts and gestures as did primitive man.

Of course, the varying degrees of environmental stimuli to which children are exposed at all age levels create a slower or faster development of language. Some children are prepared to articulate concepts and recognize symbolism by the time they enter fifth grade because they have been exposed to challenging reading and conversations with well-spoken adults at home or in their social groups. Others are still trying to master the sight recognition skills and are not yet ready to combine words in complex patterns.

Cultural Factors

In early childhood classrooms, the teacher must be sensitive to the culture that each child comes from. Culture is individual and the teacher may need to assess the child indivudally to identify cultural factors that may affect the child's development. Some of the cultural factors that may have an impact on the child's learning in school include:

- Race
- Religion
- Ethnic background
- Socio-economic status
- Gender
- Place of birth
- Language

The beliefs of the parents come through in the child's reactions to experiences in school. The teacher has to be able to determine if there is a cultural problem that may be causing the child to experience a delay in some aspect of development.

Economic Factors

The socio-economic status of the family has a direct bearing on the development of some children. For example a child that comes to school wiuth no knowledge of books or writing could come from a home where there is no extra money for books. It could also be a cultural factor in that the parenst are new immigrants and cannot read any of the books published in a different language. Children raised in poverty may not have the proper nutrition they need to develop normally and this could cause medical problems as well. In addition, parents of children with disabilities may not not have the monetary measn to provide medical care for the children or may not be aware of any social programs available to them within the community.

SEE also Skill 1.5, page 18.

Health and Nutrition

Issues of physical health include prenatal exposure to drugs, alcohol, or nicotine. In all cases, moderate to severe brain damage is possible; however, more subtle impairment, such as breathing problems and attention deficit disorder, can also occur. Because drugs, alcohol, and nicotine can impair brain development, children exposed to such substances in the womb may need significant extra classroom support. Some of these children should also be referred to the special education teacher in order to be tested for learning disabilities.

Such day-to-day issues as insufficient sleep or poor nutrition harm children in a more temporal fashion. While a child who has had sleep disruptions or insufficient nutrition can bounce back easily when these deficiencies are corrected, children living in environments where sleep and proper nutrition are not available will struggle for these necessities throughout childhood. Through federal and local funds, many schools provide free or reduced-price breakfasts and lunches for children; however, such children may not get a decent dinner and, during weekends and holidays, may struggle even more.

Symptoms of inadequate nutrition and sleep deficiencies most notably include poor concentration, particularly in the classroom. Furthermore, these children may become agitated more easily than other children.

Teachers should always pay attention to abnormalities in the behavior of children, including sudden drop-offs in achievement or attention, and notify superiors with concerns.

Economics

The family's financial situation, the ability to provide enough food and medical attention, has a tremendous effect on a child's development. The economic situation also affects the child's experiences. Does the child have access to books? Can the child attend events that provide experiences to draw on in the school situation and, therefore, help the child develop academically? For example, when the teacher talks about the circus or a fair, if the child has never attended these events, making any personal connections between the classroom and the world will be difficult. Children who come from impoverished homes are often at a disadvantage when they enter school.

Public Policy

SEE Skill 2.3

Skill 1.2 **Identify the sequence of development and the milestones (e.g., social-emotional, cognitive, language, physical) for the typically developing child**

Connection Between All Areas of Child Development

The teacher has a broad knowledge and thorough understanding of the development that typically occurs during the students' current period of life. More importantly, the teacher understands how children learn best during each period of development. The most important premise of child development is that all domains of development (physical, social, and academic) are integrated. Development in each domain does not occur alone. What happens in one area of development affects all the others. . Moreover, today's educator must also have a knowledge of exceptionalities and how these exceptionalities affect a child's development.

The early years are particularly important because the child's brain is continually developing and growing. Experiences in any one of the areas of development (socio-emotional, cognitive, language and physical) all have an impact on the typical development of a child. Growth in one area does not mean that the child will demonstrate growth in all others, but it does lay the foundation for the growth to take place at a later time. As a child develops physically, for example, and is able to do more things, it is only natural that the child will start to grasp the language associated with these activities, learn the rules of the activity, and play with other children. By playing with other children, a child develops socially and emotionally as well as developing in language and cognitive abilities and in so doing will also develop physically.

The critical areas of child development occur before the age of six. During these years children need optimum exposure to developmental experiences. A lack of these experiences could lead to impairments in all areas of development later on.

Physical Development[jmm4][v5]

The teacher must be aware of the physical stages of development and how the child's physical growth and development affect learning. The physical stage of development determines such factors as the ability to sit and attend, the need for activity, the relationship between physical skills and self-esteem, and the degree to which physical involvement in an activity, as opposed to being able to understand an abstract concept, affects learning.

It is important for the teacher to be aware of the physical stages of development and how changes to the child's physical attributes (which include internal developments, increased muscle capacity, improved coordination and other attributes as well as obvious growth) affect the child's ability to learn. Factors determined by the physical stage of development include: ability to sit and attend, the need for activity, the relationship between physical coordination and self-esteem, and the degree to which physical involvement in an activity (as opposed to being able to understand an abstract concept) affects learning and the child's sense of achievement.

By the time children reach school age there are certain physical activities they should be able to do. Careful observation of children when they first start school with regard to these activities should alert the teacher that there may be a problem with the child's physical development. These include:

- Being able to ride a tricycle
- Throwing, catching and holding a ball
- Being able to dress oneself, but still needing help with zippers and buttons
- Being able to walk on tiptoe
- Being able to use scissors to cut paper
- Being active at play outdoors and in the classroom

In addition, children with physical disabilities are not able to move as quickly as other children of the same age.

Cognitive (Academic) Development

Beginning with pre-operational thought processes and moving to concrete operational thoughts, children go through patterns of learning. Eventually they acquire the mental ability to think about and solve problems in their heads because they can manipulate objects symbolically. Children of most ages can use such symbols as words and numbers to represent objects and relationships, but they need concrete reference points. Teachers must encourage children to use and develop the thinking skills that they possess to solve problems that interest them. The content of the curriculum must be relevant, engaging, and meaningful to the students.

It is important for teachers of the early childhood grades to be aware of the warning signs of cognitive delay in children, although most of these are apparent before the children come to school. In order for a child to be diagnosed as having an impairment in cognitive development, there must be a deficiency in at least two of the following:
- Speech and communication
- Self-care
- Social and Interpersonal skills
- Functional academic skills for the grade level

Social Development

Beginning with an awareness of peers but a lack of concern for their presence, children progress through a variety of social stages. Young children engage in *parallel* activities, i.e., playing alongside their peers without directly interacting. During the primary years, children develop an intense interest in peers. They establish productive, positive social and working relationships with one another.

This stage of social growth continues to increase in importance throughout the child's school years. The teacher must recognize the importance of developing positive peer group relationships and provide opportunities and support for cooperative small group projects. These projects not only develop cognitive ability but promote peer interaction. The ability to work and relate effectively with peers contributes greatly to the child's sense of competence. In order to develop this sense of competence, children must successfully acquire the knowledge and skills recognized by our culture as important, especially those skills that promote academic achievement.

Knowledge of age-appropriate expectations is fundamental to the teacher's positive relationship with students and effective instructional strategies. The knowledge of what is individually appropriate for the specific children in a classroom is equally important. Developmentally oriented teachers approach classroom groups and individual students with a respect for their emerging capabilities. They recognize that young people grow in common patterns but at different rates, which usually cannot be accelerated by adult pressure or input. Developmentally oriented teachers know that variance in the school performance of children often results from differences in their general growth. Because of the inclusionary classes now established throughout the schools, teachers need to know the characteristics of students' exceptionalities and their implications on learning.

Children progress through a variety of social stages beginning with an awareness of self and self-concern. They soon develop an awareness of peers but demonstrate a lack of concern for their presence. For a time, young children engage in "parallel" activities, playing alongside their peers without directly interacting with one another.

During the primary years, children develop an intense interest in peers. They establish productive, positive, social and working relationships with one another. This area of social growth will continue to increase in significance throughout the child's academic career. The foundation for the students' successful development in this area is established through the efforts of the classroom teacher to plan and develop positive peer group relationships and to provide opportunities and support for cooperative small group projects that not only develop cognitive ability, but promote peer interaction. The ability to work and relate effectively with peers contributes greatly to the child's sense of competence. In order to develop this sense of competence, children need to be successful in acquiring the information base and social skill sets which promote cooperative effort to achieve academic and social objectives.

High expectations for student achievement, which are age-appropriate and focused, provide the foundation for a teacher's positive relationship with young students and are consistent with effective instructional strategies. It is equally important to determine what is appropriate for specific individuals in the classroom, and approach classroom groups and individual students with an understanding and respect for their emerging capabilities. Those who study childhood development recognize that young students grow and mature in common, recognizable patterns, but at different rates which cannot be effectively accelerated. This can result in variance in the academic performance of different children in the same classroom. With the establishment of inclusion as a standard in the classroom, it is necessary for all teachers to understand that variation in development among the student population is another aspect of diversity within the classroom. And this has implications for the ways in which instruction is planned and delivered and the ways in which students learn and are evaluated.

For information on the stages of social and emotional development:	Learn more about the stages of child development:
http://www.childdevelopmentinfo.com/development/erickson.shtml	http://www.cccf-fcsge.ca/english/resources/onefivedevelopment.htm

Skill 1.3   Identify developmental alerts

When children are emotionally neglected or have recently endured family upsets, they can react in several ways. First, the level of attention toward school can be greatly reduced. They may show signs of jealousy toward other children, or they may feel angry at other children, the teacher, or their parents. Aggression is very common among emotionally-neglected children.

The symptoms of diminished verbal interaction are often similar to those of abuse or neglect. The child exhibits a "deer in the headlights" look and maintains a very socially awkward set of behaviors. In general, such children have a drastically reduced ability to express themselves in words and, often, see aggression as the best tool to get their thoughts across.

Although cognitive ability is not lost because of such circumstances as abuse, neglect, emotional upset, and lack of verbal interaction, these children most likely do not have as much intellectual energy as he or she would if none of these issues were present. But, since the child may see the classroom as a safe place, teachers must be attentive to the needs and emotions of their students.

Skill 1.4   Identify common difficulties in emergent literacy development[jmm6][v7]

In today's educational communities, emergent literacy development poses critical issues and difficulties. Early childhood literacy development begins with exposing children to literacy enriched environments that include pictorial and written activities that provide examples of reading acquisition and cognitive development. The more common difficulties include understanding how early childhood cognitive development correlates with emerging literacy and educating the stakeholders that contribute to formal literacy development for children.

School communities struggle with finding strategies and designing curriculum for young students who lack emergent literacy skills. Phonics application, whole language understanding, alphabetical construction in word development, and literacy skills provide strong bases for reading development. Students without these skills exhibit risk factors in literacy development. We should design literacy programs that support a child's cognitive, social, and emotional development while the child develops the necessary tools for emerging literacy.

Given that literacy development begins early in a child's cognitive development and provides the foundation for emergent literacy construction, educational researchers continue to promote the importance of parents and pre-school educators. Children who acquire pre-reading and literacy constructs in early childhood before the formal schooling process begins are better equipped for literacy development.

Phonological awareness is of vital importance for children learning to read. Children who have difficulty determining letter sounds do not necessarily have a learning disability, but they do need more explicit instruction in phonics. The depth of the instruction depends on the child; some children need more, some need less.

Literacy is not something that begins when the child enters school. It begins at birth, and the experiences the child has in the home determine how ready the child is for reading. Children from homes where the parents read to them on a regular basis have a greater sense of phonological awareness than those that come from homes where books and reading are not seen as important. These children have a sense of story structure, a better vocabulary and recognize that reading and writing are essential for communication.

Common difficulties in emergent literacy development begin early in childhood development and provide the foundation for how children acquire literacy skills and apply them in reading and writing development. Providing children with the tools for successful literacy acquisition enhances the reading and writing experience and provides ongoing successful development in literacy application and comprehension.

Some of the factors that cause difficulties for children in emergent literacy include:

- They do not have the requisite phonemic awareness skills to begin reading

- They have difficulty with phonological memory

- They experience problems with lexical access and lack the ability to rapidly name colors, pictures and objects.

Exposing children to print is extremely important in emergent literacy. Classroom should be rich in books and magazines and children should have ample opportunities to check out books from the library. The teacher should engage the children in multiple reading and writing activities where they can experiment with print across the curriculum. One of the common difficulties that children experience is that they do not connect what they learn in Language Arts to what they learn in other subjects.

Not only do children need exposure to print and opportunities to use it, but they also need to interact with their classmates through discussion, group work and role play. Daily writing in journals is important, but the teacher again must allow the students to experiment with spelling and to supplement the stories they write with pictures and illustrations. One cannot expect students to grasp all the concepts of literacy at once. Therefore, concepts and strategies should be introduced as students need them and they need time to practice.

Skill 1.5   Identify the influences of substance abuse, physical abuse, and emotional distress on child development

Substance Abuse

Students use drugs and alcohol at surprisingly young ages today. Cases exist of ten-year-old alcoholics. Young people start using drugs and alcohol for one of the following four reasons:

        1) out of curiosity
        2) to party
        3) because of peer pressure
        4) to avoid dealing with problems

In the school setting, teachers and administrators consider hard signs [jmm8]of dependency very serious. Hard signs of substance abuse are those that even the inexperienced adult can recognize in children. Some of these hard signs include:

- Severe mood swings in children who usually have a stable demeanor

- Signs of excessive fatigue

- Weight loss

- Medical conditions, such as watery eyes, sneezing, etc.

- Defensiveness, irritation or agitation over seemingly unimportant situations or incidents

Another hard sign[jmm9] is irresponsible, illogical, and dangerous use. The use of any substance by young people constitutes irresponsible, illogical, and dangerous use because substances of abuse, including alcohol, are all illegal[jmm10]. Because of the inherent physical risk of ingesting street drugs; the possibility of brain damage; the drop in educational levels; and lost social development, which diminishes a student's abilities and chances in life; medical science recommends a zero tolerance for drugs. Psychologically, the use of drugs and alcohol prevents the youth from struggling with using non-chemical coping skills to solve problems. Typically, the student misses learning sophisticated anger modulation techniques usually acquired in late adolescence and is, therefore, limited in handling that most important emotion. Substance abuse also contributes to the terrible number of automobile crash deaths, teen pregnancies, overdoses on contaminated substances, and such mental disorders as activation of a latent schizophrenia caused by exposure to harsh substances.

Soft signs, less rapacious and life threatening, are the three psychosocial declines. The young substance abuser exhibits losses in previously attained social and academic functional levels. The adage *Pot makes a smart kid average and an average kid dumb* is right on the mark. In some families , pot smoking is a known habit of the parents, and the children may start their habits by stealing from the parents. Parental use makes it almost impossible to convince the child that drugs and alcohol are not good for them,

Staff at a medical facility must treat any student who exhibits hard signs associated with substance ingestion immediately. Seizures because of withdrawal are fatal 17 percent of the time. Overdoses, because of mixed substances or overuse of a single substance, including alcohol, are rapidly fatal. Never, under any circumstances, attempt to treat, protect, tolerate, or negotiate with a student who is showing signs of a physical crisis. The police or emergency medical personnel must remove the student from the school center as soon as possible. You must provide constant one-to-one supervision away from the regular classroom until the student is taken to the hospital. You must call the police because this student is a danger to self and others. If you have questions about calling for help under such circumstances, learn the protocol for each step in the process.

Typically, a student on drugs or alcohol will show the following:

- lack of muscle coordination
- wobbly, ataxic gait
- reddened, puffy eyes (reddened sclera)
- averted gaze
- dilated pupils
- dry eyes
- dry mouth (anticholinergia)
- excessive sneezing or sniffing
- gazing off into space or nervousness
- [jmm11] nervous trembling
- failure to respond to verbal prompts
- passive-aggressive behavior
- sudden sickness in class
- vomiting and chills
- slurred speech
- aggression
- sleep
- odd, sudden personality changes
- withdrawal
- an appearance of responding to internal stimuli
- the smell of alcohol or the smell of marijuana (pungent, sharp odor, similar to burning cane)
- the appearance of powder around the nasal opening, on the clothes or hands

Students in early childhood classrooms do not have the same experience with drugs and alcohol as older students. They do, however, need to have instruction about the danger of taking prescription drugs. They see the medicine cabinet at home full of pills and medicine and need to know that these drugs, while legal, are very dangerous and that they should not take them. Teachers need to make this information part of Health class so that students know they only take medicine when needed.

Physical Abuse

Often, teachers do not detect physical abuse because the clothing covers the child's bruises. The traumatic effect that physical abuse has on the child's emotional state of mind is also hidden. Fear affects how well the student learns and participates in class, and, in young children, it is often hidden under a cloak of shyness.

Some of the signs that abused children may display include the following:

- a poor self-image
- difficulty trusting adults
- aggressive and disruptive behavior in the classroom
- displays of anger and rage over little events
- self-destructive behavior
- anxiety and fears
- fear of new situations
- failure in school

Early identification is essential in order for the child to develop normally and without long-lasting effects.

Emotional Abuse

All students demonstrate behaviors that indicate emotional distress from time to time since all children experience stressful periods in their lives. However, emotionally healthy students maintain control of their behavior even during stressful periods. Teachers need to remember that the difference between typical stressful behavior and severe emotional distress is determined by the frequency, duration, and intensity of the stressful behavior.

Lying, stealing, and fighting are atypical behaviors that most children exhibit occasionally, but if a child lies, steals, or fights regularly or blatantly, then these behaviors may indicate emotional distress. Lying is especially common among young children who feel the need to avoid punishment or make themselves feel more important. As children become older, lying is often a signal that the child is feeling insecure. These feelings of insecurity may escalate to the point of being habitual or obvious and then may indicate that the child is seeking attention because of emotional distress. Fighting, especially among siblings, is a common occurrence. However, if a child fights, is unduly aggressive, or is belligerent towards others on a long-term basis, teachers and parents need to consider the possibility of emotional problems.

How can a teacher know when a child needs help with his or her behavior? The child's actions indicate the need and desire for help. Breaking rules established by parents, teachers, and other authorities and destroying property can signify that a student is losing control, especially when these behaviors occur frequently. Other signs that a child needs help include frequent bouts of crying, a quarrelsome attitude, and constant complaints about school, friends, or life in general. Anytime a child's disposition, attitude, or habits change significantly, teachers and parents should seriously consider the existence of emotional difficulties.

Emotional disturbances in childhood are common and take a variety of forms. Usually these problems present as uncharacteristic behaviors. Most of the time, children respond favorably to brief psychotherapy treatment programs. At other times, disturbances may need more intensive therapy and are harder to resolve. Teachers and parents must address all stressful behaviors and examine any type of chronic antisocial behavior as a possible symptom of deep-seated emotional upset.

Many safe and helpful interventions are available to the classroom teacher when dealing with a student who is suffering serious emotional disturbances. First, and foremost, the teacher must maintain open communication with the parents and other professionals who are involved with a student who exhibits overt behavior characteristics. Students with behavior disorders need constant behavior modification, which may involve daily, two-way communication between the home and school.

Other problems that cause emotional pain include: social awkwardness, depression, incipient major mental illnesses, personality disorders, learning disabilities, ADHD, conduct disorder, and substance abuse and dependency in family members. The most common emotional problems found in student populations are such parent-child problems as a deficit in communication, authority, and respect between parent and child. A close second is conduct disorder—a behavior set characterized by aggression; exploitation; violence; disregard for the rights of others; animal cruelty; fire setting; bed wetting; defiance; running away; truancy; juvenile arrest record; and associated ADHD, substance abuse, and parent-child problems.

The teacher must establish an environment that promotes appropriate behavior for all students and respect for one another. Teachers should explain any special needs of classmates so they can consider these needs. The teacher should also initiate a behavior modification program for any student that shows emotional or behavioral disorders. Such behavior modification plans can be an effective means of preventing deviant behavior. In the event that deviant behavior does occur, the teacher should have a safe and secure time-out place where the student can go for a respite and an opportunity to regain self-control.

Often when a behavior disorder is more severe, the student must be involved in a more concentrated program such as psychotherapy. In such instances, the school psychologist, guidance counselor, or behavior specialist is directly involved with the student and provides counseling and therapy on a regular basis. Frequently they are also involved with the student's family.

As a last resort, many families are turning to drug therapy. Once viewed as a radical step, administering drugs to children to balance their emotions or control their behavior has become a widely used form of therapy. Of course, only a medical doctor can prescribe such drugs.

Learn to recognize signs of child abuse:

http://www.co.clermont.oh.us/djfs/cps/508/ide
ntify.htm

Skill 1.6   Identify strategies for designing and implementing instructional practices to support typically and atypically developing young children[V12]

The effective teacher is cognizant of students' individual learning styles and human growth and development theory and applies these principles in selecting and implementing appropriate instructional activities.

When designing and implementing strategies to use with children, whether they have typical or atypical development, one has to start with the overall educational goal. This will determine the focus of the curriculum and thus the instruction. Along with designing the instructional strategies to use, the teacher must also be cognizant of the learning environment, the age and capability of the students, and their stage of development.

For young children, instruction should take place in small or whole group settings and with ample time to practice the skills. Some instructional strategies and methodologies teachers can use include:

- **Direct instruction** by the teacher for providing directions or step-by-step instruction of skills and concepts. It is also effective for introducing lessons, and for actively involving students in the learning process.

- **Indirect instruction** takes the form of involving the students in inquiry, problem-solving and discovery, which is essential for young children. Since they are naturally curious, this instructional strategy allows them to explore the environment, work with manipulatives and learn by doing and playing. It takes advantage of the students' interests and encourages them to find their own solutions.

- **Interactive instruction** involves the students in discussion, which may or may not be teacher directed. It relies heavily on interaction among the participants, which is not only conducive to learning skills and concepts, but also helps children to develop socially and emotionally.

- Experiential learning is learner and activity centered. For this reason, it is the instructional strategy used most often in early childhood classrooms. The students participate in activities, share the results of the activity (what they have learned), make inferences that they can use to apply to other learning situations and look back on their learning to determine where their strengths and weaknesses. The emphasis here is on the process of learning and not on the actual product.

For children who are developing in a typical fashion, the teacher can use any combination of these instructional methods. For children who have atypical development, one approach may work better than another. The strategy the teacher uses will depend, to a large part, on the problems or conditions the child has and where more instruction or practice may be needed.

Learning activities selected for younger students (below age eight) should focus on short time frames in highly simplified form. The nature of the activity and the content in which the activity is presented affects the approach that the students take in processing the information. Younger children tend to process information at a slower rate than older children (age eight and older).

On the other hand, when selecting and implementing learning activities for older children, teachers should focus on more complex ideas. Older students can understand more complex instructional activities. Moreover, effective teachers maintain a clear understanding of the developmental appropriateness of activities and choose and present these activities in a manner consistent with the level of readiness of the students.

Students may need accommodations to the instruction and/or activities in order for them to achieve the outcomes. This can include such things as providing them with visual aids, instruments to help them hear the teacher clearly, such as a phonic ear, extra time for completing work, the use of a scribe for writing assignments or an assistant to help them with reading or physical activity.

Skill 1.7   Identify the influence of brain research on theories of cognitive and social competence, the principles of how children learn, and the development and implementation of instructional strategies

We can apply several educational learning theories to classroom practices. One classic learning theory is Piaget's stages of development, which comprise the following four learning stages: sensory motor stage (from birth to age 2), pre-operation stages (ages 2 to 7 or early elementary), concrete operational (ages 7 to 11 or upper elementary), and formal operational (ages 7-15 or late elementary to high school). Piaget believed children passed through this series of stages to develop from the most basic forms of concrete thinking to sophisticated levels of abstract thinking.

Some of the most prominent learning theories in education today include brain-based learning and the Multiple Intelligence Theory. Supported by recent brain research, brain-based learning suggests that knowledge about the way the brain retains information helps educators design the most effective learning environments.

As a result, researchers have developed the following twelve principles that relate knowledge about the brain to teaching practices:

- The brain is a complex adaptive system.
- The brain is social.
- The search for meaning is innate.
- We use patterns to learn more effectively.
- Emotions are crucial to developing patterns.
- Each brain perceives and creates parts and whole simultaneously.
- Learning involves focused and peripheral attention.
- Learning involves conscious and unconscious processes.
- We have at least two ways of organizing memory.
- Learning is developmental.
- Complex learning is enhanced by challenge and inhibited by threat.
- Every brain is unique.

(Caine & Caine, 1994, Mind/Brain Learning Principles)

Educators can use these principles to design methods and environments in their classrooms that maximize student learning.

The Multiple Intelligence Theory, developed by Howard Gardner, suggests that students learn in at least seven different ways. These include visually and spatially, musically, verbally, logically and mathematically, interpersonally, intrapersonally, and bodily and kinesthetically.

The most current constructivist learning theory says that students should construct learning opportunities. Constructivist teachers believe that students create their own reality of knowledge and methods of processing and observing the world around them. Students are constantly constructing new ideas that serve as frameworks for learning and teaching. Researchers have shown that the constructivist model comprises the following four components:

1. Learner creates knowledge.
2. Learner constructs and adds meaningful new knowledge to existing knowledge.
3. Learner shapes and constructs knowledge by life experiences and social interactions.
4. Learner, teacher, and classmates establish knowledge cooperatively on a daily basis.

In *Clinical Psychology and Personality: the Selected Papers of George Kelly* (1969), Kelly holds the idea that the fact that human beings construct knowledge systems based on their observations parallels Piaget's theory that individuals construct knowledge systems as they work with others who share a common background of thought and processes[jmm14]." Constructivist learning for students is dynamic and ongoing. The classroom becomes a place where students are encouraged to interact with the instructional process by asking questions and posing new ideas to old theories. The use of cooperative learning that encourages students to work in supportive learning environments, using their own ideas to stimulate questions and propose outcomes, is a major aspect of a constructivist classroom.

The metacognition learning theory deals with "the study of how to help the learner gain understanding about how knowledge is constructed and about the conscious tools for constructing that knowledge" (Joyce and Weil 1996). The cognitive approach to learning involves the teacher's understanding that teaching the student to process his or her own learning and mastery of skill provides the greatest learning and retention opportunities in the classroom. Students are taught to develop concepts and teach themselves skills in problem solving and critical thinking. The student becomes an active participant in the learning process, and the teacher facilitates that conceptual and cognitive learning process.

Social and behavioral theories look at classroom social interactions that instruct or have an impact on learning opportunities. The psychological approaches behind both theories are subject to individual variables that are learned and applied either positively or negatively in the classroom. The stimulus of the classroom can promote conducive learning or evoke behavior that is counterproductive for both students and teachers. Students are social beings that normally gravitate to action, so teachers must establish classroom environments that provide both focus and engagement to maximize learning opportunities.

Designing classrooms that provide optimal academic and behavioral support for a diversity of students can be daunting for teachers. The ultimate goal for both students and teachers is creating a safe learning environment where students can construct knowledge in an engaging and positive classroom climate .

None of these theories will work for every classroom, and incorporating a range of learning styles is a good approach. Still, under the guidance of any theory, good educators differentiate their instructional practices and use various methods to meet the diverse needs of their students.

> **For more information about different learning styles:**
>
> http://www.funderstanding.com/index.html

Skill 1.8   **Recognize ways in which children's early experiences and culturally transmitted knowledge contribute to individual differences in development and learning**

Beginning teachers must recognize the profound effect they have as an authority figure, instructor, and behavior model for students in the early formative years. At this stage of life, children are not only continually developing physically, emotionally, and intellectually, and acquiring new skills in all of these areas, they are also beginning to retain basic concepts, modes of thinking, and behavioral models that will continue to develop and will serve them—for better or for worse—throughout life.

The influences on all aspects of a child's development come from the home, family, and the community as well as the school. But the most directed, purposeful and productive time in the average child's day is the time spent in the classroom and the school environment. Therefore, we plan, schedule, monitor and measure to very high standards. The adults into whom the children will develop are, to a considerable extent, the product of the educational system we provide for them. So, at various stages of the process, we incorporate instruction on life skills, independent thinking, social values and social interaction, at-risk behaviors, and many other non-traditional topics intended to equip our students for making appropriate choices and improving their lives, now and in the future.

For beginning teachers, this process often starts with affirming the their high expectations for the success of each student and their confidence in each student's ability to meet these expectations. Unfortunately, in some school systems, very high expectations are placed on certain students and little expectation placed on others. Often, the result is predictable: you get exactly what you expect to get. And you seldom get more out of a situation or person than you are willing to put in. A teacher is expected to provide the same standards of excellence in education for all students. This standard cannot be upheld or met unless the teacher has—and conveys—high expectations for all students.

Educators have done considerable research regarding student performance. Time and again, they have demonstrated a direct correlation between the teacher's expectations for a particular student and that student's academic performance. This action may be unintended and subtle, but the effects are manifest and measurable.

Discipline is another early issue beginning teachers must address. Children will accept appropriate discipline that may instill certain values that promote the development of self discipline in the individual. While early childhood and elementary students are generally more easily controlled—often appearing better behaved and more responsive to authority—than older students, they still have a tendency to socialize and play just for the sake of play. This socialization and play can quickly cause the classroom situation and the learning environment to deteriorate into chaos. When teachers implement a well-structured plan, with measurable milestones and specific objectives, they will quickly identify and redirect conversation and activity that is not relevant or supportive of the instructional objectives. Teachers may allow younger students a greater degree of latitude, but they must restrict their longitude.

Allowing for the differing needs of younger students does not mean abandoning classroom discipline and organized instruction. At this level, students need the reassurance of structure, organization, and discipline. If the appropriate attitudes and responses to structure and discipline are internalized at an early age, they will serve the student throughout the educational experience and provide a solid foundation upon which the individual can develop the self-discipline necessary in later life. The teacher who can instill these values in a young student will have earned the gratitude and respect of all the teachers who instruct this student in the future.

For further reading on classroom discipline:

http://teched.vt.edu/VCTTE/VCTTEMonographs/VCTTEMono2(Discipline).html

http://712educators.about.com/od/discipline/tp/disciplinetips.htm

---

COMPETENCY 2.0   KNOWLEDGE OF FOUNDATIONS

Skill 2.1   Identify theorists, theories, and benchmarks in the fields of early childhood and elementary education and their implication for the classroom teacher of young children

Jean Piaget

Jean Piaget, a European scientist who died in the late twentieth century, developed many theories about the way humans learn. Most famously, he developed a simple theory about the stages of the development of human minds. During the first stage, the *sensory-motor* stage, which lasts until the toddler years, children begin to understand their senses.

In the next stage, the *pre-operational* stage, children begin to understand symbols. For example, as they learn language, they realize that words are symbols of thoughts, actions, items, and other elements in the world. This stage lasts into early elementary school.

The third stage, which lasts until late elementary school, is the *concrete operations* stage. During this stage, children go one step beyond learning symbols. They learn how to manipulate symbols, objects, and other elements. A common example of this stage is the displacement of water. In this stage, they can reason that a wide and short cup of water and a tall and thin cup of water can actually contain the same amount of water.

The *formal operations* stage usually starts in adolescence and continues into adulthood. This stage involves such skills as critical thinking, hypothesis, and systematic organization of knowledge.

Generally, when we say that children move from a stage of concrete thinking to logical and abstract thinking, we mean that they are moving from the *pre-operational* and *concrete* stages to the *formal operations* stage. But as anyone who spends time with children knows, becoming a strong critical thinker is not without problems. And remember, just because children have moved into a particular stage does not mean that they can completely function at the new level. For example, adolescents may be able to think critically, but they need plenty of instruction and assistance to do so adequately. Critical thinking skills should not necessarily be taught out of context; rather, all lessons should contribute to the skills that help children develop critical thinking skills.

Benjamin Bloom

In 1956, Benjamin Bloom, an educational psychologist, developed a detailed classification of critical thinking and learning skills and objectives into tiered levels. These hierarchal levels ordered thinking skills from the simplest, or lower-ordered, to the more complicated or higher-ordered. Motivating teachers to teach at all levels of critical thinking and not just at the most common level—such lower-ordered thinking skills as memorize, restate, and define—was the goal of Bloom's taxonomy. For details on the taxonomy, see skill 6.14

Lawrence Kohlberg

Lawrence Kohlberg outlined what we know as *Kohlberg's stages of moral development* in 1958. Kohlberg's six stages are grouped into the following three levels: pre-conventional, conventional, and post-conventional. Each level consists of two stages.

- Pre-conventional (Egocentric: birth to age nine)
    - Punishment and obedience—morality is based on established rules. Children in this stage see that following the rules and avoiding negative consequences define moral behavior.
    - Instrumental purpose—In this stage, whatever satisfies the child's needs is considered moral by that child.
- Conventional (Socio-centric: age nine to adolescence)
    - Interpersonal—Children begin to understand that good behavior is expected, and achieving those expectations is moral.
    - Social system—Adolescents at this stage understand that they need to fulfill obligations and expectations and that this fulfillment constitutes moral behavior.
- Post-conventional (adulthood)
    - Social contract—We understand that various cultures, as well as individuals, have different definitions of morality, and good moral behavior is seen as meeting the moral standards of that person's social norm.
    - Universal Ethical Principles— At this stage, reasoning is based on ethical fairness, and individuals can judge themselves and others based on their own sense of morality.

> **For additional reference:**
>
> http://allpsych.com/psychology101/moral_development.html
> http://www.utmem.edu/~vmurrell/dissertation/Kohlberg.htm

Skill 2.2   Identify curriculum models of early childhood and elementary education programs in a variety of settings

Early curriculum models in elementary education programs have historical roots in the Head Start Programs of the early sixties that were based on a comprehensive curriculum model for preparing low-income students for success in school. During the seventies and eighties, a diversity of models that focused on the academic achievement of all students in educational environments replaced curriculum models. Longitudinal research showing that constructing curriculum models had an impact on early childhood development and academic success rekindled the resurfacing of curriculum models in the early nineties.

The No Child Left Behind (NCLB) Act has directed the growth of both federal and state mandates to construct curriculum models specific to the development of early childhood and elementary programs for academic enhancement. The statistical data demonstrating academic outcomes for underachieving children in school communities have contributed to state-financed pre K-2 curriculum models that address cognitive development and literacy acquisition. The NCLB Act requires that all teachers be highly qualified in the subject area they are teaching, and it increases school and district accountability for yearly performance. Under this legislation, schools receiving federal funding must develop measurable achievement objectives and meet them if they are to secure funding. School districts may no longer adopt a complacent attitude about low performance.

> **Read more about NCLB:**
>
> http://en.wikipedia.org/wiki/No_Child_Left_Behind

The emergence of Head Start and community centered programs has provided conceptual and actual frameworks of well defined curriculum models that are consistent in serving academically at-risk students.

Many widely known curriculum models continue to contribute to effective curriculum model development. The ones used in early childhood curriculum development include the following models:

- Head Start
- Montessori method
- Creative curriculum
- High/scope curriculum

For more information on these models:

http://ca.search.yahoo.com/search?ei=utf-8&fr=slv8-gs3&p=Head%20Start

http://www.montessori.edu/FAQ.html

http://www.circleofinclusion.org/english/approaches/creative.html

http://en.wikipedia.org/wiki/High/Scope

Theoretical research provides a definitive foundation in understanding how to develop curriculum models that frame how teachers instruct and how students learn.

Curriculum models are conceptual frameworks that are structurally organized to inform and have an impact on educational decision making and policy direction. Acting as guides for program implementation and curriculum evaluation, curriculum models are foundation constructs for early elementary programs serving all students. Curriculum models vary in structure and school implementation. Curriculum models provide consistency in instruction and create evaluation criteria for uniformity in programs designated for early childhood curriculum.

Researchers continue to show that childhood curriculum models produce effective academic outcomes. However, limitations in curriculum reform have a negative impact on implementing specifically designed curriculum models that educate and accelerate learning for at risk students. By designing early childhood curriculum models that raise academic standards and outcomes for students, experienced educators ultimately improve the quality of instruction in elementary education programs.

[jmm15]Strategies used in designing and implementing effective curriculum models should include the following:

- Lesson concepts diversified for individual student learning goals
- Differentiated instruction for group and individual academic needs
- Best practices and instructional approaches
- Enhanced curriculum design that includes rigor and relevance and is relationship oriented
- Portfolio of evaluation assessments for individual student performance
- Reading and writing level testing results for specified literacy skills and identified reading levels
- World-wide application of curriculum design and reading resources

Curriculum models should include predicative conceptual frameworks that outline specific academic expectations and evaluation components for those assessing the effectiveness of implemented programs. Early childhood and elementary education programs must incorporate cognitive and social development of young learners. As educators increase their use of curriculum models in elementary education, the ultimate educational goal and focus should be to improve curriculum programs for children.

Skill 2.3   Identify the impact of federal and state laws on education in the classroom

The Individuals with Disabilities Act (IDEA), passed in 1990, has a direct impact on classrooms. This law ensures that all children with disabilities and their families receive the help and support they need. It governs how states and public agencies provide intervention services and how schools provide special education services for these children. Part A of the law covers children from birth to age two, and Part B covers children with disabilities from ages three to twenty-one. The first step is identifying the specific learning disability and then getting the help the child needs. From the beginning, the family is involved. They work with a school team that includes outside support agencies.

> **To find out more about IDEA:**
>
> http://idea.ed.gov/

The referral of students for this process is usually relatively simple for the classroom teacher and requires little more than some initial paper work and discussion. The services and resources received as a result of the process are invaluable to the student with behavioral disorders.

At times, the teacher must go beyond the school system to meet the needs of some students. An awareness of special services and resources and how to obtain them is essential to all teachers and their students. When the school system cannot address the needs of a student, the teacher often must take the initiative and contact agencies within the community. Frequently, schools have no special policy for finding resources. The individual teacher must be creative and resourceful and find whatever help the student needs. Meeting the needs of all students is certainly a team effort that is most often spearheaded by the classroom teacher.

No Child Left Behind

SEE Skill 2.2

Family involvement

The IDEA requires parent or guardian involvement in developing the student's IEP. This involvement is absolutely essential for the advocacy of the disabled student's educational needs. Educators must tailor IEPs to meet the student's needs, and no one knows those needs better than parents, guardians, and other significant family members. Optimal conditions for a disabled student's education exist when teachers, school administrators, special education professionals, and parents or guardians work together to design and execute the IEP.

Due process

Under the IDEA, Congress provides safeguards, including the right to sue in court against schools' actions, and encourages states to develop hearing and mediation systems to resolve disputes. Authorities cannot deny due process to students, parents, or guardians because of disability.

Inclusion, mainstreaming, and least restrictive environment

Under the IDEA, inclusion, mainstreaming, and least restrictive environment are interrelated policies with varying degrees of statutory imperatives.

- Inclusion is the right of students with disabilities to be placed in the regular classroom.
- Least restrictive environment is the mandate that children be educated to the maximum extent appropriate with their non-disabled peers.
- Mainstreaming is a policy through which disabled students can be placed in the regular classroom, as long as such placement does not interfere with the student's educational plan.

Abuse Situations

Teachers and administrators must first serve the needs of the child who is being abused. A suspected case gone unreported may destroy a child's present life and subsequent life as a functional adult. Every citizen who suspects abuse and neglect has a duty to make a report, and reporting the incident is a requirement for state licensed and certified persons. All reports can be kept confidential if required, but disclosing your identity is best in case authorities require more information. This personal matter has no impact on qualifications for license or certification. Failure to make a report when abuse or neglect is suspected is punishable by revocation of certification and license, a fine, and criminal charges.

Any accused individual has the right to have counsel and make a defense in any matter of law. The procedure for reporting makes clear the rights of the accused, who stands before the court innocent until proven guilty, with the right to representation, redress, and appeal, as in all matters of United States law. The state is cautious about receiving spurious reports but investigates any that seem real enough. Some breaches of standards of decency are not reportable offenses, such as possession of pornography that is not hidden from children. Teachers should go ahead and make the report and let the counselor make the decision. Your conscience is clear, and you have followed all procedures that keep you from liability. The obligation to report is immediate when you suspect abuse.

The law does not specify an acceptable or safe period of time a teacher can wait before reporting, so hesitation to report may be a cause for legal action against you. Do not wait once your suspicion is firm. You need only a reasonable suspicion, not actual proof, which is the job for the investigators.

COMPETENCY 3.0   KNOWLEDGE OF RESEARCH, STANDARDS, AND TRENDS

Skill 3.1   Identify professional organizations, web sites, and scholarly journals in the field of early and elementary education

A variety of professional organizations, web sites, and scholarly journals and books provide vital educational information on early and elementary education programs and models. The information will be categorized according to the defined criteria and presented as resources for educators seeking quality strategies to improve early childhood education for students.

Books

Epsteing, A.S. , Schweinhart, L.J., & McAdoo.L. (1996). *Models of early childhood education.* Ypsilanti, MI: High/Scope Press.

Essa,E.L. (2006). *Introduction to early childhood education.* (5th ed.). New York: Thomson Delmar Learning.

Harvey, S. & Goudvis, A. (2000). Strategies that work: Teaching comprehension to enhance understanding. York, Maine: Stenhouse Publishers.

Goffin, S.G., & Wilson, C. (2001). *Curriculum models and early childhood education: Appraising the relationship* (2nd ed.). Upper Saddle River, NJ: Merrill/Prentice Hall.

Morrison, G.S. (2005). *Fundamentals of early childhood education.* (4th ed.). New York: Prentice Hall.

Morrison, G.S. (2001). *Early childhood education today.* (8th ed.). Columbus, OH: Merrill-Prentice Hall.

Powell, D.R. (1987). Comparing preschool curricula and practices: The state of research. In S. L. Kagan & E.F. Zigler (eds.), *Early schooling: The national debate* (pp. 190-211). New Haven, CT: Yale University Press.

Journals

Journal of Moral Education

Review of Educational Research

Teacher Magazine

Curriculum Design and Development

Educational Leadership

Marcon, R.A. (1999). Differential impact of preschool models on development and early learning of inner city children: A three-cohort study. *Developmental Psychology,* 35(2), 358-375.

Schweinhart, L.J., & Weikart, D.P. (1997). The High/Scope preschool curriculum comparison study through age 23. *Early Childhood Research Quarterly*, 12(2), 117-143.

Web Sites

Educational Archives

http://ceep.crc.uiuc,edu//eecearchive/digests/2000/goffin00.html. Goffin, S.G. The role of curriculum models in early childhood education. (2000). EDO-PS-00-8.

Educational Reform and Concerns:

http://www/edweek.org/ew/index.html.

Professional Organizations

The Southern Early Childhood Association
P.O. Box 55930-Little Rock, AR 72215-5930
800-305-7322
gbean@southernearlychildhood.org —email
http://www.southernearlychildhood.org/postion_earlyliteracy.html

National Study of School Evaluation (NSSE)
1699 East Woodfield Road, Suite 406
Schaumburg, IL 60173
847-995-9080
http://www.nsse.org - website

Center for the Improvement of Early Reading Achievement (CIERA)
University of Michigan, School of Education
610 E. University, Room 1600 SEB
Ann Arbor, MI 48109-1259
734-647-6940
http://www.ciera.org/ -website

ERIC Clearinghouse on Reading, English, and Communication

Indiana University
Smith Research Center, Suite 150
Bloomington, IN 47408-2698
800-759-4723
http://www.indiana.edu/~eric_rec/ -website

National Institute for Literacy
1775 I St. N.W., Suite 730
Washington, DC 20006-2401
202-233-2025
Andrew Hartman, Director
http://www.nifl.gov - website

Skill 3.2   Identify position statements of such organizations as the International Reading Association (IRA), Association for Childhood Education International (ACEI), National Association for the Education of Young Children (NAEYC), National Council of Teachers of Mathematics (NCTM), and the Southern Early Childhood Association (SECA) and their influence on instructional practice

The following organizations have been instrumental in providing educational support for school communities, parents, legislators, and educators. They promote educational reform, design innovative curriculum to address student academic needs, and provide a collaborative process for reform and instruction.

Position Statements

Southern Early Childhood Association
The Southern Early Childhood Association provides a number of position statements on educational reform and curriculum models promoting student educational excellence. In its *Early Literacy and Beginning to Read* position statement, the Southern Early Childhood Association promotes early literacy for children learning to read and write. The Association believes that literacy is collaborative and inclusive of all stakeholders in a young child's life—parents, teachers, invested adults, and neighborhood communities.

In promoting early literacy, the Association understands that young children must have opportunities to become active participants in activities that promote literacy skill development. The inclusion of professional development opportunities for teachers must deal not only with literacy skill and curriculum model development, but also with how cultural differences influence literacy skill acquisition of students from different ethnic and cultural backgrounds. The framework for literacy development and reading proficiency must begin in the foundational years of childhood development, pre K-2, and formal educational training.

Other position statements promoted for The Southern Early Childhood Association include the following and all are available online on the website:

- *Brain Research and Its Implications for Early Childhood Programs*
- *Assessing Development and Learning in Young Children*
- *Quality Child Care*
- *Supporting Learning with Technology in the Early Childhood Classroom*
- *Arts & Movement Education for Young Children*
- *Valuing Diversity for Young Children*
- Invest in Children, Invest in Virginia: Universal Pre-Kindergarten, the Right Investment for the Right Reasons.

For more information on the Southern Childhood Association:

http://www/southernearlychildhood.org/ position_earlyliteracy.html.

Association for Childhood Education International (ACEI)
The position statement for the Association for Childhood Education International (ACEI) is a collaborative one that extends its vision and mission of educational development for students into the global community. The position is progressive and underlies a strong commitment to students and staff in changing school communities and educational reform.

Being influential in developing professional programs and training opportunities for educators and students benefiting from progressive and intentional educational programs remains an integral aspect of the position statement of ACEI. Providing consistent educational standards and equity are the cornerstones of ACEI's position statement.

> **For further reading about ACEI:**
>
> http://www.acei.org/

International Reading Association (IRA)

The international Reading Association (IRA) provides a comprehensive professional organization for preparing teachers and educators for reading instruction. The guided mission and position for IRA includes providing support in increasing literacy skills and reading instruction for students and promoting effective instruction for parents, educators, and policymakers.

IRA studies the research and data from national organizations and school communities on effective reading instruction and strategies that promote reading acquisition.

Providing teachers with reading instruction in the newly created *Status of Reading Instruction Institution* has been beneficial in developing programs and initiatives promoting reading preparation programs for school communities. Preparing elementary teachers for reading instruction creates better readers and academic accessibility for students.

> **For further information about the International Reading Association:**
>
> Email Dr. Karen Douglas at:
> kdouglas@reading.org
>
> http://www.reading.org/

National Association for the Education of Young Children (NAEYC)
The National Association for the Education of Young Children focuses on improving and developing programs and services for children from birth through eight years. Founded in 1926, the Association is considered the world's largest educational organization with almost 100,000 members who work on behalf on the education of young children.

As a global organization, the NAEYC has a governing board that deals with educational issues relevant to childhood education policy and practices. With almost 300 affiliates, the NAEYC extends membership to anyone dedicated to promoting the educational needs of children.

The NAEYC provides position statements on a diversity of educational issues related to childhood program development, such as:

- Code of ethical conduct and statement of commitment with supplements for adult educators and program administrators
- Framework for conceptual professional development Early childhood curriculum, assessment, and program evaluation
- Early childhood mathematics and learning standards
- Learning to read and write

The influence of NAEYC on instructional practices for educators is extensive. The organization provides a comprehensive educational approach in developing and promoting educational practices and policies that have a direct impact on the learning acquisition of young children.

> **Read more about the NAEYC:**
>
> http://www.naeyc.org.

National Council of Teachers of Mathematics (NCTM)

The governing position for the National Council of Teachers of Mathematics has a direct impact on the educational decision-making of administrators, teachers, and other professional staff in school communities. The following six overarching themes that influence mathematic standards for Prekindergarten-Grade 12 govern the principal positions for the NCTM:

- Equity—curriculum design and implementation must have rigor and excellence providing opportunity for all students.
- Curriculum—consistent and structured focus on mathematical conceptual design and instruction is aligned from grade level to grade level.
- Teaching—mathematical inclusion must provide a cultural and challenging instructional implementation effective for all students.
- Learning—performance-based assessment opportunities for students must include assessments and evaluations that substantiate the student's prior knowledge and skill base.
- Assessment— congruent evaluations to mathematical conceptual learning must have real life applications for students.
- Technology—the influence of using technology to connect students with additional resources to study mathematical concepts and application

The comprehensive aspect of NCTM in providing an overview of standards for school mathematics directly influences how school communities construct curriculum design and direct teacher instruction for students in grades preK-12. With consistency in curriculum design and implementation, we can construct an alignment of evaluation tools to assess student learning of mathematical concepts and application.

> **For further reading about the NCTM:**
>
> http://www.nctm.org/

Skill 3.3 Identify current issues, trends, and educational innovations and legislation

A diversity of current issues, trends, educational innovations, and legislation have an impact on elementary school communities. National assessments and local evaluations of student academic performance in the areas of reading, writing, and mathematics show that gaps in classroom learning exist from one cultural group to another. The issue of student learning and performance has become a national debate on whether providing additional educational funding will alleviate or create academic access for students identified as at risk.

Current Trends

Differentiating Instruction
The effective teacher tries to connect all students to the subject matter through multiple techniques, with the goal that students, through their own abilities, will relate to one or more techniques and excel in the learning process. Differentiated instruction encompasses several areas:

1. Content—What is the teacher going to teach? Or, perhaps better put, what does the teacher want the students to learn? Differentiating content means that students will have access to content that piques their interest about a topic with a complexity that provides an appropriate challenge to their intellectual development.
2. Process—A classroom management technique through which instructional organization and delivery are maximized for the diverse student group. These techniques should include dynamic, flexible grouping activities, where instruction and learning occur both as whole-class, teacher-led activities and peer learning and teaching, while the teacher observes and coaches, within small groups or pairs.
3. Product—The expectations and requirements placed on students to demonstrate their knowledge or understanding. The type of product expected from each student should reflect that student's own capabilities.

Creating programs for literacy development and mathematical acquisition have become both the issues and the trends in educational innovations. Differentiating instruction for learners who come to school in the pre-K grades has become a focus for educators seeking to increase the literacy and mathematical skills of its youngest learners. The development of effective programs and subsequent funding continue to be the goals of a legislative process dedicated to promoting educational equity for students.

Multiple Intelligence Theory and Brain-based Research
SEE Skill 1.7, page 25.

Alternative Assessment
In alternative assessment, students create an answer or a response to a question or task, as opposed to traditional, inflexible assessments where students choose a prepared response from among a selection of responses, such as matching, multiple-choice, or true–false.

When implemented effectively, an alternative assessment approach includes the following characteristics, among others:

- Requires higher-order thinking and problem-solving
- Provides opportunities for student self-reflection and self-assessment
- Uses real world applications to connect students to the subject
- Provides opportunities for students to learn and examine subjects on their own and collaborate with their peers.
- Encourages students to continue learning beyond the requirements of the assignment
- Clearly defines objective and performance goals

Inquiry-based learning is performance-based learning. Students are actively involved in the learning process and in the constructing new knowledge. When students engage in inquiry-based learning in order to understand the world around them, the learning process involves the formulation of questions that convert new information into an active application of knowledge.

Find out more about alternative assessment:
http://www.emtech.net/Alternative_Assessment.html

Figure 1 shows the contextual and interactive component of inquiry-based learning for students.

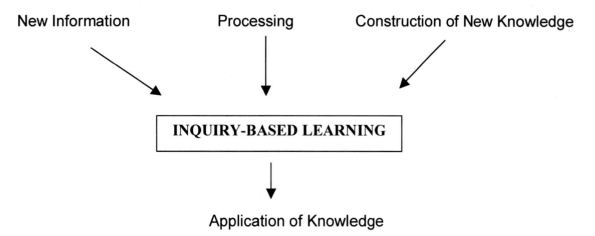

When students are given new information to process, inquiry-based learning becomes a natural extension of knowledge acquisition and understanding. In traditional classrooms, the lecture is the mode of learning for students who want to understand the context of mathematical and real-life applications of problem solving skills learned in the traditional math class. In an inquiry-based learning format, the teacher shows students how to apply mathematical learning and apply that knowledge in real-life situations. Involving students in the active processing of mathematical learning increases their ability to construct frameworks of understanding into useful applications of new knowledge.

Legislation

Legislation issues of educational funding for teachers and program development continue to have an impact on existing educational implementations. With thousands of school communities failing to meet NCLB and Adequate Yearly Progress (AYP) standards, the cost of overhaul and additional financial support for effective school communities with over-capacity issues is a major reason given for the decreased educational funding. Students continually promoted from pre-K to higher elementary grade levels who have failed to acquire the basic skills of reading, writing, and math are becoming increasingly frustrated by school systems designed to promote rather than hold accountability for student learning and evaluation.

Other Current Issues

The estimated cost of teacher turnover in school communities is 5-7 billion dollars. This figure has an additional impact on the legislature's ability to provide enough funding for all educational communities. Professional development training and required certification classes for teachers in elementary education also contribute to the comprehensive cost of educating students.

Early violence in elementary schools and classroom management issues contribute to a reduction in teaching and instructional time for young learners. Providing young learners with ethical and social strategies to improve cooperative learning and communication will go a long way in reducing the time spent on conflict and increase the time spent on learning acquisition.

Educational innovations in technology and educational reform must address the conflicting issues that influence educational development and effective curriculum implementation. Current educational reform must continue to focus on addressing educational issues that promote learning opportunities and professional development for both students and educators.

Skill 3.4   Identify ethical behavior and professional responsibilities as they relate to young children, families, colleagues, and the community

Ethical behavior and professional responsibilities for early childhood educators are principles or codes of ethics that govern the practices of educators in school communities. The educators' role in guiding and building the learning capacity of young children is extremely important in developing a culture of learning and academic success that defines optimal student and teacher performance.

Character Education and the Early Childhood Program

Developing character and ethical responsibility in today's students and providing academic and social direction are the mainstays of current instruction. Thinking about developing judgment and direction for young students who have cognitive and physiological problems that may prevent application of the learning is its own dilemma for educators.

Ethical instruction must come from a variety of alternative resources dedicated to the promotion of educational development of young learners. By including ethical dilemmas in curriculum design and instructional practice, educators can address student ethical behavior within the guise of the curriculum expectations.

In elementary classrooms, teachers can use the following diversity of activities to develop character and ethical responsibility in early childhood programs:

- Artistic designs to help students think about everyday ethical dilemmas
- Ethical journals to help students keep daily journals on daily school experiences
- Cooperative team activities to build character education such as role playing school dilemmas and outcomes
- Assessments that provide students with scenarios to evaluate and apply solutions in ethical dilemmas and character education issues.
- Classroom discussions on student centered ethical issues

When students can share their daily experiences and their understanding of their world in a safe and nurturing learning environment, they can evaluate and redirect ethical issues that occur during the school day and build character in the process.

Working well with Colleagues

Administrators should include ethical expectations for students and staff in handbooks that clearly define outlines of behavioral and ethical operatives. Progressive school communities provide professional development on ethics training and strategies on construct and implementation of ethical discussion and activities in subject area expectations.

By incorporating a core of ethical expectations for both students and staff, school communities set the tone and school climate for accountability in action. In order to help students develop an ethical compass in behavior and performance in classrooms, educational staff must include ethical issues in classroom instruction and implementation. Professional modeling of expected student behavior and ethical standards by adults in the school community will provide an adult compass for students seeking to develop their inner source of ethical values and character.

Professional development for staff on ethical concerns in curriculum and instructional practices must provide consistent implementation throughout the school community. Practical strategies for dealing with the myriad of daily expectations and dilemmas in learning environments should be the cornerstone of staff development that improves staff collaboration and ethical character.

Connecting Ethics to the Community

School-wide community building activities that provide a connective bridge of ethical character building for students, parents, staff, and community members can present effective community outreach opportunities. Ethical development for students who take part in community programs after school can align with ethical expectations from the school community.

In order to connect the existing school code of ethical character building to the community, educators can use the following strategies to maintain effective networking between schools and communities:

- Create community links and technology websites between schools and communities to develop a consistency of the school's ethical codes and expectations for students participating in community support programs.
- Share the schools' code of ethics by providing community members with a copy of the handbook or by directing members to the school's website on ethical expectations and character building.

- Develop a collaborative community and school ethics panel for consultation and as a source for speakers on the subject of student and staff ethical character building.
- Engage in community based professional development on ethics workshops and invite community members to school workshops on ethical implementation in classrooms.

COMPETENCY 4.0   KNOWLEDGE OF EFFECTIVE PRACTICES

Skill 4.1   Identify developmentally appropriate practices that guide effective instruction

The effective teacher selects learning activities based on specific learning objectives. Ideally, teachers should not plan activities that fail to augment the specific objectives of the lesson. They should plan activities with a learning objective in mind. Objective-driven learning activities tend to serve as a tool to reinforce the teacher's lesson presentation. In addition, learning objectives should be consistent with state and district educational goals that focus on National educational goals (Goals 2000) and the specific strengths and weaknesses of individual students assigned to the teacher's class.

The effective teacher takes care to select appropriate activities and classroom situations in which learning is optimized. The classroom teacher should manipulate instructional activities and classroom conditions in a manner that enhances group and individual learning opportunities. For example, the classroom teacher can organize group learning activities that place students in a situation that requires cooperation, sharing ideas, and discussion. Cooperative learning activities help students learn to collaborate and share personal and cultural ideas and values in a classroom learning environment.

The effective teacher introduces learning activities them in a meaningful instructional sequence. Teachers should combine instructional activities so that they reinforce information .

If an educational program is child-centered, then it will surely address the abilities and needs of the students because it will take its cues from students' interests, concerns, and questions. Making an educational program child-centered involves building on the natural curiosity children bring to school and asking children what they want to learn.

Teachers help students identify their own questions, puzzles, and goals and then structure widening circles of experience and investigation of those topics. Teachers manage to infuse all the skills, knowledge, and concepts that society mandates into a child-driven curriculum. But teachers respond to more than the students' explicit cues. They also draw on their understanding of children's developmental needs and enthusiasms and design experiences that lead children into new areas interest and engage them—areas they might not choose on their own. Teachers also share their own interests and enthusiasms in the classroom to motivate students

Implementing such a child-centered curriculum requires careful and deliberate planning, which helps the teacher organize instruction and influences classroom teaching. Well thought-out planning includes specifying behavioral objectives and students' entry behavior (knowledge and skills), selecting and sequencing learning activities that move students from entry behavior to objective, and evaluating the outcomes of instruction in order to improve planning.

Planning for instructional activities entails identification or selection of the activities the teacher and students will engage in during a period of instruction. Planning is a multifaceted activity that includes the following: determining the order in which activities will be completed; specifying the component parts of an activity including their order, the materials to be used for each part, and the particular roles of the teacher and students; deciding the amount of time to be spent on a given activity and the number of activities to be completed during a period of instruction; judging the appropriateness of an activity for a particular situation; and specifying the organization of the class for the activity.

Attention to learner needs during planning is foremost and includes identifying what the students already know or need to know; matching learner needs with such instructional elements as content, materials, activities, and goals; and, following instruction, determining whether or not students performed at an acceptable level.

Skill 4.2   Identify the components of effective organization and management, such as classroom rituals, routines, and schedules

Punctuality is when a "teacher begins class work promptly." If class is delayed for ten minutes each day, almost two months of instruction is lost during the school year. Therefore, beginning class on time is very important. Effective teachers are punctual because punctuality leads to more on-task time, which results in greater subject matter retention among the students.

A number of circumstances, such as attendance, discipline, or just getting students to settle down, can delay the beginning of instruction. Effective teachers have predetermined plans to deal with these distractions.

Teachers can complete the daily task of attendance efficiently and quickly with the use of a seating chart. A teacher can spot absentees in seconds by noting the empty seats rather than calling each student's name, which could take as long as five minutes. This laborious roll-calling sets up the ideal situation for deviant behaviors, which result in further off-task time. Therefore, the use of seating charts leads to more on-task time. Laminating the seating chart is another timesaving technique because the teacher can make daily notes right on the chart. The teacher can use the chart to keep track of who is volunteering and who is answering questions and use this information to create an equitable classroom climate for all students.

In today's classrooms, deviant behavior leads to more off-task time than any other factor. Effective teachers reduce the incidence of these behaviors through clear-cut rules and consistency. If the teacher is consistent, then the students know what to expect and learn very quickly that they, too, must be consistent. Beginning-teacher programs teach that effective teachers state the rules, explain the rules, and then put the students through a guided practice of the rules. This results in a clear understanding of what behaviors are expected in the classroom from each student. Moreover, reducing the occurrence of deviant behaviors is more efficient than dealing with them when they happen. Effective teachers achieve this efficiency through clear-cut rule explication and consistent monitoring.

Furthermore, effective teachers maintain a business-like atmosphere in the classroom. This atmosphere leads to the students getting on-task quickly when instruction begins. Effective teachers can use a variety of methods to begin instruction immediately. Using overhead projectors is one method.

The teacher turns on the overhead the second class begins, and the students begin taking notes. The teacher is then free to circulate for the first few minutes of class and settle down individual students as necessary. In addition, when a teacher has a regular routine for the beginning of class, students can begin without waiting for teacher instruction.

Effective teachers use class time efficiently, which results in higher student-subject engagement and more subject matter retention. One way teachers use class time efficiently is through a smooth transition from one activity to another, known as *management transition*. Using management transition, the "teacher shifts from one activity to another in a systemic, academically oriented way." One factor that contributes to efficient management transition is the teacher's management of instructional material. Management of instructional material is defined as "teacher preparation of readily available materials that are to be used for a particular segment of instruction[jmm16]." Effective teachers gather their materials during the planning stage of instruction and, therefore, avoid flipping through materials looking for the items necessary for the current lesson. Momentum is lost, student concentration is broken, and deviant behaviors escalate when teachers appear disorganized.

In conclusion, effective teachers use class time efficiently. The teacher understands that beginning class promptly is important because an enormous amount of teaching time can be lost if instruction is delayed. Therefore, effective teachers take attendance and complete other non-academic tasks routinely while maintaining on-task behavior among the students.

In addition, teachers who keep students informed of the sequencing of instructional activities maintain systematic transitions because the students are prepared to move on to the next activity. We describe sequencing of instructional activity as "teacher cites an order or pattern for a series of activities." For example, the teacher says, "When we finish with this guided practice together, we will turn to page twenty-three and each student will do the exercises. I will then circulate throughout the classroom helping on an individual basis. Okay, let's begin." Following an example such as this leads to systematic, smooth transitions between activities because the students will turn to page twenty-three when the class finishes the practice without a break in concentration.

Another method that leads to smooth transitions is moving students in groups and clusters rather than one by one or *group fragmentation*. For example, if some students do seat work while other students gather for a reading group, the teacher moves the students in predetermined groups.

Instead of calling the individual names of the reading group, which would be time consuming and laborious, the teacher simply says, "Will the blue reading group please assemble at the reading station. The red and yellow groups will quietly do the vocabulary assignment I am now passing out." As a result of this activity, the classroom is ready to move on in a matter of seconds rather than minutes.

The teacher may also employ academic transition signals. An academic transition signals is a "teacher utterance that indicate[s] movement of the lesson from one topic or activity to another by indicating where the lesson is and where it is going." For example, the teacher may say, "That completes our description of clouds; now we will examine weather fronts." Like the sequencing of instructional materials, this method keeps the students informed on what is coming next so they will move to the next activity with little or no break in concentration.

Therefore, effective teachers manage transitions from one activity to another in a systematic way through efficiently managing instructional matter, sequencing instructional activities, moving students in groups, and employing academic transition signals. This efficient use of class time increases achievement because students spend more class time engaged in on-task behavior.

Effective teachers have rules that deal with controlled interruptions. Controlled interruptions happen when a "teacher enforces rules and procedures to be followed by students who are tardy to class or who do not have their supplies, etc." Teachers who give a high level of directions run the most efficient classrooms. Rule explication and monitoring is the best way to set the tone for this classroom atmosphere. Rule explication and monitoring happen when a "teacher specifies rules of conduct, explains them, provides practice in their use, and consistently checks student conduct by the rules."

For example, when a student returns to class after being absent, he or she places his or her parent note in the box on the teacher's desk designated for this purpose. The student is aware that the teacher will deal with it after the class is engaged and when time allows. The student then proceeds to the side counter where extra copies of yesterday's work are located. The student takes the work and sits down to begin today's class work. The student is aware that the teacher will deal with individual instructions during seatwork time when it will not disrupt the class momentum. The teacher explained the procedures for this instance at the beginning of the year, and, through constant monitoring, the student is aware of what is expected of him or her in this situation. Because the teacher specified classroom procedures for controlled interruptions, the classroom momentum is maintained, and on-task time is increased. The result is increased achievement because on-task time directly correlates to student achievement.

Therefore, effective teachers have rules in place dealing with controlled interruptions. The teacher has used rule explication and monitoring to ensure that students will follow these rules. For a rule to be effective, the teacher must state the rule, explain the rule, lead the students through a guided practice of the rule and then consistently monitor the rule to insure compliance. The monitoring process is teaches the students that they must also be consistent in these matters.

Effective teachers deal with daily classroom procedures efficiently and quickly because then students will spend the majority of class time engaged in academic tasks that will likely result in higher achievement. Various studies have shown that the high achieving classrooms spend less time on off-task behavior. For example, C.W. Fisher, et al, in a 1978 study, found that, in the average classroom, students spent about eight minutes an hour engaged in off-task behavior. However, this time was reduced to about four minutes in high achieving classrooms. Therefore, effective teachers spend less time on daily housekeeping chores.

Housekeeping is when a teacher [jmm17] routinely uses the same procedures and approaches each day for activities such as passing papers out, moving to get books, writing on the board, etc., and has materials prepared, procedures worked out, and everything in order [jmm19] For example, it is advisable that teachers presort papers into rows and have the first person in the row distribute them. This procedure achieves the laborious task of passing back papers in a few minutes. This same technique is useful for distributing books. The teacher may ask the students in the first seat to pick up enough books for their row and pass them out. Using this technique keeps the majority of the students in their seats and completes the task quickly. The teacher could also place the proper number of books on the front desks while students are finishing the last lesson. In this case, students have been told not to pass the books back until instructed to do so. Regardless of the technique used by the teacher, it should planned to use as little of class time as possible. Instructing the students about daily routine activities early in the year leads to a more efficient use of class time on a daily basis.

Effective teachers have carefully planned lessons with all materials in order before class. This *management of instructional material* is "teacher preparation of materials that are to be used for a particular segment of instruction readily available." In other words, if a teacher is going to use a chart or a map in a lesson, the chart or map is already prepared and in place in the classroom before class begins. Furthermore, all materials are copied and in order ready to pass out as needed. This efficient distribution of materials results in less off-task time.

Therefore, effective teachers establish routines for daily housekeeping activities to minimize the amount of time spent on them. They have all materials prepared before class and have them in order to facilitate speedy distribution.

Learn more strategies for effective classroom management:

http://specialed.about.com/od/classroommanagement/a/consequences.htm

http://www.teachervision.fen.com/teaching-methods/classroom-management/7236.html

Skill 4.3   Identify ways to organize furniture, equipment, materials, and other resources in an indoor and/or outdoor environment

A well organized classroom often begins with the room's physical composition—the arrangement of desks, the attractiveness of bulletin boards, and the storage of supplies and materials. By identifying various ways of organizing learning space, teachers can create a caring and child-centered environment.

The physical layout of a classroom should reflect the teacher as a warm and caring professional. Teachers should give the classroom a personal touch with potted plants, colorful art, rugs, posters, and even some over-sized cozy pillows for the reading corner.

Teachers can create different learning areas within the classroom. For example, a quiet reading corner with pillows to relax on, listening stations where students can listen to music through the use of headphones while completing work, a large table for group projects, multimedia centers, several learning stations, and individual work areas. Easily accessible supplies and materials can eliminate delays and confusion as students prepare for activities.

In the majority of classrooms, student desks occupy most of the floor. Some teachers like to arrange desks in groups of four; others prefer a U-shaped arrangement that gives every student a front row seat. Most importantly, teachers should arrange the desks so that he or she can make eye contact with every student. If the arrangement of the room doesn't work, teachers should be ready to make changes.

Environmental preferences such as lighting, noise level, and room temperature are factors that can affect students in various ways and are often directly related to individual learning styles. A number of students learn best in bright light, but others learn considerably better in low-lighted areas. Bright light can actually cause some students to become restless and hyperactive. Teachers can provide listening stations with headsets for children who need sound; and quiet, comfortable study areas for those who learn best in a silent environment. Teachers should encourage students to dress according to their bodies' temperatures, so that students are not uncomfortable and can concentrate fully on their schoolwork.

SEE also Skill 4.13

> **Compare sample classroom floor plans:**
>
> http://www.learnnc.org/lp/pages/Environ6

Skill 4.4   Identify the components of a print-rich environment (e.g., word walls, classroom libraries, labeled objects, student work displayed) and the impact of such an environment on classroom instruction

A child's concept of print develops through repeated exposure to literature. Children quickly learn that stories and other texts are written from left to right, that the spaces between words matter, and that words on a page correspond with the words the reader is speaking.

Components of a print-rich environment

Classroom Libraries
Students need many opportunities to read and comprehend a wide assortment of books and other texts. Classroom libraries should offer students a variety of reading materials, and the teacher should attempt to build a collection with various genres of children's literature. The reading difficulty should vary to include multiple levels of reading; a number of the books should be easy to read while others are more challenging and of increasing difficulty and complexity. Libraries should include a variety of topics to interest all students, and diversity of books and their themes should also be considered.

Word Walls

A word wall is an organized collection of words displayed on a classroom wall to support students in correctly spelling high frequency words. The words should include the words students encounter in their daily reading and writing and words they frequently misspell. Word-wall words can be arranged alphabetically, by spelling patterns, or by themes. Activities with a word wall include clapping out the letters in a word, solving mystery words, making word cards, and organizing them by parts of speech, by letters, or by subjects and themes.

SEE also Skill 6.2

Labeling

Labeling items in the classroom takes word walls to another level. Labels provide another everyday visual of words that are commonly encountered in a classroom. Labeling can also be done in multiple languages to promote diversity.

Displays

Teachers should display the students' work throughout the room. Children can be encouraged to dictate titles for their own artwork and "stories". The students' work should be placed at the children's eye level for the other students to read, recognize, and enjoy.

Experiences with print (through writing and reading) help young children develop a better appreciation and understanding of the purposes and functions of print. A print-rich environment contributes to the students' phonological awareness and letter recognition. Children can then begin to acquire early reading proficiency by developing word-recognition skills.

Skill 4.5   Identify strategies for short- and long-term planning to set instructional goals in alignment with standards for developing teacher objectives

Instructional goals are a clear statement of the planning that is needed to develop teacher objectives in accordance with required standards.

By identifying strategies that specify the instructional goals that need to be aligned with the standards that need be achieved, teachers can plan effective objectives. The target objectives are clearer statements of the specific activities required to achieve the goals of the lessons.

After the goals have been developed, the objectives should be written for each goal. The objectives are the measurements that support the goals.

Objectives should be as follows:

1. adaptable to timelines
2. concise and to the point
3. clear
4. observable

By designing realistic instructional objectives, teachers can plan short and long term goals that are achievable.

> **For tips on writing lesson plans:**
>
> http://www.huntington.edu/education/lessonplanning/Plans.html

Skill 4.6 **Identify strategies for designing appropriate objectives and developing and implementing lesson plans**

Successful lesson plans should have a logical sequence that enables learning to take place effectively. The material should be organized in a method that encourages student comprehension and learning. Effective lesson plans aid the teacher in preparing the lessons and provide the means for implementing the instructional material.

Objectives provide the basis for the entire lesson plan. Teachers should always give careful thought into the design and development of appropriate objectives. Teachers should consider addressing all levels of learning and critical thinking when developing their lesson objectives (*see Bloom's taxonomy in Skill 6.14, page 118.*). The objectives of a lesson plan must always be student centered. The phrase, "The student will......" should be used in writing the lesson objectives. By implementing this strategy teachers can focus on what the student is expected to learn.

Implementing Lesson Plans

All lessons should have an introduction, body, and conclusion. In many instances, developing the body of the lesson before writing the introduction and conclusion is more effective By constructing the body of the lesson first, the teacher is in a better position to decide how to introduce the lesson and then conclude the lesson by emphasizing the main ideas. The body of the lesson is where the teacher decides how to organize the main points and sub points of the lesson.

Each lesson should include definitions of new words or concepts. Teachers should include examples, perhaps a personal experience that the students can relate to, in order to give the students information so they may connect with prior learning. If students are unfamiliar with the information, the teacher can do a compare-and-contrast concept.

Each lesson plan answers three questions—WHAT? HOW? WHY? The introduction outlines the lesson and tells the students what they will be learning. The introduction should spark the students' interest in the subject and motivate them to eagerly learn the lesson. The introduction should flow smoothly and effortlessly into the body of the lesson.

The conclusion should emphasize the main points of the lesson. The final summary should also emphasize the objectives of the lesson plan. Teachers should also allow extra time at the end of the lesson for questions and to clarify and explain the lesson.

Finally, teachers should reflect on a lesson when it has been completed and make notes of what to adapt and evaluate whether or not the lesson achieved the objective(s).

Skill 4.7   Identify activities that enrich and extend active learning through the selection and use of developmentally and age-appropriate instructional materials

In considering suitable learning materials for the classroom, the teacher must have a thorough understanding of the state-mandated competency-based curriculum. According to state requirements, certain objectives must be met in each subject taught at every designated level of instruction. The teacher must become well acquainted with the curriculum to which he or she is assigned. The teacher must also be aware that it is unlawful to require students to study from textbooks or materials other than those approved by the state Department of Education.

In choosing materials, teachers should also keep in mind that students not only learn at different rates, they also bring a variety of cognitive styles to the learning process. Prior experiences influence the individual's cognitive style or method of accepting, processing, and retaining information. According to Marshall Rosenberg, students can be categorized as follows:

1. rigid-inhibited
2. undisciplined
3. acceptance-anxious
4. creative

"The creative learner is an independent thinker, one who maximizes his/her abilities, can work by him/herself, enjoys learning, and is self-critical." This last category constitutes the ideal, but teachers should make every effort to use materials that will stimulate and hold the attention of learners of all types.

Keeping in mind what is understood about the students' abilities and interests, the teacher should design a course of study that presents units of instruction in an orderly sequence. The instruction should be planned so as to advance all students toward the next level of instruction; however, exit behaviors need not be identical because of the inevitability of individual differences.

Textbooks

Most teachers use textbooks that are suitable to the age and developmental level of specific student populations. Textbooks reflect the values and assumptions of the society that produces them, but they also represent the knowledge and skills considered to be essential for an educated adult. Finally, textbooks are useful to the school bureaucracy and the community because they make public and accessible the private world of the classroom.

Though these factors may favor the adoption of textbooks, the individual teacher may have only limited choice about which textbooks to use, since the school administration or the local school district (in observance of the state guidelines) often makes such decisions. If teachers are consulted about textbook selection, they probably have little training in evaluation techniques, and they are seldom granted leave time to encourage informed decisions. On those occasions when teachers are asked to assist in the selection process, they should ask, above all, whether the textbooks have real substance—is World War II accurately chronicled, does the science textbook correctly conceptualize electrical current, do literary selections reflect a full range of genre?

From time to time, controversy has arisen about the possible weakness of textbooks—the preponderance of pictures and illustrations, the avoidance of controversy in social studies textbooks, the lack of emphasis on problem-solving in science books. In the 1980's, certain books were criticized for their attention to *liberal* or *secular* values, and the creationism versus evolution argument has re-surfaced again and again. Finally, recent decades have witnessed a movement to grant more attention to women, Afro-Americans, and other groups whose contributions to our developing culture may have been overlooked in earlier textbooks. Individual teachers would be well advised to keep themselves informed of current trends or developments, in order to make better informed choices for their students and deal with the possibility of parental concern.

Focusing on the needs evident in almost any classroom population, the teacher will want to use textbooks that include activities and selections to challenge the most advanced students as well as those who have difficulty mastering the material at a moderate pace. The teacher can eliminate some of the exercises for faster learners, and students who have difficulty may need to have material arranged into brief steps or sections. For almost any class, some experience in co-operative learning is advisable. The faster learners will reinforce what they have already mastered, and those of lesser ability at the tasks in question can ask about their individual problems or areas of concern. Teachers can use most textbook exercises intended for independent work in cooperative learning, though in most cases, teachers encourage better participation he or she asks the cooperating group to hand in a single paper or project that represents their combined efforts, rather than individual papers or projects.

Technological Materials

Aside from textbooks, a wide variety of materials are available to today's teachers. Microcomputers are now commonplace, and some schools can now afford laser discs to bring alive the content of a reference book in text, motion, and sound. Hand-held calculators eliminate the need for drill and practice in number facts, and they also support mathematical problem solving and process. Videocassettes (VCRs) are common and permit the use of home-produced or commercially produced tapes.

Textbook publishers often provide films, recordings, and software to accompany the text and maps, graphics, and colorful posters to help students visualize what is being taught. Teachers can usually scan the educational publishers' brochures that arrive at their school offices on a frequent basis. Attending workshops or conferences is another way to stay current in the field. On those occasions when educational publishers are asked to display their latest productions and revised editions of materials, teachers are enthusiastically welcomed.

In addition, yesterday's libraries are today's media centers. Teachers can usually have opaque projectors delivered to the classroom to project print or pictorial images (including student work) onto a screen for classroom viewing. Some teachers have replaced chalkboards with projectors that reproduce print or images on plastic sheets known as transparencies, which the teacher can write on during a presentation or have machine-printed in advance. In either case, the teacher can easily store the transparency for later use. In an art class, photography class, or any class in which displaying visual materials is helpful, the teacher can easily project slides onto a wall or a screen.

Cameras are inexpensive enough that students can photograph and display their own work and provide a record of their achievements for teacher files or student portfolios.

Studies have shown that students learn best when information taught in lecture and textbook reading is presented more than once in various formats. In some instances, students themselves may be asked to reinforce what they have learned by completing some original production—for example, by drawing pictures to explain some scientific process, by writing a monologue or dialogue to express what some historical figure might have said on some occasion, by devising a board game to challenge the players' mathematical skills, or by acting out (and perhaps filming) episodes from a classroom reading selection. Students usually enjoy having their work displayed or presented to an audience of peers. Thus, their productions may supplement and personalize the learning experiences that the teacher has planned for them.

Factoring In Student Readiness

Keeping in mind the state requirements concerning the objectives and materials, the teacher must determine the abilities of the incoming students assigned to his or her class or supervision. Teachers must be aware of students' entry behavior—their current level of achievement in the relevant areas. Next, the teacher must look at a broad overview of what students are expected to learn before they are passed to the next grade or level of instruction. Finally, the teacher must design a course of study that will help students reach the necessary level of achievement that will be displayed in their final assessments, or exit behaviors. Teachers must select textbooks and learning materials that fit into this context.

Consulting the students' prior academic records might be helpful in determining their abilities. The teacher can take into account letter grades assigned at previous levels of instruction and scores on standardized tests. In addition, the teacher may choose to administer pre-tests at the beginning of the school year and perhaps at the initial stage of each new unit of instruction. The textbooks available for classroom use may provide suitable pre-tests, tests of student progress, and post-tests.

In selecting tests and other assessment tools, the teacher should keep in mind that different kinds of tests measure different aspects of student development. The tests included in most textbooks chosen for the classroom and in the teacher's book that accompanies them are usually achievement tests. Few of these tests are designed to measure the students' inherent ability or aptitude. Teachers will find it difficult to raise students' scores on ability tests, but students' scores on achievement tests can improve with proper instruction and application in the area being studied.

In addition to administering tests, the teacher may assess the readiness of students for a particular level of instruction by having them demonstrate their ability to perform some relevant task. In a class that emphasizes written composition, for example, students may be asked to submit writing samples. The teacher uses these samples to ensure that students are placed at the proper level and as a diagnostic tool to help students understand what aspects of their composition skills may need improvement. Students in a speech class may be asked to make an impromptu oral presentation before beginning a new level or specific level of instruction. Others may be asked to demonstrate their psychomotor skills in a physical education class or display their computational skills in a mathematics class. Whatever the chosen task, the teacher must select or devise an appropriate assessment scale and interpret the results with care.

If students are informed about their entry behaviors on such a scale, they will be better motivated, especially if they are able to observe their progress by some objective means at suitable intervals during the course. For this reason, recording the results of such assessments in the student's portfolios in the teacher's records may be advisable.

Teachers may also simply ask students about their previous experience or knowledge of the subject or task at hand. While their comments may not be completely reliable indicators of what they know or understand, such discussions do providing an idea of the students' interest in what is being taught. Teachers can have little impact unless they can demonstrate the relevancy of the material to the students' lives.

Skill 4.8 Identify a variety of methods of flexibly grouping children for the purposes of instruction

Children learn at different paces because of prior experiences, personal situations, abilities, interests, and other issues. Today, teachers use flexible grouping strategies to address the different learning needs of various students, and they are beginning to change the ways they organize their classrooms.

Depending on the lesson objectives and classroom participants, teachers are starting to consider group dynamics when planning instruction. Using flexible grouping, teachers can provide various levels of differentiating learning when it is needed. Below are some of the most common organization methods for flexible student grouping.

Teacher-led groups

- Whole class instruction such as lecture or mini-lessons
- Small group instruction such as guided reading
- Teacher-directed activities such as workshops

Student Groups

- Collaborative groups such as circle sharing
- Performance-base groups such as group study or interviews
- Student dyads (pair work) such as "think, pair, share"

The following is a small sampling of teacher-created, team building activities for elementary school children that are available for sharing with colleagues through the Internet. Thousands of similar lesson plans and activities are available to address the development of social and academic skills through teamwork among young children in the classroom setting.

Author: Group Stories

An activity where students can create stories as a group. Several variations are available.

Spider Web

In this team building activity, students can get to know each other while creating a unique design.

Trading Cards

Children can share information about themselves by creating personalized trading cards. This activity could be used as an *ice-breaker*.

Can You Build It?

Students can work together toward a common goal in this team activity. It can also be used as an *ice-breaker*.

Who Am I?

Children can use this activity to get to know each other by sharing about themselves and working together.

Ideas for Working With Kids

Suggestions for games to help students get to know each other and build group cohesion.

Mad Minute Relay

Students can learn math in a team environment with this timed activity.

All of Me

This activity can help students get to know each other by drawing pictures that show some of the different aspects of their lives and sharing the pictures with classmates.

We're Different/We're Alike

By using Venn diagrams to describe the ways in which they are similar and different, students can learn more about each other with this lesson.

Make a Class Pictogram

Children can use this activity to help them understand the nature of social groups and their roles as members of various groups.

It's Too Loud in Here!

This lesson plan gives students the opportunity to work as a team and participate in decision making processes in the classroom.

A-Z Teacher's Stuff: Teamwork

What does it mean to be a team? In this lesson plan, students define teamwork and work together in groups.

The teacher must remain current with the studies and findings published in numerous journals related to child and educational psychology and physical and intellectual development in early childhood.

For example, several studies—past and present—have shown that girls tend to be more communicative with each other, and boys are prone to be more physically active together. Boys, however, are less responsive to verbal interaction with each other. Although a generalization, this information still predicts that an effective grouping will include an approximately equal mix of girls and boys with the teacher monitoring and encouraging the participation of all in each aspect of the planned activity.

As in this example, awareness of research and findings in the study of childhood development will inform the teacher's application of appropriate groupings and goals for developing teamwork among younger students.

Skill 4.9   Identify methods for prevention of and intervention for common emergent literacy difficulties

Children begin to learn language at a very young age. Their speech and language skills become increasingly more complex as they grow and mature. They begin to use language to express their ideas and feelings and also to communicate with others. Children begin to interact with print, through books, magazines, and signs by recognizing letters and words. Children soon begin to sing rhyming words, scribble with crayons, point out logos, and recognize some letters of the alphabet. This phase, known as emergent literacy, begins in early childhood and continues through the early school years.

Early Warning Signs

Parents and teachers should be aware of early warning signs of emergent literacy difficulties. These include the following:

- failure in identifying or recognizing letters in the child's own name
- lack of interest in singsong rhymes
- difficulty learning and remembering names and shapes of letters
- trouble comprehending simple instructions

Intervention and prevention of emergent literacy difficulties is most advantageous when these difficulties are diagnosed early in the preschool period. If not caught early, they are often persistent and influence the children's language and literacy learning throughout the following school years.

Methods for intervention

- Encourage the child to name or describe objects, people, and events in their everyday lives.
- Read picture and story books that focus on sounds and rhymes.
- Introduce new vocabulary words during holidays and special activities.
- Encourage the child to describe a story about his/her drawing and write down the words.

If the teacher or parent suspects a serious problem, a certified speech-language pathologist should be contacted.

SEE also Skill 1.4 and Skill 6.3

Skill 4.10   Identify characteristics of an integrated curriculum

An integrated curriculum is a program of study that describes a movement toward integrated lessons. This program helps students make connections across curricula. This curriculum links lessons among the humanities, art, natural sciences, mathematics, music, and social studies.

Especially with young students, an integrated curriculum efficiently ties knowledge from various subjects together. Integrating subjects creates mental links between material and helps students retain the information.

The integrated curriculum teaches students to break down barriers between subjects. Teachers plan lessons around broad themes, such as the environment, with which students can identify. Major concepts are pulled from this broad theme, and teachers then plan activities that teach these concepts.

Characteristics of an integrated curriculum

- A combination of subjects
- An emphasis on projects
- Sources that go beyond textbooks
- Relationships among concepts
- Thematic units as organizing principles
- Flexible schedules
- Flexible student groupings

Integrated curriculum education is organized in such a way that it cuts across subject-matter lines and brings various aspects of the curriculum into meaningful association to focus upon broad areas of study. It views learning and teaching in a holistic way and reflects the real world, which is interactive (Humphreys, Post, and Ellis).

> **Learn more about an integrated curriculum:**
>
> http://www.nwrel.org/scpd/sir s/8/c016.html

Skill 4.11   Identify characteristics of play relating to the child's social, emotional, and cognitive development

Too often, recess and play are considered peripheral or unimportant to a child's development. People often view recess as a tradition of childhood or a way for children to release physical energy. Play is, however, very important to human development. In our country, even though we are very industrious, we believe strongly that all individuals deserve time to relax and enjoy life.

But even more importantly, for children—who will soon be active citizens of our democracy, parents, spouses, friends, colleagues, and neighbors—play is an activity that helps teach such basic values as sharing and cooperation. It also teaches that taking care of oneself, as opposed to constantly working, is good for human beings and further creates a more enjoyable society.

The stages of play development move from solitary in infancy to cooperative in early childhood, but even in early childhood, children should be able to play on their own and entertain themselves from time to time. Children who do not know what to do with themselves when they are bored should be encouraged to think about particular activities that might be of interest.

Children must also play with peers. While the emerging stages of cooperative play may be awkward, since children will at first not want to share toys, for example, children learn how to be good peers and friends with some guidance and experience.

Play—both cooperative and solitary—helps develop very important attributes in children. For example, children learn and develop personal interests and practice particular skills. The play that children engage in may even develop future professional interests.

Finally, playing with objects helps develop motor skills. The objects that children play with should be varied and age appropriate. For example, playing with a doll can actually develop hand-eye coordination. Sports for both boys and girls is equally valuable. Parents and teachers, though, need to remember that sports at young ages should only be for the purpose of development of interests and motor skills—not competition. Many children will learn that they do not enjoy sports, and parents and teachers should respect these decisions.

In general, play is an appropriate place of children to learn many things about themselves, their world, and their interests. Children should be encouraged to participate in different types of play, and they should be watched over as they encounter new types of play.

Skill 4.12 **Identify methods of observing, facilitating, and extending children's play to practice newly acquired competencies through problem solving, imitation, persistence, and creativity**

Today's hurried lifestyles, changes in family structure, and increased attention to academic, have reduced play time. We should remove barriers to children's opportunities to play. When children's lives are overscheduled with activities, sports, and classes, they do not have time to themselves and time for unstructured play. When children watch too much television, their play often mimics what they see on TV or the computer screen, and this mimicry robs them of valuable time for imagination and creativity. A child's "I'm bored" may be a cry for more unstructured time for play not less.

Through play, children create and explore a world they can master and conquer their fears while practicing their adult roles, sometimes with other children and sometimes with adult caregivers. This practice leads to increased confidence and the resiliency they will need to face challenges in the future. While adults are often involved in playing with young children, adults should be careful not to control the play. Undirected play teaches children decision-making skills, creativity, leadership, and group skills.

Adults should join in on what the child is doing and talk with the child. Children are endlessly curious and often ask "Why?" Instead of being exasperated by the continuous questioning, adults should encourage questions and answer them to the best of their ability. Adults must respect the unusual ideas of children and show them that their ideas have value. As you interact with a child at play, offer help when needed, raise questions to stimulate thought, and give wholehearted approval of the child's honest attempts.

Passive toys like computers require limited imagination. Imaginative play, allows children to create situations for themselves and work out solutions and reactions. Providing such toys as blocks, dolls, and dress up clothes encourages this kind of play. Providing such raw materials of all kinds as sand, paint and scraps of paper also supports creative play. Adventure play involves overcoming obstacles, gaining new skills, and exercising and using coordination.

Repetition is an important aspect of children's play. Doing the same thing over and over may be boring to the adult caregiver, but through repetition, the child masters the new skill and then moves on to experimentation and creativity.

Children at play reveal many things about themselves. Adults should observe and listen for the child to reveal his or her hopes, fears, and joys. With this knowledge, the adult can provide materials and opportunities for continued learning in the areas of interest.

Most importantly, adults should provide opportunities for learning and discovery without the threat of immediate evaluation. Teachers and parents should help each child experience some success every day, develop a healthy attitude toward mistakes, and gradually assume responsibilities in the care of materials. This feeling of security will leave the child free to think, imagine, select, and make decisions.

> **For further reading about how children learn through play:**
>
> http://www.teachers.ab.ca/Quick+Links/Publications/The+Learning+Team/Volume+6/Number+3/Children+learn+through+play.htm

Skill 4.13 **Identify ways to adapt and organize space, equipment, facilities, and materials to create an environment that supports early childhood curricula and the development of the whole child**

Public education should be concerned with much more than academic standards. School is a place where children learn skills of good citizenship, time management, goal setting, and decision-making. But teachers must be deliberate about teaching these skills. Like most good teaching, though, students will have much more success learning these skills if they get the opportunity to practice them. Therefore, a classroom should be like a little community where children get opportunities to help with chores and maintain responsibility for certain activities. Some of the ways teachers can provide these opportunities include setting up stations and centers throughout the classroom. In a classroom that contains various centers, student desks are only one physical component of the room. Teachers can set up student mailboxes to store certain materials. They can also arrange manipulatives and other classroom objects in various places where students are required to maintain and keep clean.

Many teachers rotate various chores each week to provide children with these opportunities. One student might be responsible for ensuring that materials get distributed to students. Another student might supervise clean-up time. Another student might help prepare manipulatives. Not only does this type of activity improve the students' time management and organizational skills, it creates a classroom community that is motivating to students. Students feel safer and more included in their classroom environment.

In addition to physical classroom arrangement and student responsibility, teachers should focus on teaching children skills for time management and goal setting. Teachers can use a variety of materials and expectations to do this. For example, many teachers have students write down class-time agendas each morning and then set personal goals for the school day. Then, they might have their students reflect on whether or not they met these goals and whether or not they successfully completed all agenda items.

Teachers can also discuss longer-term goals. Teachers might work with students on an individual basis to set personal academic goals. Students should be encouraged to come up with their own goals with the assistance of teachers. Teachers can help students focus on goals that might be related to current performance and interests. Then, students should have frequent opportunities to reflect on their goals, consider their work toward those goals, and alter goals as they go along.

Finally, learning centers, although usually for teaching content-area skills, can be great tools for teaching responsibility and independence. Teachers can use this time particularly to work independently with students. While they do so, students in small groups travel from one center to another, completing various learning activities. For example, one center might ask students to read a story together and answer a few questions. Another center might have computers and require that students complete various computer-based learning activities. These activities promote independent and group learning skills and give students opportunities to set and monitor short-term goals.

The effective teacher is aware of students' individual learning styles and human growth and development theory and applies these principles in selecting and implementing appropriate instructional activities.

Learning activities selected for younger students, below age eight, should focus on short time frames and highly simplified forms. The nature and content of the activity affects the approach that the students will take in processing the information. Younger children tend to process information at a slower rate than children over the age of eight.

SEE also Skill 4.3

COMPETENCY 5.0 KNOWLEDGE OF ISSUES AND STRATEGIES FOR FAMILY AND COMMUNITY INVOLVEMENT

Skill 5.1 Identify strategies for encouraging and facilitating family and community partnerships in all phases of school programs

Connecting School to the Outside World

According to Campbell, Campbell, and Dickinson (1992) *Teaching and Learning Through Multiple Intelligences*, "The changing nature of demographics is one of the strongest rationales for multicultural education in the United States." The Census Bureau prediction about the changing demographic for the American population and school communities between 1990 and 2030 states that "while the white population will increase by 25 percent, the African American population will increase by 68 percent, the Asian-American, Pacific Island, and American Indian by 79 percent, and the Hispanic-American population by 187 percent." This prediction reinforces the premise that learning beyond the classroom must include a diversity of instructional and learning strategies for any adult role models in a student's life.

Mentoring has become an instrumental tool in addressing student achievement and access to learning. Adult mentors work individually with identified students on specific subject areas to reinforce learning through tutorial instruction and application of knowledge. Providing students with role models to reinforce learning has become a crucial instructional strategy for teachers seeking to maximize student learning beyond the classroom. Students who work with adult mentors from culturally diverse backgrounds are given a multicultural aspect of learning that is cooperative and multi-modal in personalized instruction.

The interpersonal use of technology provides a mentoring tutorial support system and different conceptual learning modalities for students seeking to understand classroom material. Technology provides a networking opportunity for students to find study buddies, peer study groups, and free academic support that will help them problem-solve and develop critical thinking skills that are imperative in acquiring knowledge and conceptual learning. Distance Learning is a technological strategy that keeps students and teachers interactively communicating about issues in the classroom and beyond. Using technology, students will communicate more freely with teachers or adult mentors than they will in a classroom of peers.

The Community as a Resource

The community is a vital link to increased learning experiences for students. Community resources can supplement the minimized and marginal educational resources of school communities. With state and federal educational funding becoming increasingly subject to legislative budget cuts, school communities welcome the financial support that community resources can provide in terms of discounted prices on such high-end equipment as computers, printers, and technology supplies and free notebooks, backpacks and student supplies for low income students who may have difficulty obtaining basic school supplies.

Community stores can provide cash rebates and teacher discounts for educators in struggling school districts and compromised school communities. Both professionally and personally, communities can enrich the student learning experiences by including the following support strategies:

- Provide programs that support student learning outcomes and future educational goals
- Create mentoring opportunities that provide adult role models in various industries to students interested in studying in that industry
- Provide financial support for school communities to help low-income or homeless students begin the school year with the basic supplies
- Develop paid internships with local university students to provide tutorial services for identified students in school communities who are having academic and social difficulties processing various subject area content.
- Provide parent-teen-community forums to create public voices for change in communities
- Offer parents without computer or Internet connections stipends to purchase technology to create equitable opportunities for students to do research and complete requirements for papers written in Microsoft word.
- Visit classrooms and ask teachers and students what's needed to promote academic progress and growth.

Community resources are vital in providing that additional support to students, school communities, and families struggling to remain engaged in declining educational institutions competing for federal funding and limited district funding. The commitment that a community shows to its educational communities is a valuable investment in the future. Community resources that provide additional funding for tutors in marginalized classrooms or help schools reduce the number of students needing additional remedial instruction have a direct impact on educational equity and facilitation of teaching and learning for both teachers and students.

Promoting a Sense of Community

The bridge to effective learning for students begins with a collaborative approach by all stakeholders that support educational needs. Underestimating the power and integral role of community institutions in influencing the current and future goals of students can carry high stakes for students beyond the high school years who are competing for college access, student internships, and entry level jobs in the community. Researchers have shown that schools that are involved and connected with community institutions have greater number of students who graduate and go on to higher education. We must reevaluate the current disconnect and autonomy that is commonplace in today's society in terms of promoting tomorrow's citizens.

When community institutions provide students and teachers with meaningful connections and input, the commitment is apparent in terms of volunteering, loyalty, and professional promotion. Providing students with placements in leadership positions in such organizations as the Associated Student Body (ASB), the Parent Teacher Student Association (PTSA), school boards, neighborhood sub-committees addressing political or social issues, and government boards that influence school communities creates valuable learning experiences. In these positions, students can explore ethical, participatory, collaborative, and transformational leadership that they can apply to all areas of their educational and personal lives.

Through community liaisons, students experience accountability and responsibility. They learn about life and how organizations use effective communication and how teams work together to accomplish goals and objectives. Teaching students skills of inclusion and social and environmental responsibility and creating public forums that represent student voice and vote foster student interest. They can develop and reflect on individual opinions and begin to understand the dynamics of the world around them.

When a student sees that the various support systems are in place and consistently working as a team to provide resources and avenues of academic promotion and accountability, they are more willing to take risks and, for example, become a teen voice on a local committee about teen violence or volunteer in a local hospice for young children with terminal illnesses. The community institutions provide role models of the world of which the student will soon become an integral and vital member. Being a part of that world as a student makes the transition to young adulthood easier.

Skill 5.2   Identify contemporary family systems and how to provide for their needs

Teachers today cope with an increasingly diverse group of cultures in their classrooms. While this diversity is exciting for most teachers, it creates new challenges in meeting a variety of family expectations for school and teachers.

First, teachers must show respect to all parents and families. They must set a tone that suggests that their mission is to develop students into the best people they can be. Then they need to realize that ideas about how children should be educated vary among cultures

Second, teachers have better success when they talk personally to parents about their children. Even though teachers may have many students, when they share personal things about each child, parents feel more confident that their child is in the right hands.

Third, it is very important that teachers act as if they are partners in the children's education and development. Parents know their children best, and feedback, information, and advice from parents is important.

Finally, teachers must be patient with difficult families and realize that certain methods of criticism, such as verbal abuse, are unacceptable. Such circumstances require that the teacher get assistance from an administrator. This situation, however, is very unusual, and most teachers will find that, when they really try to be friendly and personal with parents, the parents usually reciprocate and assist in the educational program.

COMPETENCY 6.0 KNOWLEDGE OF DEVELOPMENTALLY APPROPRIATE CURRICULUM

Skill 6.1 Identify the implications of teacher read alouds and how they directly relate to the academic success of children at all grade levels

Storybook reading affects children's knowledge about, strategies for, and attitudes toward reading. Of all the strategies intended to promote growth in literacy acquisition, none is as commonly practiced nor as strongly supported across the emergent literacy literature as storybook reading. Children in different social and cultural groups have differing degrees of access to storybook reading. For example, it is not unusual for a teacher to have students who have experienced thousands of hours of story reading time and other students who have had little or no such exposure.

During storybook reading teachers can show students how to recognize the fronts and backs of books, locate titles, or look at pictures and predict the story, rather than assume children will learn this through incidental exposure. Or teachers can use daily storybook reading to discuss book-handling skills and direction concepts that are particularly important for children who are unfamiliar with printed texts.

Teachers can also use repeated readings to give students multiple exposures to unfamiliar words and extended opportunities to look at books with predictable patterns. By modeling the behaviors associated with reading, reading aloud provides support. By adjusting their demands—asking increasingly complex questions or encouraging children to take on portions of the reading—or by reading more complex text as students gain knowledge, teachers can act as scaffolds during these storybook reading activities.

> **Read more about the value of reading aloud to children:**
>
> www.journal.naeyc.org/btj/200 303/ReadingAloud.pdf

Skill 6.2   Identify techniques for creating a print-rich environment (e.g., word walls, classroom libraries, labeling objects, student work displayed) reflecting diverse cultures

The concept that print carries meaning is demonstrated every day in the elementary classroom as the teacher holds up a selected book to read it aloud to the class. The teacher explicitly and deliberately thinks out loud about how to hold the book, how to focus the class on looking at its cover, where to start reading, and in what direction to begin. Even in writing the morning message on the board, the teacher provides a lesson on print concepts. The children see that the message is placed at the top of the board and then followed by additional activities and a schedule for the rest of the day.

When the teacher challenges children to take a single letter and make the items in the classroom, their home, or their knowledge base that start with that letter, the children are making the abstraction that print carries meaning concrete.

Teachers must look for the following five basic behaviors in students:

- Do students know how to hold the book?
- Can students match speech to print?
- Do students know the difference between letters and words?
- Do students know that print conveys meaning?
- Can students track print from left to right?

To understand concepts of print, students must be able to recognize text and understand the various mechanics that text contains. These mechanics include the following:

- All text contains a message.
- The English language has a specific structure.
- In order to decode words and read text, students must understand that structure.

The structure of the English language consists of rules of grammar, capitalization, and punctuation. Younger children must be able to recognize letters and form words. Older children must recognize different types of text, such as lists, stories, and signs, and know the purpose of each one.

When reading to children, teachers point to words as they read them. Illustrations and pictures also contribute to understanding the text. Therefore, teachers should also discuss illustrations related to the text.

When reading to students, teachers also discuss the common characteristics of books such as author, title page, and table of contents. Asking students to predict the story based on the cover teaches students about the importance of the book cover to the story. Pocket charts, big books, and song charts provide ample opportunity for teachers to point to words as they read.

Instructional Strategies

1. Using big books in the classroom

   The teacher gathers the children in a group with the big book placed on a stand so that all children can see the words and pictures. The teacher reads and points to each word. By using a pointer, the teacher does not cover any other words or part of the page. When students read from the big book on their own, they can also use the pointer for each word.

   When students begin reading from smaller books, they can transfer what they have learned about pointing to the words; they can use their fingers to track the reading. Observation is a key point in assessing a student's ability to track words and speech.

2. A classroom rich in print

   Having words from a familiar rhyme or poem in a pocket chart lends itself to the following activity: the students arrange the words in the correct order and then read the rhyme. This instructional strategy reinforces concepts of print. It also reinforces punctuation and capitalization and matching print to speech.

   Using highlighters or sticky tabs to locate upper and lower case letters or specific words can help students isolate words and develop concepts about the structure of language that they need for reading.

   The classroom should have plenty of books for children to read on their own or in small groups. While students read on their own, the teacher should note how the child holds the book and tracks and reads the words.

3. Word Wall

   The use of a word wall is a great teaching tool for words in isolation and with writing. Each of the letters of the alphabet is displayed with words under each one that begin with that letter. Students are able to find the letter on the wall and read the words under each one.

4.   Sounds of the letters

In addition to letter names, students should learn the corresponding sound of each letter. This skill is a key feature of decoding when a student is beginning to read. The use of rhyming words is an effective way to teach letter sounds.

Teachers should expose students to daily opportunities for viewing and reading texts. By engaging the students in discussions about books during shared, guided, and independent reading times, teachers provide this exposure. The teacher should draw the students' attention to the conventions of print and discuss with them the reasons for choosing different books. For example, teachers should let the students know that it is perfectly acceptable to return a book and select another if they think the first book is too hard for them.

Predictable books help engage the students in reading. Once the students realize which words are repeated in the text, they will eagerly chime in to repeat the words at the appropriate time during the reading. Rereading of texts helps the students learn the words and helps them read these lines fluently.

A Diverse Classroom Environment

Classrooms that value people of all cultures integrate multicultural materials into many different areas of the classroom. In the art area are multicolored crayons, paints, and clay; teachers post art prints on the walls showing scenes and people from many different racial and ethnic backgrounds and people with disabilities. Occasionally in the block area, teachers will post a variety of pictures showing many different kinds of houses from different cultures. This area includes such things as miniature play people. Rhythm instruments from a variety of cultures are in the music area. In the dramatic play area, teachers provide items and clothing from different cultures integrated together.

For example, a sombrero and a construction hard hat might be available; a tortilla press and a play mixer might be in the kitchen area. Dolls of various ethnicities should be available for dramatic play. Many teachers also use persona dolls to represent ethnicities not present in the classroom. The book area should be rich with examples so that children can see themselves in the stories and learn about others and their cultures. This area is a major, important part of the classroom.

Children's Literature as a Springboard to Cultural Awareness

Many fine children's books show how people in the world are alike. Differences then become interesting and tantalizing. Allowing children to see their own culture reflected in the books and activities in the classroom is deeply affirming. The following books give all children a glimpse of the delights and challenges we all face at times:

- ✓ Linda Jacobs Altman's *Amelia's Road* (migrant farm workers)
- ✓ Paul Goble's *The Girl Who Loved Wild Horses* (Native American)
- ✓ Bill Martin's *Knots On a Counting Rope* (Native American)
- ✓ Eve Bunting's *Going Home* (from California to Mexico)
- ✓ Pat Mora's *Uno, Dos, Tres: One, Two, Three* (shopping in a Mexican market)
- ✓ Gary Soto's *Too Many Tamales* (did a wedding ring get lost in the tamales?)
- ✓ Joseph Bruchac's *Crazy Horse's Vision* (Native American)
- ✓ Carole Boston Weatherford's *Freedom on the Menu* (sit-in movement at lunch counters.

Classroom Activities

1. Make a graph about the sizes of families represented in the classroom.
2. Take snapshots of the children in your classroom, laminate them, and make a Concentration game.
3. Enlarge the children's pictures and make face puzzles of them.
4. Make classroom books about My Family after reading a book such as Rebecca Doltich's *A Family Like Yours*.
5. Provide children with playdough and a variety of powdered colors, along with a mirror. Let them match their skin colors. This activity provides an opportunity to learn new descriptive words and demystifies skin color.
6. After reading *Hairs/Pelitos* by Sandra Cisneros (different kinds of hair within Latino cultures) and Camille Yarborough's *Cornrows* (an African American hairstyle), provide a microscope through which children can look at their hair, comparing and contrasting their hair with others.
7. Have older children make a family tree after interviewing their relatives.
8. Do creative dramatics—act out powerful stories such as Eloise Greenfield's *Rosa Parks*.
9. Use persona dolls to tell stories of such difficulties as teasing or name-calling. Use class discussion to help children recognize the unfairness of this and brainstorm ways students can stand up for themselves.

10. Use oral stories and pictures to tell the story of such local, regional, and national heroes as Barack Obama.

11. Bake different kinds of breads in the classroom after reading Ann Morris's *Bread, Bread, Bread.*

12. Use Mitsumasa Anno's *All in a Day* (which shows eight children from eight different countries at the same time each day for two days) as inspiration for essays about a typical day in their lives.

13. Create a shoe store in the dramatic play area after reading Ann Morris's *Shoes, Shoes, Shoes.* Or assemble an interesting collection of different kinds of shoes and allow children to make shoeprints in art.

14. Use Karin Luisa Badt's *Good Morning, Let's Eat!* (breakfast in different cultures) as a lead in to a math graphing activity of different foods children eat for breakfast.

15. After reading Laura Ingalls Wilder's *Little House on the Prairie* and Louise Erdrich's *The Birchbark House* (about an Ojibway girl who lives on Madelaine Island on Lake Superior in about the same time period as Laura), have children use a Venn diagram to show similarities and differences between the two characters and stories.

Skill 6.3   Identify various approaches for developing pre-reading and early literacy skills that include oral language and listening, phonological awareness, alphabet knowledge, background knowledge, and print concepts

In 2000, the National Reading Panel released its now well-known report on teaching children to read. In a way, this report put to rest the debate between phonics and whole-language. It argued, essentially, that both word-letter recognition and reading comprehension were important. The report's *big 5* critical areas of reading instruction are as follows:

- Phonemic Awareness
- Phonics
- Fluency
- Comprehension
- Vocabulary

Methods used to teach these skills are often featured in a *balanced literacy* curriculum that focuses on the use of skills in various instructional contexts. For example, with independent reading, students choose and read books that are at their reading levels; with guided reading, teachers work with small groups of students to help them with their particular reading problems; with whole group reading, the entire class reads the same text, and the teacher incorporates activities to help students learn phonics, comprehension, fluency, and vocabulary. In addition to these components of balanced literacy, teachers incorporate writing so that students can learn to communicate through text.

Emergent literacy research examines early literacy knowledge and the contexts and conditions that foster that knowledge. Despite differing viewpoints on the relation between emerging literacy skills and reading acquisition, the literature strongly supports the important contribution that early childhood exposure to oral and written language makes to the facility with which children learn to read.

> **Learn more about the National Reading Panel:**
>
> http://www.nationalreadingpanel.org/

Approaches to Early Reading

When students practice fluency, they practice reading connected pieces of text. In other words, instead of looking at a word as just a word, they read the complete sentence. In order to comprehend what they are reading, students must be able to piece words in a sentence together quickly. Students who are not fluent in reading sound out each letter or word slowly and pay more attention to the phonics of each word. A fluent reader, on the other hand, might read a sentence out loud and use appropriate intonations. Having a student read something out loud, preferably a few sentences in a row is, in fact, the best way to test for fluency. Most new readers will probably not be very fluent; but with practice, they will increase their fluency. Even though fluency is not the same as comprehension, it is a good predictor of comprehension. If students are focusing on sounding out each word, they won't be paying attention to the meaning.

Learning approach

SEE Skill 1.1

Linguistic approach

SEE Skill 1.1

Cognitive approach

Researchers in the 1970s proposed that language knowledge derives from both syntactic and semantic structures. Drawing on the studies of Piaget and other cognitive learning theorists, supporters of the cognitive approach maintained that children acquire knowledge of linguistic structures after they have acquired the cognitive structures necessary to process language. For example, joining words for specific meaning necessitates sensory motor intelligence. Children must be able to coordinate movement and recognize objects before they can identify words to name the objects or word groups to describe the actions performed with those objects. Children must have the mental abilities for organizing concepts and concrete operations, predicting outcomes, and theorizing before they can assimilate and verbalize complex sentence structures, choose vocabulary for particular nuances of meaning, and examine semantic structures for tone and manipulative effect.

Socio-cognitive approach

SEE also Skill 1.1

During the preschool years, children acquire cognitive skills in oral language that they later apply to reading comprehension. Reading aloud to young children is one of the most important things that an adult can do because adults are teaching them how to monitor, question, predict, and confirm what they hear in the stories. Reid (Reid 1988, p. 165) described four metalinguistic abilities that young children acquire through early involvement in reading activities:

1. Word consciousness. Children who have access to books can tell the story through the pictures before they can read. Gradually they begin to realize the connection between the spoken words and the printed words. The beginning of letter and word discrimination begins in the early years.

2. Language and conventions of print. During this stage children learn how to hold a book, where to begin to read and the left to right motion, and how to continue from one line to another.

3. Functions of print. Children discover that print can be used for a variety of purposes and functions, including entertainment and information.

4. Fluency. Through listening to adult models, children learn to read in phrases and use intonation.

Importance of Background Knowledge

All children bring some level of background knowledge to beginning reading. Teachers can use this background knowledge to help children link their personal literacy experiences to beginning reading instruction and also close the gap between students with rich experiences and those with impoverished literacy experiences. Activities that draw upon background knowledge include incorporating oral language activities that discriminate between printed letters and words into daily read-alouds and frequent opportunities to retell stories, look at books with predictable patterns, write messages with invented spellings, and respond to literature through drawing.

Many children with impoverished literacy experiences have difficulty making connections between old and new information. Teachers can apply strategic integration to help link old and new learning. For example, in the classroom, the teacher can provide access to literacy materials in writing centers and libraries. Students should also have opportunities to integrate and extend their literacy knowledge by reading aloud, listening to other students read aloud, and listening to tape recordings and videotapes in reading corners.

Phonemic Awareness

Phonemic awareness is the ability to hear, identify, and manipulate the individual sounds or phonemes in spoken words. English has approximately 40 phonemes. Phonological awareness is a broader term that includes phonemic awareness.

Language games that encourage phonological and phonemic awareness help students understand that language is a series of sounds that form words and ultimately, sentences.

- *Listening games* sharpen a student's ability to hear selective sounds.
- *Counting syllables* games help students discover that many words are made of smaller chunks
- *Rhyming games* draw a student's attention to the sound structure of words
- *Word and sentence building games* help students understand that language consists of words connected to form sentences.

Structured computer programs can also help teach or reinforce these skills. Daily reading sessions with the students (one-on-one or group) help develop their understanding of print concepts.

Activities that develop phonemic awareness include the following:

- identifying phonemes
- categorizing phonemes
- blending phonemes to form words
- deleting or adding phonemes to form new words

SEE also Skill 6.6

Alphabet Knowledge

SEE Skill 6.8

Skill 6.4 Identify strategies that facilitate the development of effective oral language communication (e.g., vocabulary, grammar, syntax, pragmatics) and listening skills

Semantic Cues

The following are prompts that the teacher can use to alert the children to semantic cues:

- You said (the child's statement and incorrect attempt). Does that make sense to you?
- If someone said (repeat the child's attempt), would you know what he or she meant?
- You said (child's incorrect attempt). Would you write that?

Children need to use meaning to predict what the text says so that the relevant information can prompt the correct words to surface as they identify the words. If children come to a word they can't immediately recognize, they should use their past reading (or being read to) experiences, background knowledge, and context to figure it out.

Syntactic Cues

- You said (child's incorrect attempt). Does that sound right?
- You said (child's incorrect attempt). Can we say it like that?

Pragmatics

 Pragmatics is concerned with the difference between the writer's meaning and the literal meaning of the sentence based on social context. A student competent in pragmatics can understand the writer's intended meaning or what the writer is trying to convey. In a simpler sense, we can consider pragmatics the social rules of language.

For example, a young girl sitting beside her mother at a fancy restaurant after her great-grandmother's funeral looks over to the table next to them. She sees a very elderly woman eating her dessert. "Mom?" she asks, patiently waiting for response. When her mother addresses her, she states loudly, "That woman is old like Grandma. Is she going to die soon too?" Of course, embarrassed, the mother hushes her child. However, this statement is a simple example of immature pragmatics. The child has the vocabulary, the patience to wait her turn, and some knowledge of conversational rules; however, she is not aware that certain topics are socially inappropriate and, therefore. does not adapt her language to the situation.

Vocabulary

SEE Skill 6.11

Grammar

Students should learn the following basic grammar concepts:

Sentence completeness
Avoid fragments and run-on sentences. Recognition of sentence elements necessary to make a complete thought, proper use of independent and dependent clauses, and proper punctuation will correct such errors.

Capitalization
Capitalize all proper names of persons (including specific organizations or agencies of government); places (countries, states, cities, parks, and specific geographical areas); things (political parties, structures, historical and cultural terms, and calendar and time designations); and religious terms (any deity, revered person or group, sacred writings).

> Percy Bysshe Shelley, Argentina, Mount Rainier National Park, Grand Canyon, League of Nations, the Sears Tower, Birmingham, Lyric Theater, Americans, Midwesterners, Democrats, Renaissance, Boy Scouts of America, Easter, God, Bible, Dead Sea Scrolls, Koran

Capitalize proper adjectives and titles used with proper names.

> California gold rush, President John Adams, French fries, Homeric epic, Romanesque architecture, Senator John Glenn

Note: Some words that represent titles and offices are not capitalized unless used with a proper name.

Capitalized	Not Capitalized
Congressman McKay	the congressman from Florida
Commander Alger	commander of the Pacific Fleet
Queen Elizabeth	the queen of England

Capitalize all main words in titles of works of literature, art, and music.

Verbs
A verb is the action word in a sentence, such as in "The boy **ran** down the road." Verbs can also link the subject and predicate of a sentence and do not perform an action. For example, in the sentence "I am a teacher", the verb is "am" because it links the subject "I" to the predicate "a teacher"

There are three main forms of verb tense_ Past, present and future to demote time. The present form of the verb is tells what is happening now. To form the past, some changes have to be made to the present tense. In the case of regular verbs, this means adding the suffix"-ed" to the verb, as in talk – talked. Some irregular verbs involve changing the spelling of the word to form the past tense, as in teach – taught and bring – brought. To form the future tense, it is necessary to add words denoting the future, such as will, shall, or should. An example of a sentence using the future tense is "I **will talk** to the teacher tomorrow."

Verb conjugation
The conjugation of verbs follows the patterns used in the discussion of tense above. However, the most frequent problems in verb use stem from the improper formation of the past and past participial[jmm22].

Regular verb: believe, believed, (have) believed
Irregular verbs: run, ran, run; sit, sat, sat; teach, taught, taught

Two other verb problems stem from misusing the preposition *of* for the verb auxiliary *have* and misusing the verb ought (now rare).

| Incorrect: | I should of gone to bed. |
| Correct: | I should have gone to bed. |

| Incorrect: | He hadn't ought to get so angry. |
| Correct: | He ought not get so angry. |

Use of pronouns

A pronoun used as the subject of a sentence is in the nominative case.

> *She* was the drum majorette

A pronoun used as a predicate nominative is in the nominative case.

> The lead trombonists were Joe and *he.*

A pronoun used as the subject of a predicate nominative is in nominative case.

> The band director accepted *whoever* could march in step.

A pronoun used as a direct object, indirect object, or object of a preposition is in the objective case.

> The teacher praised *him*. She gave *him* an A on the test. Her praise of *him* was appreciated. The students *whom* she did not praise will work harder next time.

Common pronoun errors occur from misuse of reflexive pronouns:

> Singular: myself, yourself, herself, himself, itself
> Plural: ourselves, yourselves, themselves.
>
> Incorrect: Jack cut hisself shaving.
> Correct: Jack cut himself shaving.
>
> Incorrect: They backed theirselves into a corner.
> Correct: They backed themselves into a corner.

Use of adjectives
An adjective should agree with its antecedent in number.

> Those apples *are* rotten. This one *is* ripe. These peaches *are* hard.

Comparative adjectives end in -*er* and superlatives in –*est*. Some exceptions are worse and worst. *More* and *most* precede some adjectives that are not easily inflected.

> Mrs. Carmichael is the better of the two basketball coaches.
> That is the hastiest excuse you have ever contrived.

Avoid double comparisons.

> Incorrect: This is the *worstest* headache I ever had.
> Correct: This is the *worst* headache I ever had.

When comparing one object to others in a group, exclude the object under comparison from the rest of the group.

> Incorrect: Joey is larger than any baby I have ever seen. (Since you have seen him, he cannot be larger than himself.)
> Correct: Joey is larger than <u>any other</u> baby I have ever seen.

Include all necessary words to make a comparison clear in meaning.

> I am as tall as my mother. I am as tall as she (is).
> My cats are better behaved than those of my neighbor.

For additional information, **SEE** also Skill 6.8

Short tutorials on all aspects of English grammar:

http://www.englishclub.com/grammar/

Skill 6.5 Select literature from a variety of narrative and expository text that builds language skill and concept development

What actually constitutes *children's literature*? It is usually defined as literature that is selected and read by children rather than literature that the powers-that-be, such as teachers, reviewers, and parents, deem appropriate. Sometimes, it is defined as literature written especially for children, but that definition tends to break down when we look at some of the major books that are read primarily by children, such as Mark Twain's *The Prince and the Pauper* and *Huckleberry Finn*, which were written specifically for adults. Publishers have difficulty deciding whether or not to categorize and market a book as children's literature, young adult literature, or adult literature. Many books cross the line in all directions.

Of course, much of what has been traditionally regarded as children's literature has multiple levels of meaning, and adults who read *Alice in Wonderland*, for example, as a child, will read it again as an adult and find meaning they did not see and could not understand as a child.

Students should be able to distinguish between fiction and non-fiction in order to determine the book's perspective. Generally fiction is divided into three main areas:

- Story
- Novel
- Novella

Works of fiction usually have a main character, setting, plot, climax, and resolution. Non-fiction on the other hand is usually intended to inform the reader. Common types of non-fiction include:

- Essays
- Documentaries
- Biographies
- Autobiographies
- Informational books

The author or narrator communicates meaning in the words of the text. In works of fiction, abstract themes of love, hate, friendship, honor, good, justice, and power become real through the concrete words and actions of the characters. To find and understand the author's perspective, students need the teacher's help in analyzing the work. Through discussion and direct teaching, the students can look at the characters, actions, problems, and dialogue and discover how they are related to or help develop the theme.

Selecting Appropriate Literature

While having a selection of quality literature in the classroom for children to read independently is essential, using literature in instruction is also important for developing language skills and concepts. Through literature, students see how the skills they learn are applied in writing and how they can use these skills in speaking and reading.

During the first month of school in the early grades, the teacher assesses students to find their reading levels. Based on these findings, the teacher plans instruction that will take the students from where they are to the next level. When planning the day's lesson, the teacher should choose a book to read to the class as shared reading. In this part of the classroom routine, the teacher reads a book, a big book if possible, to the class while showing the pictures and stops at appropriate points to ask questions about the reading or to point out the use of words or punctuation.

Through guided reading sessions with small groups of students, the teacher uses literature to help them develop reading strategies. Each child should have a book, and the teacher begins the lesson by showing the students the book and letting them skim through it and make predictions about the subject of the book. After reading the book, the teacher uses strategies to teach word skills that the students within the group need. These lessons should include a variety of fiction and non-fiction books.

Literature circles are another method of using literature in the classroom to help students develop, not only in language and concept skills, but also in critical literacy. In small groups of students, the children learn how to discuss books and ask questions about what they are reading.

Basal readers contain short stories and quality reading material that can serve as a resource for teaching the skills students need at various levels of development. The use of literature is not just for teaching reading. Teachers can also use literature to teach writing skills, such as paragraphing, use of quotation marks, plot development, and writing endings for stories.

Through a reading and interest survey, teachers can also learn what topics students like to read about. When book topics appeal to students, they are more likely to choose them for independent reading. Using literature in the classroom requires a lot of planning. Bins of books at all reading levels that include topics that will appeal to all students in that group should be available for guided reading. Because they will be reading material at their instructional level, the students will be successful. When students have books they can read independently, they are less likely to get turned off of reading.

Sample authors to choose for books in the classroom:

- Eric Carle
- Mem Fox
- Betsy Byars
- Tomie de Paola
- Leo Lionni
- Kristine O'Connell George
- Joan Holub
- Kevin Henkes

Skill 6.6   Identify activities that build phonemic awareness

Phonemic awareness is the acknowledgement of sounds and words. For example, a child's realization that some words rhyme Is phonemic awareness. Onset and rhyme, for example, are skills that help students learn that they can exchange the sound of the letter *b* in the word *bad* with the sound *d* to make it *dad*. You can teach this skill to children with their eyes closed. In other words, phonemic awareness is about sounds not ascribing written letters to sounds.

Knowledge of Phonemes

In everyday language, we attach affective meanings to words unconsciously; we exercise more conscious control of informative connotations. In the process of language development, the student must grasp not only the definitions of words, but also the affective connotations and how listeners process these connotations. Gaining this conscious control over language makes it possible to use language appropriately in various situations and to evaluate its uses in literature and other forms of communication.

The manipulation of language for a variety of purposes is the goal of language instruction. Advertisers and satirists are especially conscious of the effect word choice has on their audiences. By evoking the proper responses from readers and listeners, we can prompt them to take action.

A *phoneme* is the smallest contrastive unit in a language system and represents a sound; it is the smallest meaningful psychological unit of sound. The phoneme is said to have mental, physiological, and physical substance; our brains process the sounds; human speech organs produce the sounds; and the sounds are physical entities that we can record and measure. Consider the English words *pat* and *sat*, which appear to differ only in their initial consonants. This difference, known as *contrastiveness* or *opposition*, is adequate to distinguish these words, and, therefore, the *P* and *S* sounds are considered different phonemes in English. A pair of words, identical except for such a sound, is known as a *minimal pair*, and the two sounds are separate phonemes.

Where no minimal pair exists to demonstrate that two sounds are distinct, they may be *allophones*. *Allophones* are variant phones, or sounds, that speakers do not recognize as distinct. They are not meaningfully different in the language and so are perceived as being the same. The heavy sounding *L* at the end of the word *wool* as opposed to the lighter sounding *L* that starts the word *Leaf* is an example of an *allophone*." This example demonstrates allophones of a single phoneme. While it may exist and be measurable, the difference is unrecognizable and meaningless to the average English speaker. Identifying phonemes and applying their use is a step in the process of developing language fluency.

Examples of Common Phonemes Applied

Phoneme	Uses
/A/	a (table), a_e (bake), ai (train), ay (say)
/a/	a (flat)
/b/	b (ball)
/k/	c (cake), k (Key), ck (back)
/d/	d (door)
/E/	e (me), ee (feet), ea (leap), y (baby)
/e/	e (pet), ea (head)
/f/	f (fix), ph (phone)
/g/	g (gas)
/h/	h (hot)
/I/	i (I), i_e (bite), igh (light), y (sky)
/i/	i (sit)
/j/	j (jet), dge (edge), g (gem)
/l/	l (lamp)
/m/	m (map)
/n/	n (no), kn (knock)
/O/	o (okay), o_e (bone), oa (soap), ow (low)
/o/	o (hot)
/p/	p (pie)
/kw/	qu (quick)
/r/	r (road), wr (wrong), er (her), ir (sir), ur (fur)
/s/	s (say), c (cent)
/t/	t (time)
/U/	u (future), u_e (use), ew (few)
/u/	u (thumb), a (about)
/v/	v (voice)
/w/	w (wash)
/gz/	x (exam)
/ks/	x (box)
/y/	y (yes)
/z/	z (zoo), s (nose)
/OO/	oo (boot), u (truth), u_e (rude), ew (chew)
/oo/	oo (book), u (put)
/oi/	oi (soil), oy (toy)
/ou/	ou (out), ow (cow)
/aw/	aw (saw), au (caught), al (tall)
/ar/	ar (car)
/sh/	sh (ship), ti (nation), ci (special)
/hw/	wh (white)
/ch/	ch (chest), tch (catch)
/th/	th (thick)
/<u>th</u>/	th (this)
/ng/	ng (sing)

Phonemically aware readers and listeners can recognize and manipulate specific sounds in spoken words. The majority of phonemic awareness tasks, activities, and exercises are oral.

Since the ability to distinguish between individual sounds, or phonemes, within words is a prerequisite to association of sounds with letters and manipulating sounds to blend words—a fancy way of saying reading, teaching phonemic awareness is crucial to emergent literacy or early childhood K-2 reading instruction. Children need a strong background in phonemic awareness for effective phonics instruction—sound and spelling relationships in printed materials.

Theorist Marilyn Jager Adams who researches early reading outlined five basic types of phonemic awareness tasks.

Task 1—Ability to hear rhymes and alliteration.
For example, children listen to a poem, rhyming picture book, or song and identify the rhyming words they hear. The teacher records or lists the words on an experiential chart.

Task 2- Ability to do oddity tasks (recognize the member of a set that is different [odd] among the group.)
For example, the children look at the pictures of a blade of grass, a garden and a rose and identify the word that starts with a different sound.

Task 3—The ability to orally blend words and split syllables.
For example, the children can say the first sound of a word and then the rest of the word and put the sounds together as a single word.

Task 4—The ability to orally segment words.
For example, the ability to count sounds. The children would be asked as a group to count the sounds in "hamburger."

Task 5—The ability to do phonics manipulation tasks.
For example, the students can replace the r sound in rose with a p sound to get the word pose.

The following Instructional methods may be effective for teaching phonemic awareness:

- Clapping syllables in words
- Distinguishing between a word and a sound
- Using visual cues and movements to help children understand when the speaker goes from one sound to another
- Oral segmentation activities which focus on easily distinguished syllables rather than sounds
- Singing such familiar songs as *Happy Birthday* and *Knick Knack Paddy Wack* and replacing key words in the song with words having a different ending or middle sound (oral segmentation)
- Dealing children a deck of picture cards and having them sound out the words for the pictures on their cards or calling for a picture by asking for its first and second sound.

SEE also Skill 6.3

For further reading of phonemic awareness activities:

http://www.sasked.gov.sk.ca/docs/ela/
e_literacy/awareness.html

Skill 6.7   Identify strategies for instruction in letter-sound relationships and phonics

Unlike the study of phonemic awareness, children must study phonics with their eyes open. Phonics is the connection between sounds and the letters on a page. In other words, students learning phonics see the word *bad* and sound out each letter slowly until they realize that they just said the word.

Phonological awareness is the ability of the reader to recognize the sound of spoken language. This recognition includes how those sounds can be blended together, segmented (divided up), and manipulated (switched around). This awareness leads to phonics, a method of teaching children to read. It helps them *sound out words*.

Development of phonological skills may begin during the pre-kindergarten years. By the age of five, a child who has been exposed to rhyme can recognize a rhyme. By filling in the missing rhyming word in a familiar rhyme or rhymed picture book, such a child can demonstrate phonological awareness.

Children gain phonological awareness when they learn the sounds made by the letters and the sounds made by various combinations of letters and when they can recognize individual sounds in words.

Phonological awareness skills include the following:

1. Rhyming and syllabification
2. Blending sounds into words—such as *pic-tur-bo-k*
3. Identifying the beginning or starting sounds of words and the ending or closing sounds of words
4. Breaking words down into sounds, also called *segmenting* words
5. Recognizing other smaller words in the big word by removing starting sounds, for example seeing the word *ear* in the work *hear*.

> **Read more about phonological awareness:**
>
> http://www.kidsource.com/kidsource/content2/disability.phonological.html

Skill 6.8   Identify the processes, skills, and phases of word recognition—pre-alphabetic, partial alphabetic, full alphabetic, graphophonemic, morphemic, syntactic, semantic—that lead to decoding

Monitoring a student's progress is particularly important for the primary teacher. The teacher must adapt instruction to account for children's differences. For those children with previous knowledge of the alphabetic principle, instruction extends their knowledge as they learn more about the formal features of letters and their sound correspondences. Other students with fewer prior experiences must be taught the beginning alphabetic principle—that the alphabet comprises a limited set of letters and that these letters stand for the sounds of spoken words. These students will require more focused and direct instruction. In all cases, however, children need to interact with a rich variety of print

If a student's alphabetic skills fail to make expected progress in literacy learning or if their literacy skills are extremely advanced, teachers must prepare more individualized instructional strategies to meet each student's needs.

Alphabetic Principle

The alphabetic principle is sometimes called *graphophonemic awareness*. This technical reading foundation term represents the understanding that written words are composed of patterns of letters that represent the sounds of spoken words.

The alphabetic principle has the following two parts:

- Words are made up of letters and each of these letters has a specific sound
- The correspondence between sounds and letters leads to phonological reading—reading regular and irregular words and performing advanced word analyses.

Since the English language is dependant on the alphabet, the ability to recognize and sound out letters is the first step for beginning readers. Relying simply on memorization for recognition of words is not feasible as a way for children to learn to read. Therefore decoding is essential. Teaching students to decode text so that they can read fluently and with understanding is the beginning reading teacher's most important goal.

The following are the four basic features of the alphabetic principle:

1. Students must be able to take spoken words apart and blend different sounds together to make new words
2. Students must apply letter sounds to all their reading
3. Teachers must use a systematic, effective program in order to teach children to read
4. The teaching of the alphabetic principle usually begins in kindergarten.

Teachers must remember that some children already know the letters and sounds before they come to school. Others may catch on to this quite quickly, and still others need one-on-one instruction in order to learn to read.

Students need to learn the following critical skills :

How to recognize letter–sound correspondences
- How to sound out words
- How to decode text to make meaning

Morphology, Syntax & Semantics

Morphology is the study of word structure. When readers develop morphemic skills, they begin to understand the patterns they see in words. For example, English speakers realize that cat, cats, and caterpillar share some similarities in structure. Using this skill, readers recognize words faster and more easily because they don't decode each word individually.

Syntax refers to the rules or patterned relationships that create phrases and sentences from words. When readers develop an understanding of syntax, they begin to understand sentence structure and, eventually, grammar.

Example: "I am going to the movies." This statement is syntactically and grammatically correct.

Example: "They am going to the movies." This statement is syntactically correct since all the words are in their correct place, but it is grammatically incorrect with the use of the word *They* instead of *I*.

The meaning expressed when words are arranged in a specific way is called *semantics*. Eventually, knowledge of semantics, the connotation and denotation of words, will have a role with readers.

All of these skill sets are important for building the effective word recognition skills that help emerging readers develop fluency.

Decoding

Decoding refers to the students' abilities to sound out a word by translating different letters or groups of letters (graphemes) into sounds (phonemes). If students do not have the ability to hear, identify, and manipulate individual sounds in spoken words and do not understand that spoken words and syllables are made up of sequences of speech sounds, they will have difficulty connecting sounds with letters or groups of letters.

Tasks for assessing word-analysis and decoding skills can be grouped into three categories:

- comparing sounds
- blending phonemes into words
- segmenting words into phonemes

Procedures for assessing how students compare sounds are the easiest to use. Teachers can ask the student which words begin with the same sound or ask them to find words that rhyme. Teachers need to assess the students' general level of phonemic awareness in order to adjust the instructional time and effort in accordance with students' prior knowledge and needs.

Teachers can present a list of words and ask the students to read the them. When students have difficulty, the teacher asks them to sound out the word and makes note of the strategies used. Another informal assessment is to use cards with letters on them. Ask the students to make the sound of the letter. Teachers can also use cards with nonsense words on them that contain various combinations of consonants and vowels. A checklist of various phonemes is also helpful in recording students' needs. The checklist includes such items as the following:

- identify individual phonemes
- identify patterns of phonemes
- categorize phonemes
- identify blends
- segment words into phonemes
- add phonemes
- substitute phonemes

Using decodable texts for informal reading tests is the best way to assess students' reading needs. Beginning readers are encouraged to sound out words and rely on phonetic cues. Once the strategies are in place, these readers can read short texts easily and quickly.

Skill 6.9 Identify the components of reading fluency—accuracy, automacity, rate, prosody

Accuracy

Assessing student accuracy is one way to evaluate reading fluency, and teachers can assess this accuracy by keeping running records of students during oral reading. Calculating the reading level lets teachers know whether the book is at an appropriate level—a level where the child can comfortably read independently or with guidance—or at a level that frustrates the child.

As part of the informal assessment of primary grade reading, the teacher should record the child's word insertions, omissions, requests for help, and attempts to get the word. In informal assessment, the teacher can estimate the rate of accuracy from the ratio of errors to total words read.

Results of running record informal assessment can be used for teaching based on text accuracy. If students read from 95 to100 percent correctly, they are ready for independent reading. If they read from 92 to 97 percent correctly, they are ready for guided reading. Students who are correct less than 92 percent of the time need read-aloud or shared reading activities.

Automacity

Fluency in reading is dependent on automatic word identification, which helps the student comprehend the material. Even slight difficulties in word identification can significantly increase the time it takes a student to read material, may require rereading parts or passages of the material, and reduces the level of comprehension expected. If students experience reading as a constant struggle or an arduous chore, they will avoid reading whenever possible and consider it a negative experience. Obviously, the ability to read for comprehension and learning in general, will suffer if all aspects of reading fluency are not presented to students as acquirable skills that they can readily develop with the appropriate effort.

Automatic reading involves developing strong orthographic representations, which allow fast and accurate identification of whole words made up of specific letter patterns. Most young students move easily from the use of alphabetic strategies to the use of orthographic representations that can be accessed automatically. Initially they base word identification on the application of phonic word-accessibility strategies or letter-sound associations. These strategies are in turn based on the development of phonemic awareness, which to the student must have to relate speech to print.

One of the most useful devices for developing automaticity in young students is the visual pattern provided in the six syllable types.

Examples of the Six Syllable Types

1. **NOT**—closed
   <u>Closed</u> in by a consonant—vowel makes its **short** sound

2. **NO**—open
   <u>Ends</u> in a vowel—vowel makes its **long** sound

3. **NOTE**—silent *E*
   <u>Ends</u> in a vowel consonant *e*—vowel makes its **long** sound

4. **NAIL**—vowel combination
   <u>Two vowels together</u> make the sound

5. **Bird**—*R* controlled
   <u>Contains</u> a vowel plus 4—vowel sound is changed

6. **Table**—consonant *L-E*
   <u>Applied</u> at the end of a word

These orthographic patterns signal vowel pronunciation to the reader. Students must learn to use their knowledge of these patterns to recognize the syllable types and see these patterns automatically and, ultimately, to read words as wholes. The move from decoding letter symbols and identifing recognizable terms to automatic word recognition is a substantial move toward fluency. Anna Gillingham developed a significant aid for helping students move through this phase when she incorporated the phonetic word cards activity into the Orton-Gillingham lesson plan (Gillingham and Stillman, 1997). During this activity, students practice reading words and non words on cards as wholes. They begin with simple syllables and move systematically through the syllable types to complex syllables and two-syllable words. The words are divided into groups that correspond to the specific sequence of skills being taught.

The student's development of the elements necessary for automaticity continually moves through stages. Another important stage involves automatically recognizing single graphemes as a critical first step to recognizing letter patterns that make up words or word parts. English orthography includes the following four basic word types:

1. Regular, for reading and spelling—<u>cat</u> and <u>print</u>
2. Regular, for reading but not for spelling—<u>float</u> and <u>brain</u> could be spelled <u>flote</u> and <u>brane</u>
3. Rule based—<u>canning</u>—doubling rule, <u>faking</u>—drop e rule)
4. Irregular—<u>beauty</u>.

To be effective readers, students must recognize all four types of words. Repeated practice in pattern recognition is often necessary. Practice techniques may include speed drills. The students read lists of isolated words with contrasting vowel sounds that are signaled by the syllable type. For example, several closed syllable and vowel-consonant-e words containing the vowel *a* are arranged randomly on pages containing about 12 lines. The student reads for one minute. The teacher establishes individual goals and keeps charts of the number of words read correctly in successive sessions. The same word lists are repeated in sessions until students achieve the goal for several succeeding sessions. The list should include high-frequency words within a syllable category because this technique increases the likelihood of generalization to text reading.

True automaticity should be linked with prosody and anticipation to acquire full fluency. Such things as which syllable is accented and how word structure can be predictive are necessary for true automaticity and essential to complete fluency.

Rate

A student with a slow, halting, or inconsistent reading rate has not developed reading fluency. According to an article by Mastropieri, Leinart, & Scruggs (1999), some students develop accurate word pronunciation skills but read at a slow rate. They have not moved to the phase where decoding is automatic, and their limited fluency may affect performance in the following ways:

1. They read less text than peers and have less time to remember, review, or comprehend the text.
2. In trying to identify individual words, they expend more cognitive energy than their peers.
3. They may be less able to retain text in their memories and less likely to integrate those segments with other parts of the text.

The simplest means of determining a student's reading rate is to have the student read aloud from a prescribed passage that is at the appropriate reading level for age and grade and contains a specified number of words. The passage should not be too familiar for the student—some will try to memorize or work out difficult bits ahead of time—and should not contain more words than can be read comfortably and accurately by a normal reader in one or two minutes. Count only the words <u>correctly</u> pronounced on first reading, and divide this word count into elapsed time to determine the student's reading rate. To determine the student's standing and progress, compare this rate with the norm for the class and the average for all students who read fluently at that specific age and grade level.

Teachers can apply the following general guidelines for reading lists of words in a one-minute speed drill: 30 correct words per minute for first- and second-grade children; 40 for third-grade children; 60 for mid-third-grade; and 80 for students in fourth grade and higher.

Various techniques are useful with students who have acquired some proficiency in decoding skill but whose levels of skill are lower than their oral language abilities. Such techniques have the following common features:

1. Students listen to text as they follow along with the book.
2. Students follow the print using their fingers as guides.
3. The teacher uses reading materials that students would be unable to read independently.

Experts recommend that a beginning reading program incorporate partner reading, practice reading difficult words prior to reading the text, timings for accuracy and rate, opportunities to hear books read, and opportunities to read to others.

Prosody

Prosody is the science or study of poetic meters and versification. Prosody, because it includes such matters as which syllable of a word is accented, translates reading into the same experience as listening. It involves intonation and rhythm through such devices as syllable accent and punctuation.

In their article for *Perspectives* (Winter, 2002), Pamela Hook and Sandra Jones proposed that teachers can begin to develop awareness of the prosodic features of language by introducing a short three-word sentence with each of the three words underlined for stress. *He is sick. He is sick. He is sick.* The teacher models the three sentences and discusses the possible meaning for each variation. The students practice reading them with different stress until they are fluent. Teachers can modify and expand these simple three-word sentences to include various verbs, pronouns, and tenses. *You are sick. I am sick. They are sick.* Teachers can increase the length of phrases and emphasize different meanings *Get out of bed. Get out of bed. Get out of bed now.* Teachers can also practice fluency with phrases that frequently occur in text. Prepositional phrases are good syntactic structures for this type of work—*on the _____, in the _____, over the _____.* Teachers can pair these printed phrases to oral intonation patterns that include variations of rate, intensity, and pitch. Students infer the intended meaning as the teacher presents different prosodic variations of a sentence. For example, when speakers want to stress a concept they often slow their rate of speech and may speak in a louder voice—*Joshua, get-out-of-bed-**NOW!***).

Practicing oral variations and then mapping the prosodic features onto the text help students make the connection when reading. Teachers can also use this strategy to alert students to the prosodic features present in punctuation marks. In the early learning stages, using the alphabet helps students focus on the punctuation marks without dealing with meaning. The teacher models for the students and then has them use the intonation patterns that correctly fit the punctuation marks—ABC. DE? FGH! IJKL? or ABCD! EFGHI? KL. Teachers can then move to simple two-word or three-word sentences. The sentences are punctuated with periods, question marks, and exclamation points, and the class discusses the differences in meaning that occur with each different punctuation mark. *Chris hops. Chris hops? Chris hops!* The teacher points out that that the printed words convey the fact that someone named Chris is engaged in the physical activity of hopping, but the intonation patterns get their cue from the punctuation mark.

The meaning extracted from an encounter with a punctuation mark depends on the reader's prior experiences or background knowledge. These experiences help students project an appropriate intonation pattern onto the printed text. Keeping the text static while changing the punctuation marks helps students watch for prosodic patterns.

Students who read word-for-word may benefit initially from practicing phrasing with the alphabet rather than words. Letters do not tax the meaning system. The letters are grouped, an arc is drawn underneath, and students recite the alphabet in chunks, for example, ABC DE FGH IJK LM NOP QRS TU VW XYZ). Once students understand the concept of phrasing, teachers should help students chunk text into syntactic (noun phrases, verb phrases, prepositional phrases) or meaning units until they are proficient themselves. Syntactic units are most commonly used for chunking.

For better readers, teachers can mark the phrasal boundaries with slashes for short passages. Eventually, they can use the slashes only at the beginning of long passages, and then ask students to continue phrase reading even after the marks end. Teachers and students can mark phrases together, or students on an independent level can divide passages into phrases by themselves. Teachers can make comparisons to clarify reasons for differences in phrasing. Providing tasks that require students to identify or supply a paraphrase of an original statement is another way to encourage students to focus on phrase meaning and prosody.

Skill 6.10 Identify instructional methods, for example, practice with high-frequency words, and timed readings, for developing reading fluency

Strategies that teachers can use to help students develop fluency in reading include the following:

- modeling fluent reading
- explaining to students what fluent reading sounds like as opposed to reading word by word
- using paired reading
- reading out loud, including using dramatic scripts to encourage expression
- focusing on maintaining flow rather than correcting small mistakes
- keeping reading fun by allowing for personal choice in reading materials
- encouraging serial and chapter books

Once students know these strategies, teachers can ensure success in reading by making sure that students choose texts at their instructional levels for independent reading. The guided reading model of Fountas and Pinnell rates texts according to difficulty. Teachers can assess students' reading abilities and assign readings at appropriate levels.

Repeated readings of the same text ensure that students recognize the words readily and can read at a normal pace. Some might argue that the students have memorized the text, but teachers can easily check this by choosing pages at random for the students to read aloud.

In paired reading, the teacher pairs a good reader with a struggling reader. One student reads a page and then the other reads a page. The struggling reader can then see what fluent reading looks and sounds like.

During language arts classes, students should sometimes read silently. During this time, the teacher can select students and ask them to read aloud quietly from where they are. This exercise gives teachers information on whether or not students are reading texts at their appropriate levels. Silent reading periods should begin as short periods and lengthen gradually throughout the year. Thus, if students are not reading at home, time is provided for them to do so in school.

SEE also Skill 6.9

Skill 6.11 Identify instructional methods and strategies to increase vocabulary acquisition—word analysis, choice of words, context clues, multiple exposures—across the curriculum

The explicit teaching of word analysis requires that teachers pre-select words from a given text for vocabulary learning. They should choose words appropriate to the storyline and main ideas of the text. The educator may even want to create a story map for a narrative text or develop a graphic organizer for an expository text. Once the story mapping or graphic organizing is completed, the educator can compile a list of words that relate to the storyline and main ideas. Next, the educator should decide which key words are already well defined in the text. Obviously, these words will not need explicit class review.

First the teacher identifies the words that the child can determine through use of prefixes, suffixes, or base words. Again these words will not require direct teaching. Then the teacher reflects on the words in relation to the children's background, prior knowledge base, and language experiences, including native language and dialect words. Based on the above steps, the teacher decides which words to teach.

Only two or three words should require explicit teaching. If the number is higher, the children need guided reading, and the teacher needs to break the text down into smaller sections for teaching. When broken down into smaller sections, each text section should have only two to three words that need explicit teaching. Some researchers, including Tierney and Cunningham, believe that a few words should be taught as a means of improving comprehension. The teacher decides whether the vocabulary selected needs review before reading, during reading, or after reading.

✳ Introduce vocabulary before reading if

- Children are having difficulty constructing meaning on their own. Children themselves have previewed the text and indicated words they want to know.
- The teacher has seen that some words within the text are definitely keys necessary for reading comprehension
- The text, itself, in the judgment of the teacher, contains difficult concepts for the children to grasp.

✳ Introduce vocabulary during reading if

- Children are already doing guided reading.
- The text has words that are crucial for comprehension, and the children will have trouble comprehending the text, if they are not helped with it.

✳ Introduce vocabulary after reading if. . .

- The children themselves have shared words that they found difficult or interesting
- The children need to expand their vocabulary
- The text itself is one that is particularly suited for vocabulary building.

Use the following strategies to support word analysis and as vehicles for enhancing and enriching reading comprehension:

- A graphic organizer such as a word map
- Semantic mapping
- Semantic feature analysis
- Hierarchical and linear arrays
- Previews in context
- Contextual redefinition
- Vocabulary self-collection

As students are being taught to read, they must learn the strategies of careful reading, which include sounding out words, focusing on fluency, and obtaining meaning. However, at points in the learning-to-read process, teachers can help students learn that people read for various reasons. Sometimes people read for pleasure, in which case they can decide whether to skim through quickly for the content or read slowly to savor ideas and language. Other times, people simply want to find information quickly in which case they will skim or scan. In some texts, re-reading is necessary to comprehend information fully.

When skimming, readers read quickly and pay little attention to specific words. They often skim when they want a full picture of a text but do not want to focus on details. Readers can skim with a preview or a review purpose. When skimming for a preview, they are often trying to find out what to expect from the text. When skimming for review, they hope the quick reading will remind them of the main points of the text.

Scanning is not the same as skimming. In skimming, readers read connected text quickly. In scanning, readers go straight to specific ideas, words, sections, or examples. They pick and choose what they will read within a text. Readers scan when they do not need to know everything from a text.

Most people think that in-depth reading is the only legitimate type of reading. Strangely, though, all types of people do all types of reading—all the time! When readers want to enjoy a text or learn from it thoroughly, they read the text in depth. For the most part, these readers move forward quickly and do not stop to focus on a specific word or idea unless this focus is necessary. In this type of reading, readers do not skip over or read fast to get information. They read everything carefully and thoroughly.

The final type is re-reading, which comes in many forms. Sometimes, when the text is difficult, readers must re-read whole texts for the concepts. Re-reading can also be valuable when reading in-depth. For example, the reader may need to review a word, concept, or a few ideas before continuing. Sometimes people re-read whole texts months or years after reading them the first time. When readers realize that, because of their life experiences since the first reading, they will view the text in a different light, they read the text again.

Language development definitively parallels the physiological development of the learner. The cognitive processes that occur during physical development have been documented in the writings of Piaget and Kohlberg's cognitive learning theories.

Piaget's developmental intellectual stages project that children possess schemas that include various concepts and intellectual stages. As children develop physically, their cognitive development incorporates the experiences of the environment and facilitates learning into specific schemas. Children acquire life experiences that they assimilate into projected behaviors, new information is assimilated with new experiences, and cognitive development becomes more complex.

If we apply Piaget's theories of the process of *learning to read* and *reading to learn,* children develop and assimilate environmental and educational cues and learning that build reading skills as they get older. Once the cognitive development accommodates even greater amounts of learning, the child reverses the experience to assimilate reading into a learning experience that then becomes foundational. The exposure of the child to learning experiences increases the assimilation of the experience into that child's cognitive development.

Context Clues

This strategy helps children use context more effectively by presenting them with sufficient context before they begin reading. It models the use of contextual clues to make informed guesses about word meanings.

To apply this strategy, first select two or three unfamiliar words for teaching. Then write a sentence that supplies sufficient clues to help the student figure out the meaning. Among the types of context clues you can use are compare and contrast, synonyms, and direct definitions.

Then present the words only on the experiential chart or as letter cards. As the children pronounce the words, challenge them to define each word. After they offer more than one definition, encourage the children to decide as a group what the definition is and write down their agreed-upon definition with no comment about its true meaning.

Then share with the children the contexts —sentences the teacher wrote with the words and explicit context clues. Ask the children to read the sentences aloud and have them define each word. Do not comment as they present their definitions. Ask them to justify their definitions by making specific references to the context clues in the sentences.

As the discussion continues, direct the children's attention to their previously agreed upon definition of the word. Help them discuss the differences between their guesses about the word when they saw only the word itself and their guesses about the word when they read it in context. Finally, have the children use a dictionary to check their use of context skills to correctly define the word.

Skill 6.12 **Identify instructional methods and strategies —summarizing, monitoring comprehension, question answering, question generating, use of graphic and semantic organizers, recognizing story structure, use multiple strategy instruction— to facilitate students' reading comprehension**

Students need to be aware of their comprehension, or lack of it, in particular texts. So teaching students what to do when the text suddenly stops making sense is important. For example, students can go back and re-read the description of a character, or go back to the table of contents or the first paragraph of a chapter to see where they are headed

Comprehension means that the reader can ascribe meaning to text. Even though students may be good with phonics and know what the words on a page mean, they may not understand what they are reading because they do not know the strategies that would help them comprehend. For example, students should know that stories often have structures, such as a beginning, middle, and end. They should also know that, when they are reading a text and it does not make sense, they need to employ strategies that help them go back into the text they just read and look for clues. Various strategies are available to teach comprehension; these strategies include questioning, asking students to paraphrase or summarize, using graphic organizers, and focusing on mental images.

The point of comprehension instruction is not necessarily to focus just on the texts students are using at the very moment of instruction but to help them learn the strategies that they can use independently with any other text. The following are some of the most common methods of teaching comprehension:

Summarization: Either in writing or verbally, students go over the main point of the text and strategically choose details that highlight the main point. Summarizations are not the same as paraphrasing, which is voicing the same information in different words. Teaching students how to summarize is very important; it will help them look for the most critical areas in a text. For example, it will help them distinguish between main arguments and examples. In fiction, it helps students learn how to focus on the main characters and events and distinguish those from the lesser characters and events.

Question answering: While this strategy tends to be over-used in many classrooms, it is still a valid method of teaching students to comprehend. As the name implies, students answer questions regarding a text, either out loud, in small groups, or individually on paper. The best questions are those that cause students to have to think about the text rather than just finding an answer within the text.

Question generating: Question generation is the opposite of question answering; however, teachers may ask students to answer their own questions or the questions of peer students. In general, we want students to constantly question texts as they read because this questioning results in more critical readers. Teaching students to generate questions helps them learn the types of questions they can ask and how best to be critical of texts.

Graphic organizers: Graphic organizers are graphical representations of content within a text. For example, Use of Venn diagrams can highlight the difference between two characters in a novel or two similar political concepts in a social studies textbook. A teacher can use flow-charts with students to talk about the steps in a process, for example, the steps for setting up a science experiment or the chronological events of a story. Semantic organizers are similar in that they graphically display information. The difference, usually, is that semantic organizers focus on words or concepts. For example, a word web can help students make sense of a word by mapping from the central word all the similar and related concepts of that word.

Text structure: Often in non-fiction, particularly in textbooks, and sometimes in fiction, text structures give important clues to readers about what to look for. Often, students do not know how to make sense of all the headings in a textbook and do not realize that, for example, the side-bar story about a character in history is not the main text on a particular page in the history textbook. Teaching students how to interpret text structures gives them tools for tackling other similar texts.

Monitoring comprehension: Students need to be aware of their comprehension, or lack of it, in particular texts. So, teaching students what to do when a text suddenly stops making sense is important. For example, students can go back and re-read the description of a character, or they can go to the table of contents or the first paragraph of a chapter to see where they are headed.

Textual marking: When using textual marking, students interact with the text as they read. For example, armed with Post-it notes, students can insert questions or comments regarding specific sentences or paragraphs in the text. This activity helps students focus on the importance of the small things, particularly when they are reading larger works such as novels in high school. It also gives students a reference point to which they can return when they need to review.

Discussion: Small group or whole-class discussion stimulates thoughts about texts and gives students a larger picture of the impact of those texts. For example, teachers can strategically encourage students to discuss concepts related to the text. Students learn to consider texts within larger societal and social concepts. Teachers can also encourage students to provide personal opinions in discussion. By listening to various students' opinions, the students in a class see the wide range of possible interpretations and thoughts regarding one text.

Skill 6.13   Identify prewriting and writing skill strategies to develop print awareness concepts, including spelling and punctuation

Candidate teachers should know the proper rules and conventions of punctuation, capitalization, and spelling. Competency exams generally test the ability to apply the more advanced skills; thus, some more frustrating rules are presented here. Rules should be applied according to the American style of English, that is, *theater* instead of *theatre* and placing terminal marks of punctuation almost exclusively within other marks of punctuation. The most common conventions are discussed in this section.

Writing

Children develop writing skills through a series of steps. The following are the steps and their characteristics:

Role Play Writing
In this stage, the child writes in scribbles and assigns a message to the symbols. Even though an adult would not be able to read the writing, the child can read it and might not read it the same every time. The child can read the writing because of prior knowledge that print carries a meaning. The child will also dictate to adults who can write a message or story.

Experimental Writing
In this stage children write in simple forms of language. They usually write with letters according to the way they sound, such as the word *are* may be written as *r*. However, they do display a sense of sentence formation and write in groups of words with a period at the end. They are aware of a correspondence between written words and oral language.

Early Writing

Children start to use a small range of familiar text forms and sight words in their writing. The topics they choose for writing are ones that have some importance for them, such as their families, friends, or pets. Because they listen to stories, they have a sense of how a story sounds and begin to write simple narratives. They learn that they have to correct their writing so that others can easily read it.

Conventional Writing

By the time students reach this stage of writing, they have a sense of audience and purpose for writing. They can proofread their writing and edit it for mistakes. They can transfer between reading and writing and get ideas for writing from what they read. By this time students also have a sense of what correct spelling and grammar look like, and they can change the order of events in the writing so that it makes sense for the reader.

Spelling

Spelling instruction should include words misspelled in daily writing, generalized spelling knowledge, and mastery of objectives in progressive phases of development. The following are developmental stages of spelling:

1. **Pre-phonemic spelling**—Children know that letters stand for a message, but they do not know the relationship between spelling and pronunciation.

2. **Early phonemic spelling**—Children are beginning to understand spelling. They usually write the beginning letter correctly and finish with consonants or long vowels.

3. **Letter-name spelling**—Some words are consistently spelled correctly. The student is developing a sight vocabulary and a stable understanding of letters as representing sounds. Long vowels are usually used accurately, but silent vowels are omitted. The child spells unknown words by attempting to match the name of the letter to the sound.

Concentration in this section will be on spelling plurals and possessives.

The knowledge of the multiplicity and complexity of spelling rules based on phonics, letter doubling, and exceptions to rules that are not mastered by adulthood should be replaced by a good dictionary. Learning the use of a dictionary and thesaurus is a rewarding use of time.

Most plurals of nouns that end in hard consonants or hard consonant sounds followed by a silent *e* are made by adding s. Some words ending in vowels only add *s*.

    fingers, numerals, banks, bugs, riots, homes, gates, radios, bananas

Nouns that end in soft consonant sounds *s, j, x, z, ch*, and *sh*, add *es*. Some nouns ending in *o* add *es*.

    dresses, waxes, churches, brushes, tomatoes, potatoes

Nouns ending in *y* preceded by a vowel just add *s*.

    boys, alleys

Nouns ending in *y* preceded by a consonant change the *y* to *i* and add *es*.

    babies, corollaries, frugalities, poppies

Some nouns plurals are formed irregularly or remain the same.

    sheep, deer, children, leaves, oxen

Some nouns derived from foreign words, especially Latin, make their plurals in two different ways, one of them anglicized. Sometimes, the meanings are the same; other times, the two plurals are used in slightly different contexts. It is always wise to consult the dictionary.

    appendices, appendixes   criterion, criteria
    indexes, indices   crisis, crises

Make the plurals of closed (solid) compound words in the usual way except words ending in *ful*, which make their plurals on the root word.

    timelines, hairpins, cupsful

Make the plurals of open or hyphenated compounds by adding the change in inflection to the word that changes in number.

    fathers-in-law, courts-martial, masters of art, doctors of medicine

Make the plurals of letters, numbers, and abbreviations by adding *s*.

    fives and tens, IBMs, 1990s, *p*s and *q*s (Note that letters are italicized.)

Punctuation

In a quoted statement that is either declarative or imperative, place the period inside the closing quotation marks.

"The airplane crashed on the runway during takeoff."

If the quotation is followed by other words in the sentence, place a comma inside the closing quotations marks and a period at the end of the sentence.

"The airplane crashed on the runway during takeoff," said the announcer.

In most instances, when a quoted title or expression occurs at the end of a sentence, the period is placed before either the single or double quotation marks.

"The middle school readers were unprepared to understand Bryant's poem 'Thanatopsis.'"

Early book-length adventure stories like Don Quixote and The Three Musketeers were known as "picaresque novels."

If the content of the sentence is about a speech or quote and the meaning would be confused by the placement of the period, the final quotation mark precedes the period.

The first thing out of his mouth was "Hi, I'm home."
but
The first line of his speech began "I arrived home to an empty house".

In interrogatory or exclamatory sentences, the question mark or exclamation point is positioned outside the closing quotation marks if the quotation itself is a statement, command, or cited title.

Who decided to lead us in the recitation of the "Pledge of Allegiance"?

Why was Tillie shaking as she began her recitation, "Once upon a midnight dreary..."?

I was embarrassed when Mrs. White said, "Your slip is showing"!

In sentences that are declarative but the quotation is a question or an exclamation, place the question mark or exclamation point inside the quotation marks.

> The hall monitor yelled, "Fire! Fire!"

> "Fire! Fire!" yelled the hall monitor.

> Cory shrieked, "Is there a mouse in the room?" (In this instance, the question supersedes the exclamation.)

For information on **concepts of print**, **SEE** Skill 6.3

Skill 6.14   Identify strategies that facilitate the development of literal, interpretive, and critical listening and thinking skills

Some basic principles apply to the analysis of any text, whether magazine articles, newspaper articles, or children's literature.

Understanding the *literal* meaning of written or spoken expression requires comprehending the vocabulary, the grammar, and the context. This concept may be difficult for young children, so teachers must check that students understand what they are reading and hearing. One way to make this assessment is through discussions in which children are asked to restate what they understand.

When literal interpretation is difficult, teachers should encourage children to use context clues, to guess at the meaning of words, and to use glossaries and dictionaries to check their knowledge and understanding. Teachers can check comprehension verbally or by administering a formalized quiz or other written assessment.

Interpretive thinking skills require that children fit what they are hearing and reading into their own mental framework, perhaps relying on already-acquired knowledge. They must move beyond a literal, objective understanding to a more subjective one. This activity is sometimes referred to as *meaning-making* in which the intended recipient of communication plays a role in assigning meaning to it.

Obviously, the younger a child is, the more the focus will be on merely understanding the literal meaning of the text. Interpretive thinking skills develop partly through maturity and through having other experiences and thoughts with which to compare new ones. Modeling is one way teachers can promote the development of interpretive thinking skills. According to Bloom's taxonomy, interpretive skills are higher order thinking skills than understanding, so expecting small children to exhibit these skills is unrealistic.

The six levels of Bloom's taxonomy and the skills each entails, from simplest to most complex, are as follows:

1. **Knowledge:** This level is the most basic level of learning. Students learn terminology and specific facts; tasks at this level ask students to define, label, recall, memorize, and list.

2. **Understanding and Comprehension:** This level of learning requires that students grasp the meaning of a concept; tasks at this level ask students to classify, explain, identify, locate, and review

3. **Application:** This level of learning requires that students take previous learning and use it in a new way; tasks at this level ask students to demonstrate, illustrate, distinguish, solve, write, choose, and dramatize

4. **Analysis:** This level of learning involves breaking down material to its component parts and using those parts; tasks at this level ask students to calculate, categorize, compare, contrast, criticize, distinguish, examine, and experiment

5. **Synthesis:** This level of learning requires that students take the analyzed parts from the previous level and converge them into creative new wholes; tasks at this level ask students to collect, compose, design, manage, plan, organize, and formulate

4. **Evaluation:** The highest level of learning on the taxonomy, according to research, is the level that is least often achieved. This level of learning requires that students judge the value of material based on experience, prior knowledge, opinions, and the end product; tasks at this level ask students to assess, appraise, predict, rate, support, evaluate, judge, and argue

Critical Listening Strategies

Oral speech can be very difficult to follow. First, we have no written record that we can re-read if we didn't hear or understand the material. Second, oral speech can be much less structured than written language. Yet, aside from re-reading, many of the skills and strategies that help us in reading comprehension can help us in listening comprehension. For example, as soon as we start listening to something new, we should tap into our prior knowledge in order to attach new information to what we already know. This activity will not only help us understand the new information more quickly, it will also help us remember the material.

We can also look for transitions between ideas. Sometimes, in oral speech, this exercise is pretty simple when voice tone or body language changes. Of course, we don't have the luxury of looking at paragraphs in oral language, but we do have the animation that comes with live speech. Human beings have to try very hard to be completely non-expressive in their speech. Listeners should take advantage of this and notice how the speaker changes character and voice to signal a transition of ideas.

Listeners can also better comprehend the underlying intents of speakers when they notice nonverbal cues. Simply looking at the expression on the face of a speaker can do more to signal irony, for example, than trying to extract irony from actual words. And often in oral speech, unlike written text, elements such as irony are not indicated by the actual words, but rather by the tone and nonverbal cues.

One good way to follow oral speech is to take notes and outline major points. Because oral speech can be more circular, as opposed to linear, than written text, keeping track of an author's message can be very helpful. In the classroom, students can learn this strategy by taking notes of the teacher's oral messages and other students' presentations and speeches.

Other classroom methods can help students learn good listening skills. For example, students can practice following complex directions. They can also orally retell stories or retell (in writing or in oral speech) oral presentations of stories or other materials. These activities give students direct practice in the very important skills of listening and are outlets through which they can slowly improve their comprehension of oral language and take decisive action based on oral speech.

Effective Listening

Teachers should relate the specific purpose of their reading assignment to the students. This information will help them do the following:

- ASSOCIATE—Relate ideas to each other.
- VISUALIZE— See pictures in your mind as you read.
- CONCENTRATE—Have a specific purpose for reading.
- REPEAT—Keep reminding yourself of important points and associate details to these points.

Oral language (listening and speaking) involves receiving and understanding messages sent by other people and then expressing our own feelings and ideas. Listening is a communication process, and, in order to be successful, students must participate. In active listening, students comprehend and evaluate a message before they can respond to the teacher.

Conversation requires more than just listening. It involves feedback and active involvement, which is particularly challenging because, in our culture, we learn to move conversations along, discourage silence in a conversation, and always have the last word. In a discussion, for example, when we are preparing our next response rather than listening to what others are saying, we are not actually participating in a conversation. Children must learn that listening carefully to others in discussions actually promotes better responses on the part of subsequent speakers. Expecting students to respond directly to the previous student's comments before moving ahead with their new comments encourages active listening. Used in both large and small group discussions, this practice teaches students to consider the thoughts of the previous speaker before posing their new comments.

Thinking Skills[jmm23][v24]

Reasoning skills are higher order skills that involve recalling information, forming basic concepts and creative ideas, and critical thinking. These skills are essential across the curriculum, and they can be fostered through the language arts.

Children need to be equipped with thinking skills and strategies to help them develop these skills. Thinking skills help to promote resiliency in children as well as help them apply what they learn in one situation to other, similar situations.

Phonics is one skill level that promotes critical thinking skills in children. This is because they learn many aspects of language that will help them in many other forms of formal logic, which is the foundation of thinking. Compacting the curriculum is another way of encouraging and facilitating thinking skills in children as they have to think across several different domains. Applying what they learn in Language Arts to subjects such as Math, Science or Social Studies encourages children to think about what they have learned and see connections between the school subjects.

In early childhood classrooms, the development of higher-order thinking skills is of paramount importance in helping them learn to read. When teachers read aloud to the students they can ask them questions about the text. Although asking literal questions is important to know whether students actually comprehend the material, asking inferential questions forces them to think about the answer. Skills such as predicting are very important for reading, which is why teachers should always ask "What do you think will happen?" or "What do you think the character will or should do?" Once children have the opportunity to analyze what they read, they no longer become passive learners, but are actively engaged in the learning process.

One way language arts teachers can encourage the development of these skills is through the use of such age-appropriate detective novels as the following:

Private Eyes Club mysteries by Crosby Bonsall

Nate the Great by Marjorie Sharmat.

Cam Jansen by David Adler and Susanna Natti

These books require children to notice details, evaluate all aspects of a situation, guess at what is significant and what will happen next, relate clues to the environment, and solve problems. Students must form associations, rely on past knowledge, and overlook irrelevant information. Their thinking may have to proceed through two or more steps to arrive at a conclusion. These factors are essential to developing critical thinking skills. Of course, students can apply these critical thinking skills to reading and interpreting any written work or to dissecting any conversation.

Skill 6.15   Identify strategies for presenting concepts for mathematical proficiency, including understanding mathematical ideas and concepts, fluent computations, problem solving, and logical reasoning progressing from concrete to semi-concrete to abstract

Presenting Concepts for Mathematical Proficiency

Children are born with an innate curiosity about the world around them. Toddlers group their toys and explore early mathematical concepts through their play as they complete their shape sorters or manipulate their building blocks into piles or towers. Some of the most up-to-date research in the area of mathematics indicates children may have an inborn number sense that helps them solve some complex problems before they understand the number and symbol system used in later mathematics. This intuitive ability to understand numbers and problems is typically referred to as a child's *number sense*.

Number Sense

Number sense is the foundation upon which all future math topics are built, and providing young children with the opportunity to interact with objects across multiple contexts helps them develop number sense. During this beginning area of mathematics, students progress at different levels at different times. For example, one student may be able to count and identify a group of five but not recognize the pattern of five on a die. Another student may count the group, recognize the pattern, and understand the concept of grouping things into piles of five and counting by the groups.

While in this beginning stage, children can identify how many objects are in a group. Typically, students will have some beginning oral counting system (1-10 or 1-20). These preschool children will also begin to identify the relationships between groups of objects such as size, quantity, more, less, bigger, and smaller.

In order to formalize the meaning of whole numbers, preschool children must develop an understanding of one-to-one correspondence and be able to link a single number name with one object at a time. For example, a child counts four blocks in a row and says the number as each block is touched. Getting a carton of milk for each of the other children at a table is another example of practicing this concept.

Preschool children should also be able to use one-to-one correspondence to compare the size of a group of objects. For example, a child should be able to compare the number of cars with the number another child has and say, "I have more…or less."

Number sense develops into the understanding of place value and number relationships. The students identify and explain how they can group numbers into *tens*, *ones*, and, eventually, *hundreds* or more. Using trading games, place value mats, and base ten blocks, students can develop these skills. These activities will progress until the student understands that the *one* in *sixteen* represents *ten*, not simply *one*.

Children first learn to count using the counting numbers (1, 2, 3). Preschool children should be able to recite the names of the numerals in order or sequence (rote counting). Activities that practice this skill include singing counting songs. Eventually, students should be able to attach a number name to a series of objects. A preschool child should understand that the last number spoken when counting a group of objects represents the total number of objects.

In kindergarten, children learn to read the numbers 0 through 10, and, in first grade, they should be able to read through the number 20. At first, this activity could involve connecting a pictorial representation of the number with a corresponding number of items. This exercise may or may not involve assistive technology Assistive technology is defined as the use of devices that help students, such as calculators, an abacus or manipulatives, such as blocks. As students advance, they should be able to read the numbers as sight words.

Students should be taught that we have a naming procedure for our number system. The numbers *0* through *12* have unique names. The numbers *13* through *19* are the *teens*. These names are a combination of earlier names, and the *ones* place is named first. For example, fourteen is short for *four ten*, which means *ten plus four*. The numbers *20* through *99* are also combinations of earlier names, but the *tens* place is named first. For example, forty-eight means *four tens plus eight*. The numbers *100* through *999* are combinations of hundreds and previous names. Once a number has more than three digits, groups of three digits are set off by commas.

Eventually, children develop the necessary skills to extrapolate these beginning concepts to more difficult situations and problems. They will make generalizations about number situations, even when they cannot use traditional computational methods to solve problems. For example, young children may be able to solve a multiplication problem, such *as four rows of three chairs, how many chairs*, using manipulatives and their number sense; however, they would not be able to solve the more traditional problem of *4 X 3*.

Using a variety of materials, teachers should present concepts of numeracy and other math concepts to children across situations until they reach levels of proficiency. As concepts of math build upon one another, the appropriate foundation must be in place for future learning to progress. By presenting concepts and ideas early, teachers give students the opportunity to experience and construct their own competencies.

Teachers can use a number line to help students understand addition and subtraction. Suppose we want to show *6 + 3* on a number line.

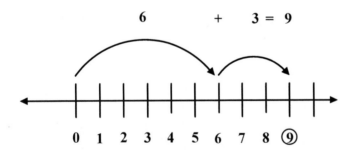

We can think of addition as starting from 0 and counting 6 units to the right on the line in the positive direction and then counting 3 more units to the right. The number line shows that this activity is the same as counting 9 units to the right.

In the same way, we can use a number line to represent subtraction. Suppose we have *6 – 3* or rather *6 + (–3)*.

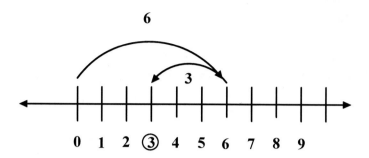

If *3* is shown by counting 3 positions to the right, then we can show *–3* as 3 positions to the left. We start from 0 and count 6 positions to the right and then count 3 positions to the left. This activity illustrates that *6 + (–3) = 3.*

As students gain an understanding of numbers and can read them, we should teach them to apply these concepts to everyday life. For example, once children can read the numbers *1* through *12*, they can learn how to tell time. At the very basic level, if shown a clock or a diagram of a clock, a child must understand that the big hand represents minutes and the little hand represents hours. The child begins to recognize that when the big hand is on the *12* and the little hand is on the *2*, it is 2 o'clock. As children learn to count by 5s, the teacher expands the concept so that they understand that the distance between 2 consecutive numbers is an interval of 5 minutes. They then begin to recognize that, when the big hand is on the *4* and the little hand is on the *2*, it is 20 minutes after the hour of 2 o'clock.

Another real-life application is money. In kindergarten, students learn to recognize a penny, nickel, dime, quarter, and one-dollar bill. In first grade, they learn how different combinations of coins have equivalent values; for example, 10 pennies are the same as 1 dime. Teaching children that money has value can start with the simple exercise of counting pennies to understand their monetary value and advance to counting nickels, dimes, and other coins. Then students can combine different coins and compute the value of the combination. As students advance in their understanding of the value of money, teachers can introduce shopping math. Students learn that money has value in exchange for goods. They can also learn to make and count change.

Understanding Mathematical Ideas and Concepts

Properties are rules that apply for addition, subtraction, multiplication, or division of real numbers. These properties are commutative, associative, and distributive.

Commutative: You can change the order of the terms or factors as follows.

> For addition: $a + b = b + a$
> For multiplication: $ab = ba$

> Since addition is the inverse operation of subtraction and multiplication is the inverse operation of division, no separate laws are needed for subtraction and division.

> Example: $5 + 8 = 8 + 5 = 13$

> Example: $2 \times 6 = 6 \times 2 = 12$

Associative: You can regroup the terms as you like.

> For addition: $a + (b + c) = (a + b) + c$
> For multiplication: $a(bc) = (ab)c$

> This rule does not apply to division and subtraction.

> Example: $(2 + 7) + 5 = 2 + (7 + 5)$
> $9 + 5 = 2 + 12 = 14$

> Example: $(3 \times 7) \times 5 = 3 \times (7 \times 5)$
> $21 \times 5 = 3 \times 35 = 105$

Identity: Finding a number so that when added to a term results in that number (additive identity); finding a number such that when multiplied by a term results in that number (multiplicative identity).

> For addition: $a + 0 = a$ (zero is additive identity)
> For multiplication: $a \cdot 1 = a$ (one is multiplicative)

> Example: $17 + 0 = 17$

> Example: $34 \times 1 = 34$

The product of any number and one is that number.

Inverse: Finding a number such that when added to the number it results in zero; or when multiplied by the number results in 1.

For addition: $a - a = 0$
For multiplication: $a \cdot (1/a) = 1$

$(-a)$ is the additive inverse of a; $(1/a)$, also called the reciprocal, is the multiplicative inverse of a.

Example: $25 - 25 = 0$

Example: $5 \times \frac{1}{5} = 1$ The product of any number and its reciprocal is one.

Distributive: Using this technique, we can operate on terms inside the parentheses without first performing operations inside the parentheses. This technique is especially helpful when you cannot combine the terms inside the parentheses.

$a\ (b + c) = ab + ac$

Example: $6 \times (4 + 9) = (6 \times 4) + (6 \times 9)$
$6 \times 13 = 24 + 54 = 78$

To multiply a sum by a number, multiply each addend by the number, then add the products.

Addition of whole numbers

The above properties and others lay the groundwork for a child's understanding of addition. Once children know these properties, they can use them as thinking strategies and remember addition facts for *0* through *9*. If we think of these facts in terms of a table, a child must learn 100 addition facts.

+	0	1	2	3	4	5	6	7	8	9
0	0	1	2	3	4	5	6	7	8	9
1	1	2	3	4	5	6	7	8	9	10
2	2	3	4	5	6	7	8	9	10	11
3	3	4	5	6	7	8	9	10	11	12
4	4	5	6	7	8	9	10	11	12	13
5	5	6	7	8	9	10	11	12	13	14
6	6	7	8	9	10	11	12	13	14	15
7	7	8	9	10	11	12	13	14	15	16
8	8	9	10	11	12	13	14	15	16	17
9	9	10	11	12	13	14	15	16	17	18

Knowing the properties helps that process.

1. **Commutativity**: If children understand commutativity, when they learn the first 55 addition facts, they will automatically know the remaining 45 facts; that is, *4 + 1 = 5* just as *1 + 4 = 5*, as highlighted in the table.

+	0	1	2	3	4	5	6	7	8	9
0		1	2	3	4	5	6	7	8	9
1			3	4	5	6	7	8	9	10
2				5	6	7	8	9	10	11
3					7	8	9	10	11	12
4						9	10	11	12	13
5							11	12	13	14
6								13	14	15
7									15	16
8										17
9										

2. **Adding zero**: Teaching children that $a + 0 = a$ adds another 10 addition facts; that is, $0 + 0 = 0, 1 + 0 = 1 \ldots 9 + 0 = 9$.

+	0	1	2	3	4	5	6	7	8	9
0	0	1	2	3	4	5	6	7	8	9
1	1		3	4	5	6	7	8	9	10
2	2			5	6	7	8	9	10	11
3	3				7	8	9	10	11	12
4	4					9	10	11	12	13
5	5						11	12	13	14
6	6							13	14	15
7	7								15	16
8	8									17
9	9									

3. **Counting on by 1 and 2**: Children find close sums, or sums obtained by adding 1 or 2, by counting on; for example, to find 8 + 2, think 8, then 9, 10.

[v30]

+	0	1	2	3	4	5	6	7	8	9
0	0	1	2	3	4	5	6	7	8	9
1	1	2	3	4	5	6	7	8	9	10
2	2	3	4	5	6	7	8	9	10	11
3	3	4	5		7	8	9	10	11	12
4	4	5	6			9	10	11	12	13
5	5	6	7				11	12	13	14
6	6	7	8					13	14	15
7	7	8	9						15	16
8	8	9	10							17
9	9	10	11							

4. **Combinations to ten**: Children use combinations of their ten fingers to find such sums as *7 + 3*, *6 + 4*, and *5 + 5*. There is now overlap in the table.

+	0	1	2	3	4	5	6	7	8	9
0	0	1	2	3	4	5	6	7	8	9
1	1	2	3	4	5	6	7	8	9	10
2	2	3	4	5	6	7	8	9	10	11
3	3	4	5		7	8	9	10	11	12
4	4	5	6			9	10	11	12	13
5	5	6	7			10	11	12	13	14
6	6	7	8		10			13	14	15
7	7	8	9	10					15	16
8	8	9	10							17
9	9	10	11							

5. **Doubles**: Children easily learn such addition facts as *1 + 1 = 2, 2 + 2 = 4,* and *3 + 3 = 6* because they are also the results of counting by twos.

+	0	1	2	3	4	5	6	7	8	9
0	0	1	2	3	4	5	6	7	8	9
1	1	2	3	4	5	6	7	8	9	10
2	2	3	4	5	6	7	8	9	10	11
3	3	4	5	6	7	8	9	10	11	12
4	4	5	6		8	9	10	11	12	13
5	5	6	7			10	11	12	13	14
6	6	7	8		10		12	13	14	15
7	7	8	9	10				14	15	16
8	8	9	10						16	17
9	9	10	11							18

6. **Associativity**: When children understand associativity as regrouping, they can understand that *8 + 7 = 15* is the same as *8 + (2 + 5) = 15* is the same as *(8 + 2) + 5 = 15* is the same as *10 + 5 = 15*. This completes the table.

+	0	1	2	3	4	5	6	7	8	9
0	0	1	2	3	4	5	6	7	8	9
1	1	2	3	4	5	6	7	8	9	10
2	2	3	4	5	6	7	8	9	10	11
3	3	4	5	6	7	8	9	10	11	12
4	4	5	6	7	8	9	10	11	12	13
5	5	6	7	8	9	10	11	12	13	14
6	6	7	8	9	10	11	12	13	14	15
7	7	8	9	10	11	12	13	14	15	16
8	8	9	10	11	12	13	14	15	16	17
9	9	10	11	12	13	14	15	16	17	18

*Doubles ± 1 and ± 2: **As an example, 7 + 8 = 7 + 7 + 1 = 14 + 1 = 15. This procedure overlaps with the other procedures.***

Subtraction of Whole Numbers

Subtraction is expressed as *a – b*, read "*a* minus *b*," where *a* is the minuend and *b* is the subtrahend. Just as properties and methods aid students in understanding addition, conceptual models can help students with subtraction.

1. Take-Away:
   Start with 10 objects.
   Take away 4 objects.
   How many objects are left?

2. Missing Addend:
   Start with 4 objects.
   How many more objects are needed to give a total of 10 objects?

3. Comparison:
   Start with two sets of objects with 10 objects in one set and 4 in the other set.
   How many more objects are in the larger set?

4. Number–Line:
   Move forward (to the right) 10 units.
   Move backward (to the left) 4 units.
   What is the distance from 0?

Multiplication of Whole Numbers

Multiplication is one of the four basic number operations. In simple terms, multiplication is the addition of a number to itself a specified number of times.

Multiplication is simply repeated addition. This relationship explains the concept of variable addition. We can show that the expression $4x + 3x = 7x$ is true by rewriting 4 times x and 3 times x as repeated addition, yielding the expression $(x + x + x + x) + (x + x + x)$. Thus, because of the relationship between multiplication and addition, variable addition is accomplished by coefficient addition.

For example, 4 multiplied by 3 is the equal to $4 + 4 + 4$ or $3 + 3 + 3 + 3$. Thinking in terms of groups is another way of conceptualizing multiplication. For example, if we have 4 groups of 3 students, the total number of students is 4 multiplied by 3. We call the solution to a multiplication problem the *product*.

The basic algorithm for whole number multiplication begins with aligning the numbers by place value with the number containing more places on top.

$$\begin{array}{r} 172 \\ \times\ 43 \\ \hline \end{array}$$

⟶ Note that we placed 172 on top because it has more places than 43 does.

Next, we multiply the ones' place of the second number by each place value of the top number sequentially.

$$\begin{array}{r} (2) \\ 172 \\ \times\ 43 \\ \hline 516 \end{array}$$

⟶ {3 x 2 = 6, 3 x 7 = 21, 3 x 1 = 3}

Note that we had to carry a 2 to the hundreds column because $3 \times 7 = 21$. Also, we add, not multiply, carried numbers to the product.

Next, we multiply the number in the tens' place of the second number by each place value of the top number sequentially. Because we are multiplying by a number in the tens' place, we place a zero at the end of this product.

$$\begin{array}{r} (2) \\ 172 \\ \times\ 43 \\ \hline 516 \\ 6880 \end{array}$$

⟶ {4 x 2 = 8, 4 x 7 = 28, 4 x 1 = 4}

To determine the final product, we add the two partial products.

$$
\begin{array}{r}
172 \\
\times\ \ 43 \\
\hline
516 \\
+\ 6880 \\
\hline
7396
\end{array}
$$

→ The product of 172 and 43 is 7396.

Example: A student buys 4 boxes of crayons. Each box contains 16 crayons. How many total crayons does the student have?

The total number of crayons is *16 x 4*.

$$
\begin{array}{r}
16 \\
\times\ \ 4 \\
\hline
64
\end{array}
$$

Total number of crayons equals 64.

Division of Whole Numbers

Division, the inverse of multiplication, is another of the four basic number operations. When we divide one number by another, we determine how many times we can multiply the divisor (number divided by) before we exceed the number we are dividing (dividend). For example, 8 divided by 2 equals 4 because we can multiply *2* four times to reach *8 (2 x 4 = 8 or 2 + 2 + 2 + 2 = 8)*. Using the grouping conceptualization we used with multiplication, we can divide *8* into 4 groups of 2 or 2 groups of 4. We call the answer to a division problem the quotient.

If the divisor does not divide evenly into the dividend, we express the leftover amount either as a remainder or as a fraction with the divisor as the denominator. For example, 9 divided by 2 equals 4 with a remainder of 1 or 4 ½.

The basic algorithm for division is long division. We start by representing the quotient as follows:

$14\overline{)293}$ → 14 is the divisor and 293 is the dividend.

This represents 293 ÷ 14.

Next, we divide the divisor into the dividend starting from the left.

$14\overline{)293}^{\ \ \ 2}$ → 14 divides into 29 two times with a remainder.

Next, we multiply the partial quotient by the divisor, subtract this value from the first digits of the dividend, and bring down the remaining dividend digits to complete the number.

$$
\begin{array}{r}
2 \\
14\overline{)293} \\
-28 \\
\hline
13
\end{array}
$$
→ 2 x 14 = 28, 29 – 28 = 1, and bringing down the 3 yields 13.

Finally, we divide again (the divisor into the remaining value) and repeat the preceding process. The number left after the subtraction represents the remainder.

$$
\begin{array}{r}
20 \\
14\overline{)293} \\
-28 \\
\hline
13 \\
-0 \\
\hline
13
\end{array}
$$
→ The final quotient is 20 with a remainder of 13. We can also represent this quotient as 20 13/14.

Addition and Subtraction of Decimals

When adding and subtracting decimals, we align the numbers by place value as we do with whole numbers. After adding or subtracting each column, we bring the decimal down, placing it in the same location as in the numbers added or subtracted.

Example: Find the sum of 152.3 and 36.342.

$$
\begin{array}{r}
152.300 \\
+\ 36.342 \\
\hline
188.642
\end{array}
$$

Note that we placed two zeroes after the final place value in 152.3 to clarify the column addition.

Example: Find the difference of 152.3 and 36.342.

```
      2 9 10            (4)11(12)
   152.300            152.300
  -  36.342     ───▶    36.342
        58            115.958
```

Note how we borrowed to subtract from the zeroes in the hundredths' and thousandths' place of 152.300.

Multiplication of Decimals

When multiplying decimal numbers, we multiply exactly as with whole numbers and move the decimal in from the left the total number of decimal places contained in the two numbers multiplied. For example, when multiplying 1.5 and 2.35, we place the decimal in the product 3 places in from the left (3.525).

Example: Find the product of 3.52 and 4.1.

```
        3.52        Note that the 2 numbers have 3 total decimal places
      x 4.1
        352
   + 14080
      14432          We place the decimal 3 places in from the left.
```

Thus, the final product is 14.432.

Example: A shopper has 5 one-dollar bills, 6 quarters, 3 nickels, and 4 pennies in his pocket. How much money does he have?

```
5 x $1.00 = $5.00     $0.25     $0.05     $0.01
                       x 6       x 3       x 4
                      $1.50     $0.15     $0.04
```

Note the placement of the decimals in the multiplication products. Thus, the total amount of money in the shopper's pocket is

```
    $5.00
     1.50
     0.15
   + 0.04
    $6.69
```

Addition and Subtraction of Fractions

Key Points

1. You need a common denominator in order to add and subtract reduced and improper fractions.

   Example: $\dfrac{1}{3} + \dfrac{7}{3} = \dfrac{1+7}{3} = \dfrac{8}{3} = 2\dfrac{2}{3}$

   Example: $\dfrac{4}{12} + \dfrac{6}{12} - \dfrac{3}{12} = \dfrac{4+6-3}{12} = \dfrac{7}{12}$

2. Adding an integer and a fraction of the <u>same</u> sign results directly in a mixed fraction.

   Example: $2 + \dfrac{2}{3} = 2\dfrac{2}{3}$

   Example: $^{-}2 - \dfrac{3}{4} = ^{-}2\dfrac{3}{4}$

3. Adding an integer and a fraction with different signs involves the following steps:

   - get a common denominator
   - add or subtract as needed
   - change to a mixed fraction if possible

   Example: $2 - \dfrac{1}{3} = \dfrac{2 \times 3 - 1}{3} = \dfrac{6 - 1}{3} = \dfrac{5}{3} = 1\dfrac{2}{3}$

   Example: Add $7\dfrac{3}{8} + 5\dfrac{2}{7}$

   Add the whole numbers, add the fractions, and combine the two results:

   $$7\dfrac{3}{8} + 5\dfrac{2}{7} = (7 + 5) + (\dfrac{3}{8} + \dfrac{2}{7})$$
   $$= 12 + \dfrac{(7 \times 3) + (8 \times 2)}{56} \quad \text{(LCM of 8 and 7)}$$
   $$= 12 + \dfrac{21 + 16}{56} = 12 + \dfrac{37}{56} = 12\dfrac{37}{56}$$

Example: Perform the operation.

$$\frac{2}{3} - \frac{5}{6}$$

We first find the LCM of 3 and 6, which is 6.

$$\frac{2 \times 2}{3 \times 2} - \frac{5}{6} \rightarrow \frac{4-5}{6} = \frac{^-1}{6}$$ (Using method A)

Fluent Computations

Students who progress through the normal mathematical developmental process will be asked to complete computations on a regular basis. For children in grades kindergarten through third grade, this activity mostly involves learning basic computational facts and skills.

Understanding the conceptual learning behind addition, subtraction, multiplication, and division is important, but students must be fluent in completing these basic computations. As students first learn the concepts, they use manipulatives to ensure that understanding is in place. However, students should not continue to use manipulatives (including their fingers) on an ongoing basis.

Removal of this scaffolding is necessary to increase the students' problem solving skills. This unique balancing act requires concerted effort on the part of the educator. True understanding of each operation is a complex process for young students to demonstrate. It involves number sense and the ability to reason out answers. Students who cannot use their skills to understand the correctness or reasonableness of answers are not showing true understanding of the operations.

Often, students and teachers both become so involved in the steps or process for completing different computations that they lose sight of the underlying mathematical reasoning behind the computation. So, once the conceptual understanding is ensured, the focus must shift to fluency of these computations.

Students who are fluent at solving calculations, particularly those that involve basic facts, can more easily focus on the reasoning behind the problems. True fluency is not memorization but the combination of understanding operations and how they relate, number relationships, and the base ten system. Students gain fluency by achieving a true understanding of mathematical concepts or developing what has been termed as a *mathematical memory* (Russell, 1999).

We can measure fluency. The most common method, which is used in progress monitoring assessments across the country, is *digits correct per minute*. Under this model, we give students a timed assessment that is generally a mixture of all problems within the curriculum at their grade level. The amount of time allowed for the assessment varies according to the company that developed the test.

We score the students' work to determine how many digits correct they achieved in one minute. Data from assessments such as these have been gathered and compiled to determine appropriate grade level norms for different periods throughout the school year (typically fall, winter, and spring). Two examples of companies who provide such materials are MBSP (published by Pro-Ed) and AIMS Web.

Russell, S. J., Smith, D., Storeygard, J., & Murray, M. (1999). *Relearning to teach arithmetic: Multiplication and division. Parsippany*, NJ: Dale Seymour Publications.

Math Strategies to Use in Early Childhood:

http://mathcentral.uregina.ca/RR/database/RR.09.97/sauter2.html

---

Problem Solving

Too often, the term *problem solving* is misinterpreted as mathematical *word problems*. In fact, if a child is unaware of the answer, any problem presented is a problem to be solved. From the very beginning, children need to experience a variety of mathematical situations across all subject areas. Exposing children to a variety of contexts in which to solve problems allows the child to develop their own constructs upon which they can build new learning.

Problem solving is not about a specific strategy or right way to get an answer; it is about letting students of varying mathematical skills and abilities look at the same situation and find a way to solve it. In a group of five children, we can reasonably expect each child to use a different method to solve the problem. Providing students with the means to investigate a problem, rather than restricting them to one mode of solution, lets them be flexible in their approach. For example, a kindergartener has the following problem: If you have three pies and twelve people to feed, how can you easily divide the pies? This student can easily use pieces of real pie to work out an appropriate solution, which is one way to find the answer. However, the parent or teacher who insists that the student use the division algorithm to solve the problem may automatically set this same student up for failure.

We should incorporate real-world problem solving into daily classroom activities so that students will understand, appreciate, and value the process. Having the students help with lunch count and attendance, count the number of days left in the school year, or calculate the time left until recess are examples of including realistic problem solving in the classroom.

Teachers should incorporate problem-solving activities into all subject areas. In science, children can graph the daily temperatures and make predictions for future temperatures. In social studies, they can gather, tabulate, and calculate the data related to the topic presented (how many classmates agree that drugs are bad for your body). In language arts, children can solve problems found in children's literature. Charting favorite books, calculating ages of characters in stories, and drawing maps of the setting(s) of books are examples of connecting language arts and math. Numerous exciting books have a mathematical basis and can be used to cover both subjects in a fun manner.

Teachers are important role models. Thinking aloud as you come across a problem in the course of the day will help the students realize the necessity and real-world implications of solving problems. Encouraging students to be reflective will also help build the necessary mathematical language. Also, students can share their ideas and methods with each other, which is an excellent strategy for learning about problem solving.

Typically, Problem solving has five steps. Teachers should teach each of the following steps explicitly and model them regularly:

1. Identify the problem.
2. Determine the question.
3. Find a strategy to solve the problem.
4. Gather the materials and method to record your work.
5. Solve the problem.
6. Explain the method used to solve the problem.

Direct observation is the most effective method of assessing problem-solving skills. Teachers need to observe students to determine what strategies they are implementing. Watching students solve problems can give teachers insight into future teaching opportunities and the skills students have already mastered. Educators have difficulty assigning grades to problem solving in isolation from other skills, but the information gained from the process is critical to future teaching.

Logical Reasoning

Reasoning is the crux of all mathematics. Without the ability to reason, students cannot make adequate progress through future mathematical processes. Young children have already developed reasoning skills before they come to school, but they may be unable to identify or classify those skills.

Children use reasoning skills to explore, justify, and use mathematical knowledge. The underlying premise for mathematical reasoning is that students make conjectures, use models to investigate their conjectures, and draw logical conclusions from the entire process.

- **Making Conjectures**—Conjectures are assumptions, hypothesis, predictions, or estimates about the problem presented. When making conjectures, students should be able to justify their thinking. At the very young level, they may use objects, pictures, and words. As students become more confident, they incorporate numbers or algorithms into their justification. As part of the process of making a conjecture, the children should be able to describe a plan for validating their suppositions.

- **Using Models**—At this stage, the students use objects or models to investigate their conjectures, and children aged four through ten must have access to pictures, objects, or other tangibles. This part of the process directly involves working through the plan developed to prove or disprove the conjecture. The process may be simplistic at this level but should not be skipped; working through the entire process is important for building later reasoning skills.

- **Drawing Logical Conclusions**—Students have completed the plan and have a solution. By working through the entire process, the children determine whether or not the conjecture made at the beginning is an accurate hypothesis. Children should be able to explain how they arrived at the conclusion and make appropriate connections to all of the previous steps.

Progressing from Concrete to Semi-Concrete to Abstract

Teaching young children mathematics requires a progression from the tangible to the abstract. As new concepts are introduced, the teacher should use concrete objects so that the students can manipulate, touch, and explore and be actively engaged in the learning. In this way, students can construct their own foundations, questions, and concepts related to numbers.

Providing the students with concrete and meaningful learning experiences is more involved than simply passing out blocks or beans to help introduce a concept. It involves using and developing the language of math. Through inquiry-based learning, the students can not only explore the materials and concepts, but they can begin to organize the information so that they can communicate their ideas of mathematics.

Without this concrete level of exploration, students may be able to memorize rote processes for solving problems (algorithms), but they may lack the foundational understanding necessary to make mathematical connections to everyday situations and experiences. Some students will be unable to see the broader generalizations found throughout math unless they are exposed to the concepts through concrete learning experiences.

Mathematics has its own language, which requires practice and development. Often students who are struggling with the concepts lack the appropriate vocabulary and exposure to mathematical language they need to be successful. Teachers should promote the development of this vocabulary in the same way they promote vocabulary for reading and other subjects.

Successful math teachers introduce their students to multiple problem-solving strategies and create a classroom environment in which they encourage free thought and experimentation. Teachers can promote problem solving by giving students multiple chances to solve problems, giving them credit for reworking test or homework problems, and encouraging idea sharing through class discussion. Once the students are successful at completing problem solving activities at the concrete level, they should be exposed to the semi-concrete (use of pictures and symbols) level and, finally, to the abstract level (use of symbols or letters to represent numbers or concepts). Teachers should be familiar with several specific problem-solving skills.

Using the **guess-and-check** strategy, students can make an initial guess at the solution, check the answer, and use the outcome to guide the next guess. With each successive guess, the student gets closer to the correct answer. Constructing a table from the guesses can help organize the data.

Example: There are 100 coins in a jar, and 10 are dimes. The rest are pennies and nickels. The jar holds twice as many pennies as nickels. How many pennies and nickels are in the jar?

The jar holds 90 nickels and pennies in the jar (100 coins – 10 dimes).

Twice as many pennies as nickels are in the jar. The student makes guesses that fulfill the criteria and adjusts the number based on the answer found. They continue until they have the correct answer—60 pennies and 30 nickels.

Number of Pennies	Number of Nickels	Total Number of Pennies and Nickels
40	20	60
80	40	120
70	35	105
60	30	90

When solving a problem that gives the final result and the steps to reach the result, students must **work backwards** to determine what the starting point must have been.

Example:
John subtracted 7 from his age and divided the result by 3. The final result was 4. What is John's age?

Work backward by reversing the operations:
4 x 3 = 12
12 + 7 = 19
John is 19 years old.

Estimation and testing for **reasonableness** are related skills students should use before and after solving a problem. These skills are particularly important when students use calculators to find answers.

Example:
Find the sum of 4387 + 7226 + 5893.

4300 + 7200 + 5800 = 17300	Estimation.
4387 + 7226 + 5893 = 17506	Actual sum.

By comparing the estimate to the actual sum, students can determine that the answer is reasonable.

Throughout the process, teachers should encourage students to develop methods for recording their information through the use of pictures, symbols, numbers, or other more appropriate methods. Venn diagrams are excellent for comparing mathematical concepts. By learning to use pictures and numbers together to represent an idea, students develop a method of communicating the concepts they are learning. By using these pictures or student-created models and labeling them with the correct mathematical name for the idea, teachers build the vocabulary and thinking skills of their students. Together these student-created and teacher-labeled representations are not only a communication tool, but a concrete method for explaining conjectures to each other.

Manipulatives

Manipulatives are hands-on materials that make abstract concepts concrete for students. However, not all manipulatives can be used to model a mathematical idea.

Good teachers use many different types of manipulatives. Manipulatives can be such everyday items as Popsicle™ sticks, dried beans, smooth stones, egg cartons, or poker chips; or they can be commercially prepared items such as geoboards, algebra tiles, and base ten blocks. The manipulative must represent the concept or operation that the students are trying to learn.

Example:
Use tiles to demonstrate both geometric ideas and number theory.

Give each group of students 12 tiles and instruct them to build rectangles. Students draw their rectangles on paper.

12×1

1×12

3×4

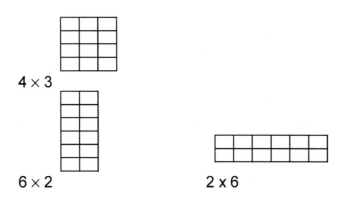

4×3

6×2

2×6

Skill 6.16   Identify strategies, including technology, for presenting social studies processes and concepts

The Internet and other research resources provide a wealth of information on thousands of interesting topics for students preparing presentations or projects. Using such search engines as Google, Microsoft, and Infotrac, students can search multiple Internet resources or databases. Before beginning a search, students should have an outline of the purpose of a project or research presentation that includes the following:

- Purpose—identity the reason for the search.
- Objective—have a clear thesis for a project so that you can be specific on Internet searches.
- Preparation—when using resources or collecting data, create folders for sorting through the information. Providing labels for the folders will create a system of organization that will make construction of the final project or presentation easier and less time consuming.
- Procedure—organize folders and make a procedural list of what the project or presentation needs to include. This activity will create A+ work for students and A+ grading for teachers.
- Visuals or artifacts—choose data or visuals that are specific to the subject content or presentation. Make sure that poster boards or Power Point presentations can be visually seen from all areas of the classroom. Teachers can provide laptop computers for Power Point presentations.

When teachers model and instruct students in the proper use of search techniques, they minimize time wasted in preparing projects and wasted paper from students who print every search. In some school districts, students are allowed a maximum number of printed pages per week. Since students have Internet accounts for computer use, the school's librarian and classroom teachers can easily monitor the printing.

Having the school's librarian or technology expert as a guest speaker in classrooms provides another method of sharing and modeling proper use of technology in presentation preparation. Teachers can also appoint technology experts from the students in a classroom to work with students on projects and presentations. In high schools, technology classes provide students with upper-class teacher assistants who fill the role of technology assistants.

Internet usage agreements define a number of criteria for technology use to which students must agree in order to have access to school computers. Students must exercise responsibility and accountability in using technology during the school day. Students who violate any part of the computer usage agreement are subject to having all access to school computers or other educational technology denied or blocked. For the student who needs to use the school computer and printer to print a paper, this discipline could make the difference in handing assignments in on time or receiving a lower grade for late assignments.

An **atlas** is a collection of maps usually bound into a book and containing geographic features; political boundaries; and perhaps social, religious, and economic statistics. Atlases can be found in most libraries, but they are widely available on the Internet.

Statistical **surveys** are used in the social sciences to collect information on a sample of the population. With any kind of information, students must take care to record data accurately so the results are not skewed or distorted.

Opinion Polls represent the opinions of a population. The polling company asks a number of people a series of questions about a product, place, person, or event and then uses the results to apply the answers to a larger group or population. Polls, like surveys, are subject to errors in the process. Errors can occur based on who is asked the question and where they are asked. The time of day and the biases of the polling company also affect the poll results.

Maps, Graphs, and Charts

Physical locations of the earth's surface features include the four major hemispheres and continents of each hemisphere. Political locations are the political divisions, if any, within each continent. Both physical and political locations are precisely determined in the following two *ways:* (1) Surveying determines boundary lines and distance from other features. (2) Imaginary lines of latitude (parallels) and longitude (meridians) precisely determine exact locations. The intersection of these lines at right angles forms a grid, making it possible use any two grid coordinates to pinpoint the exact location of any place.

The process of putting the features of the Earth onto a flat surface is called **projection**. All maps are really map projections. Each type of map projection deals with the problem of distortion in a different way. Complicated mathematics are used to make some map projections. However, looking at the three most common types can help you understand the basic ideas behind map projections

(1) **Cylindrical Projections**—To create this projection, map makers take a cylinder of paper and wrap it around a globe and then use a light to project the globe's features onto the paper. Distortion is least where the paper touches the globe. For example, if you wrapped the paper so that it touched the globe at the equator, the map from this projection would have just a little distortion near the equator. However, if you move north or south of the equator, the distortion increases as you move further away from the equator. The Mercator **Projection** is the best known and most widely used cylindrical projection. Gerardus Mercator, a Flemish mapmaker, developed it in 1569.

(2) **Conical Projections**—To create this projection, map makers use a cone of paper. The cone is made so that it touches a globe at the base of the cone only. It can also be made so that it cuts through part of the globe in two different places. Again, the least distortion occurs where the paper touches the globe. If the cone touches at two different points, there is some distortion at both points. Conical projections are most often used to map areas in the **middle latitudes**. Maps of the United States are most often conical projections because most of the country lies within these latitudes.

(3) **Flat-Plane Projections**—Made with a flat piece of paper that touches the globe at one point only, flat-plane projections are often used to show the areas of the north and south poles. Areas near the point where the paper touches the globe show little distortion. A **Gnomonic Projection** is one such flat projection. On this kind of map all meridians appear as straight lines, Gnomonic projections are useful because any straight line drawn between points on it forms a **Great-Circle Route**.

Great-Circle Routes can best be described by thinking of a globe. On the globe, you can find the shortest route between two points by simply stretching a string from one point to the other. However, if the string were extended in reality so that it took into effect the globe's curvature, it would then make a great-circle. A great-circle is any circle that cuts a sphere, such as the globe, into two equal parts. Because of distortion, most maps do not show great-circle routes as straight lines, Gnomonic projections, however, do show the shortest distance between the two places as a straight line; they are, therefore, valuable for navigation. They are called Great-Circle Sailing Maps.

To analyze a given map properly, we must be familiar with the various parts and symbols that most modern maps use. These mostly standardized parts and symbols include the following:

The Title—All maps should have a title, just like all books should. The title tells us what information we can find on the map.

The Legend—Most maps have a legend. A legend tells the reader about the various symbols used on that particular map and what the symbols represent. The legend is also called a *map key*.

The Grid—A grid is a series of lines used to find exact places and locations on the map. Several different kinds of grid systems are currently in use; however, most maps use the longitude and latitude system, known as the **Geographic Grid System**.

Directions—Most maps have some directional system to show which way the map is being presented. Often on a map, we will see a small compass with arrows showing the four basic directions—north, south, east, and west.

The Scale—This symbol is used to show the relationship between a unit of measurement on the map versus the real-world measure on the Earth. Maps are drawn to many different scales. Some maps show a lot of detail for a small area. Others show a greater span of distance. We should always be aware of just what scale is being used. For instance the scale might be something like 1 inch = 10 miles for a small area, or, for a map showing the whole world, the scale might be 1 inch = 1,000 miles.

Maps have four main properties. They are (1) the size of the areas shown on the map, (2) the shapes of the areas, (3) consistent scales, and (4) straight line directions. A map can be drawn so that it is correct in one or more of these properties. No map can be correct in all of them.

Equal areas—One property maps can have is equal areas. In an equal area map, the meridians and parallels are drawn so that the areas shown have the same proportions as they do on the Earth. For example, Greenland is about 118th the size of South America; therefore, it will be show as 118th the size of South America on an equal area map. The **Mercator projection** is an example of a map that does not have equal areas. In it, Greenland appears to be about the same size as South America because the distortion is very bad at the poles and Greenland lies near the North Pole.

Conformal Map—A second map property is conformal or correct shapes. No maps can show very large areas of the earth in their exact shapes. Only globes can really do that; however, conformal maps are as close as possible to true shapes. The United States is often shown on a Lambert Conformal Conic Projection Map.

Consistent Scales—Many maps attempt to use the same scale on all parts of the map. Generally, this attempt is easier when maps show a relatively small part of the earth's surface. For example, a map of Florida might be a Consistent Scale Map. Generally maps showing large areas are not consistent-scale maps because of distortion. Often such maps will have two scales noted in the key. One scale, for example, would be accurate to measure distances between points along the Equator. Another would be used to measure distances between the North Pole and the South Pole.

Maps showing physical features often try to show information about the elevation or **relief** of the land. **Elevation** is the distance above or below the sea level. The elevation is usually shown with colors; for instance, all areas on a map that are at a certain level are shown in the same color.

Relief Maps—These maps show the shape of the land surface—flat, rugged, or steep. Relief maps usually give more detail than simply the overall elevation of the land's surface. Relief is also sometimes shown with colors, but **contour lines** are another way to show relief. These lines connect all points of a land surface that are the same height.

Thematic Maps—These maps are used to show more specific information, often on a single **theme** or topic. Thematic maps show the distribution or amount of a feature over a certain given area in such topics of interest as population density, climate, economic information, cultural, and political information.

Although maps have advantages over globes and photographs, they do have a major disadvantage. Most maps are flat, and the Earth is a sphere. We cannot reproduce exactly on a flat surface an object shaped like a sphere. In order to put the earth's features onto a map, they must be stretched. This stretching is called **distortion.**

Distortion does not mean that maps are wrong; it simply means that they are not perfect representations of the Earth or its parts. **Cartographers,** or mapmakers, understand the problems of distortion. They try to design maps with as little distortion as possible.

To apply information obtained from **graphs**, we must understand why graphs are used. Graphs are used for the following major reasons:

1. To present a model or theory visually in order to show how two or more variables interrelate.

2. To present real world data visually in order to show how two or more variables interrelate.

Graphs themselves are most useful to show the sequential increase or decrease of a variable or specific correlations among two or more variables in a given circumstance. **Bar graphs** and **line graphs** are used most often, with the most common one being the bar graph.

A **bar graph** clarifies the differences in a given set of variables. However, it is limited because it cannot really show the actual proportional increase or decrease of each given variable to each other. In order to show a decrease, a bar graph must show the *bar* under the starting line. In this configuration, the graph cannot really show how the variables relate to each other.

To show a decrease, we must use a **line graph**. Line graphs can be **linear** or **non-linear**. A linear line graph uses a series of straight lines; a non-linear line graph uses a curved line. Though the lines can be either straight or curved, all of the lines are called **curves**.

A line graph uses a number line or **axis.** The numbers are generally placed in order, equal distances from one another. The number line represents a number, degree, or some other variable at an appropriate point on the line. We use two lines, which intersect at a specific point. They are the X-axis and the Y-axis. The Y-axis is a vertical line; the X-axis is a horizontal line. Together they form a **coordinate system**. The difference between a point on the line of the X-axis and the Y-axis is called the **slope** of the line, or the change in the value on the vertical axis divided by the change in the value on the horizontal axis. The Y-axis number is called the rise and the X-axis number is called the **run**; therefore, the equation for slope is

SLOPE = RISE—Change in value on the vertical axis
          RUN—Change in value on the horizontal axis

The slope tells the amount of increase or decrease of a given **specific** variable. When using two or more variables, we can plot the difference between them in any given situation. This complexity makes presenting information on a line graph more involved. It also makes it more informative and accurate than a simple bar graph. Knowledge of the term slope and what it is and how it is measured helps describe verbally the pictures we are seeing visually. For example, if a curve is said to have a slope of *zero,* you should picture a flat line. If a curve has a slope of *one*, you should picture a rising line that makes a 45-degree angle with the horizontal and vertical axis lines.

The preceding examples are of **linear**, or straight line, curves. With **non-linear** curves (the ones that really do curve), the slope of the curve is constantly changing, so the slope of the non-linear curved line will be at a specific point. How is this done? The slope of a straight line that intersects the curve at that specific point determines the slope of a non-linear curve. In all graphs, an upward sloping line represents a direct relationship between the two variables. A downward slope represents an inverse relationship between the two variables. In reading any graph, we must always understand what is being measured, what can be deduced, and what cannot be deduced from the given graph.

[jmm31][v32]To use **charts** correctly, we must understand that, while graphs and charts are similar, they have different uses. The choice is usually based on which, a graph or chart, can best portray the information. The **Pie-chart**, one of the most common charts, is easy to read and understand, even for the lay person. You often see pie-charts used to illustrate the differences in percentages among various items or to demonstrate the divisions of a whole.

Collecting, describing, and analyzing data are fun activities in the early childhood classroom. There are numerous exciting and playful methods for collecting data to be used in various classroom lessons. Some fun ways to collect data include:

- Have students drop a piece of cereal into a bowl that is their favorite color.
- Have students draw a tally mark under their lunch choices on a bulletin board.
- Utilize a thumbs-up or thumbs-down approach for students' responses when asking whole group questions.
- Use wipe boards.
- Have the students themselves stand in lines to form a human graph to show a particular set of data.

Ideas for collecting data to organize, describe, and analyze:

- Favorite colors
- Birthdays
- Hair/eye/clothing colors
- Favorite foods
- Favorite books
- Ending to a story (like/don't like)
- Shoe size (type/color/style)
- Favorite songs

Once the data has been collected, it needs to be organized into a format easily analyzed by the students. This can involve tables, tally charts, and graphs. Using the real objects to form the bars of the graphs can provide the students with immediate results. This can be very important to young children. It also provides a concrete representation whereas transferring the data to paper to create the graph/table or chart is more abstract of a concept.

Once the graph, table, or chart is completed, it is important to utilize mathematical language to describe and analyze the information. Comparing two different bars on the graph, finding the greatest, finding the smallest/least or other types of analysis help students to develop their critical thinking skills. The students need to be exposed to vocabulary terms that mean the same thing (such as smallest and least).

Gathering, organizing, and analyzing data is an easy to incorporate daily routine in the early childhood classroom. An entire activity can be completed in five to ten minutes of the math class on a regular basis and provide students with a fun, real-life, critical thinking activity which increases not only mathematical understanding and skills but builds vocabulary skills as well. This area of math can help to tie together many other subject areas in an easy way.

BAR, LINE, PICTO-, AND CIRCLE GRAPHS

	Test 1	Test 2	Test 3	Test 4	Test 5
Evans, Tim	75	66	80	85	97
Miller, Julie	94	93	88	97	98
Thomas, Randy	81	86	88	87	90

Bar graphs are used to compare various quantities.

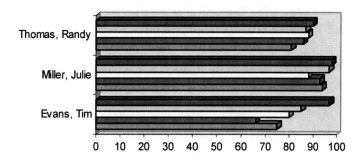

Line graphs are used to show trends, often over a period of time.

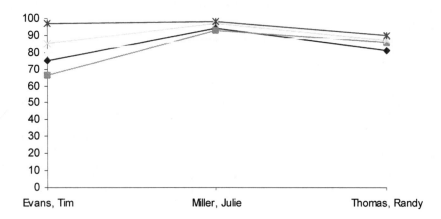

A **pictograph** shows comparison of quantities using symbols. Each symbol represents a number of items.

Circle graphs show the relationship of various parts to each other and the whole. Percents are used to create circle graphs.

> Julie spends 8 hours each day in school, 2 hours doing homework, 1 hour eating dinner, 2 hours watching television, 10 hours sleeping and the rest of the time doing other things.

When it comes to statistics, data collection, description, and analysis vocabulary, math word walls, posters, and wall displays may be the most effective method for increasing vocabulary. Interactive bulletin boards are great ways for students to explore their vocabulary. Graphs, charts, or tables can be included on a bulletin board with vocabulary posted next to the board. Students can use this as a center activity where they will then match the vocabulary term with the appropriate display on the bulletin board. The teacher can use this activity to determine a student's level of accuracy and mastery with their vocabulary as well as making the activity more valuable.

As children become more and more skilled at collecting data, they will inevitably require various methods for representing the data. With charts, tables and graphs, teachers can help further the children's understanding of the information collected.

It is important for students to be taught in an explicit manner how the individual data collected are represented on the chart, table, or graph. This is similar to the teaching of one-to-one correspondence. Having students help in the creation of the chart/table/graph is an excellent method for helping students to see the specific correlation between the data and the visual representation of that data.

With very young children, matching up the tangible data and the representation in a one-to-one way can help students to see the correspondence. This alignment is important for students to learn, as they will later need to translate data independently into a visual representation.

Another activity that can be of benefit to young children is to provide them with the visual representation and have the students count out manipulatives to show the amount on the graph/chart/table. For example, if the graph shows how many of each color block was found in the block tray, students could count out that many blocks and lay them on top of the graph. This process of showing the students a direct correlation between the data and the visual representation is a crucial beginning step to further understanding of data analysis.

Once this beginning level of understanding is achieved, less explicit methods can be employed and introduced. General questioning procedures, as well as having the students create visuals from data sets provided, are good methods teachers can implement to help students make the transition to the next level of statistical analysis.

For students in Pre-Kindergarten through third grade, it is important to provide tangible objects often for repetition and practice. Though third grade, students typically have advanced to a level of being able to interpret tables and graphs without the need for manipulatives. Skills that are more complex can be incorporated with students using them and deepening their understanding of statistical analysis. For instance, some graphs/charts/tables do not count by ones to represent their data sets. Providing the students with concrete items and the visual representations can help students to discover and learn this concept more rapidly than simply explaining it verbally.

Skill 6.17   Identify strategies, including technology, for presenting science processes and concepts

Scientists use a variety of tools and technologies to perform tests, collect and display data, and analyze relationships. Examples of commonly used tools include computer-linked probes, spreadsheets, and graphing calculators. Scientists use spreadsheets to organize, analyze, and display data. Spreadsheet use simplifies data collection and manipulation and facilitates the presentation of data in a logical and understandable format. Graphing calculators have many applications. For example, biologists use algebraic functions to analyze growth and development, chemists must determine pH and balance concentration equations, and astronomers measure distance. Graphing calculators can manipulate algebraic data and create graphs for analysis and observation.

We must communicate scientific information and experimental results by using accurate data; visual presentations including bar, line, and pie graphs; tables and charts; diagrams; artwork; power point presentations; and other appropriate media to describe the data clearly. We should use modern technology whenever it is necessary. The method of communication must be suitable to the audience. Written communication is as important as oral communication. Good written communication is essential for submitting research papers to scientific journals, newspapers, and other magazines.

For teaching purposes, models are a great resource for conveying science in the classroom.

Physical Models

A physical model provides a physical representation of an object, concept, or system. To create a physical model, we first determine what aspects of a concept we want to represent and at what scale. A physical model of a large object or concept is usually smaller than the original, and relative size may be a very important concept in generating the model. For example, while a physical model of the solar system is clearly smaller than the actual solar system, we scale down planet sizes and distances relative to each other. However, in many smaller scale models, size is only approximate or may even be intentionally distorted. A physical model of a very small object usually provides a larger view of the object. The purpose of such models may be to show the structure of an object—for example, the wing of an insect, which is not normally visible or properly visible to the human eye. For this reason, a consideration of detail is crucial when creating larger scale models.

A physical model may represent inner parts of an object or system that are concealed by an exterior casing. For example, we create physical models of human anatomy so that students can study the body layer by layer, moving from the exterior skin to the internal organs. When generating such models, the sequential layering of the body must be accurately noted and portrayed. In general, the creation of physical models is critically based on the interrelationships of a system's or object's parts.

Graphical Models

Graphical models combine probability theory and graph theory to provide a natural tool for dealing with uncertainty and complexity, two major issues in applied mathematics and science. This type of model may provide a visual representation of dependencies and correlations among random variables or a computer generated and easily manipulated representation of a system to be studied.

We can use a computer aided design (CAD) system to generate graphical models of 2- or 3-dimensional objects. Using these programs, we can input variable dimensions and create graphic models that represent moving parts, portray various scenarios, and support interaction between operator and model. The operator enters quantitative data, such as geometry and dimension observations, into such programs through such standard input means as keyboards and graphic tablets. Following data entry, the system plots models and drawings according to the CAD's particular analysis method and purpose.

Simulations

With computer models, biologists can use the data and information they collect in the field to make predictions and projections about the future of ecosystems and organisms. Because ecosystems are large and change very slowly, direct observation is not a suitable strategy for ecological studies. For example, while scientists cannot reasonably expect to observe and gather data over an entire ecosystem, they can collect samples and use computer databases and models to make projections about the ecosystem as a whole.

Skill 6.18   Identify activities that support the development of both fine and gross motor skills

Motor development is defined as how spontaneous actions within the structured central nervous system and environmental and social fields temporarily link muscle groups to do different and sequential kinds of work. Although the sequence of motor development is fairly uniform across children, individual differences still may exist. A baby may develop slowly in one stage but then catch up in the next. Concern arises if a child's motor development is delayed in more than one motor skill area.

Listed below are the stages, sequences, and characteristics of motor development and motor learning and the general ages each stage occurs:

1. Newborn to 2 months: while laying on the stomach, an infant pushes up on arms and lifts and holds head up
2. 2 to 6 months: Uses hands to support self in sitting, rolls from back to stomach, and, while standing with support, accepts entire weight with legs
3. 7 to 8 months: Sits and reaches for toys without falling, moves from stomach or back into sitting position, and creeps on hands and knees with alternate arm and leg movement (crawling)
4. 9 to 11 months: Pulls to stand and cruises along furniture, stands alone, and takes several independent steps
5. 12 months on: Walks independently and seldom falls, squats to pick up toy(s)

Age appropriate specific motor skills development:

- By age 3, walking is automatic
- By age 4, the child has mostly achieved an adult style of walking
- By age 4-5, a child can run, stop, and turn
- By age 5-6, a child's running is in the style of an adult running
- Between ages 3 and 6, a child should be able to climb using ladders
- By age 6, children can hop and jump longer distances

After age six, it becomes increasingly more difficult to describe changes and differences in motor skills among children. Changes are usually to fine motor skills only and are more subtle. By age nine, eye-hand coordination normally has developed to a good point and growth continues slowly from this point. The motor skills that have been achieved are stabilized and perfected.

Motor-development learning theories that pertain to a general skill, activity, or age level are important and necessary for effective lesson planning. Motor-skill learning is unique to each individual but follows a general sequential skill pattern, starting with general gross-motor movements and progressing to specific or fine motor skills. Teachers must begin instruction at a level where all students are successful and proceed through the activity to the point where frustration for the majority is hindering the activity. Students must learn the fundamentals or basics of a skill or subsequent learning of more advanced skills becomes extremely difficult. Students must spend time learning and practicing beginning skills until those skills are second nature. Teaching in small groups with enough equipment for everyone is essential. Practice sessions that are too long or too demanding can cause physical and mental burnout. Teaching skills over a longer period of time but with slightly different approaches keeps students attentive and involved as they internalize the skill. The instructor can then begin to teach more difficult skills while continuing to review the basics. If the skill is challenging for most students, the teacher should schedule plenty of practice time so that they retain it before having to use it in a game situation.

Visualizing and breaking the skill down mentally is another way to enhance motor movement learning. Instructors can teach students to picture the steps involved and see themselves executing the skill. Start by teaching the skill with a demonstration of the necessary steps. Beginning with the first skill taught, introduce key language terms and have students visualize themselves performing the skill. For example, when teaching dribbling in basketball, begin by demonstrating the skill and the component steps. Show students how to push the ball down toward the ground, let it bounce back up, and push it down again. Next, give students equipment to practice with while standing still. Then, add movement while dribbling. Finally, demonstrate how to control the dribbling while being guarded by another student.

The development of motor skills in children is a sequential process. We can classify motor skill competency into stages of development by observing children practicing physical skills. The sequence of development begins with simple reflexes and progresses to learning postural elements, locomotor skills, and, finally, fine motor skills. The stages of development consider both innate and learned behaviors.

Stages of Motor Learning

Stage 1—Children progress from simple reflexes to such basic movements as sitting, crawling, creeping, standing, and walking.

Stage 2—Children learn more complex motor patterns including running, climbing, jumping, balancing, catching, and throwing.

Stage 3—During late childhood, children learn more specific movement skills. In addition, the basic motor patterns learned in stage 2 become more fluid and automatic.

Stage 4—During adolescence, children continue to develop general and specific motor skills and master specialized movements. At this point, factors including practice, motivation, and talent begin to affect the level of further development.

Locomotor Skills

Locomotor skills move an individual from one point to another.

1. **Walking**—with one foot contacting the surface at all times, walking shifts one's weight from one foot to the other while legs swing alternately in front of the body.

2. **Running**—an extension of walking that has a phase where the body is propelled with no base of support (speed is faster, stride is longer, and arms add power).

3. **Jumping**—projectile movements that momentarily suspend the body in midair.

4. **Vaulting**—coordinated movements that allow one to spring over an obstacle.

5. **Leaping**—similar to running, but leaping has greater height, flight, and distance.

6. **Hopping**—using the same foot to take off from a surface and land.

7. **Galloping**—forward or backward advanced elongation of walking combined and coordinated with a leap.

8. **Sliding**—sideward stepping pattern that is uneven, long, or short.

9. **Body Rolling**—moving across a surface by rocking back and forth, by turning over and over, or by shaping the body into a revolving mass.

10. **Climbing**—ascending or descending using the hands and feet with the upper body exerting the most control.

Nonlocomotor skills

Nonlocomotor skills are stability skills. The skill requires little or no movement of one's base of support and does not result in change of position.

1. **Bending**—movement around a joint where two body parts meet.

2. **Dodging**—sharp change of direction from original line of movement such as away from a person or object.

3. **Stretching**—extending or hyper-extending joints to make body parts as straight or as long as possible.

4. **Twisting**—rotating body or body parts around an axis with a stationary base.

5. **Turning**—circular movement of the body through space releasing the base of support.

6. **Swinging**—circular or pendular movements of the body or body parts below an axis.

7. **Swaying**—same as swinging but movement is above an axis.

8. **Pushing**—applying force against an object or person to move it away from one's body or to move one's body away from the object or person.

9. **Pulling**—executing force to cause objects or people to move toward one's body.

Manipulative skills

Manipulative skills use body parts to propel or receive an object, controlling objects primarily with the hands and feet. Two types of manipulative skills are receptive (catch + trap) and propulsive (throw, strike, kick).

1. **Bouncing or Dribbling**—projecting a ball downwards.

2. **Catching**—stopping momentum of an object (for control) using the hands.

3. **Kicking**—striking an object with the foot.

4. **Rolling**—initiating force to an object to instill contact with a surface.

5. **Striking**—giving impetus to an object with the use of the hands or an object.

6. **Throwing**—using one or both arms to project an object into midair away from the body.

7. **Trapping**—without the use of the hands, receiving and controlling a ball.

Knowledge of activities for body management skill development

Sequential development and activities for <u>locomotor skills acquisition</u>

Sequential Development = crawl, creep, walk, run, jump, hop, gallop, slide, leap, skip, step-hop.

- **Activities to develop walking skills** include walking slower and faster in place; walking forward, backward, and sideways with slower and faster paces in straight, curving, and zigzag pathways with various lengths of steps; pausing between steps; and changing the height of the body.

- **Activities to develop running skills** include having students pretend they are playing basketball, trying to score a touchdown, trying to catch a bus, finishing a lengthy race, or running on a hot surface.

- **Activities to develop jumping skills** include alternating jumping with feet together and feet apart, taking off and landing on the balls of the feet, clicking the heels together while airborne, and landing with a foot forward and a foot backward.

- **Activities to develop galloping skills** include having students play a game of Fox and Hound, with the lead foot representing the fox and the back foot the hound trying to catch the fox (alternate the lead foot).

- **Activities to develop sliding skills** include having students hold hands in a circle and slide in one direction, then in the other direction.

- **Activities to develop hopping skills** include having students hop all the way around a hoop and hopping in and out of a hoop reversing direction. Students can also place ropes in straight lines and hop side-to-side over the rope from one end to the other and change (reverse) the direction.

- **Activities to develop skipping skills** include having students combine walking and hopping activities leading up to skipping.

- **Activities to develop step-hopping skills** include having students practice stepping and hopping activities while clapping hands to an uneven beat.

Sequential development and activities for <u>nonlocomotor skill acquisition</u>

Sequential Development = stretch, bend, sit, shake, turn, rock and sway, swing, twist, dodge, and fall.

- **Activities to develop stretching** include lying on the back and stomach and stretching as far as possible; stretching as though one is reaching for a star, picking fruit off a tree, climbing a ladder, shooting a basketball, or placing an item on a high self; waking and yawning.

- **Activities to develop bending** include touching knees and toes then straightening the entire body and straightening the body halfway; bending as though picking up a coin, tying shoes, picking flowers or vegetables, and petting animals of different sizes.

- **Activities to develop sitting** include practicing sitting from standing, kneeling, and lying positions without the use of hands.

- **Activities to develop falling skills** include first collapsing in one's own space and then pretending to fall like bowling pins, raindrops, snowflakes, a rag doll, or Humpty Dumpty.

Sequential development and activities for <u>manipulative skill development</u>:

Sequential Development = striking, throwing, kicking, ball rolling, volleying, bouncing, catching, and trapping.

- **Activities to develop striking** begin with a participant striking stationary objects that are in a stationary position. Next, the person remains still while trying to strike a moving object. Then, both the object and the participant are in motion as the participant attempts to strike the moving object.

- **Activities to develop throwing** include throwing yarn or foam balls against a wall, then at a big target, and finally at targets decreasing in size.

- **Activities to develop kicking** include alternating feet to kick balloons or beach balls, then kicking them under and over ropes. Change the type of ball as proficiency develops.

- **Activities to develop ball rolling** include rolling different size balls to a wall and then to targets decreasing in size.

- **Activities to develop volleying** include using a large balloon and first, hitting it with both hands, then one hand (alternating hands), and then using different parts of the body. Change the object as students progress (balloon, to beach ball, to foam ball).

- **Activities to develop bouncing** include starting with large balls and first, using both hands to bounce and then using one hand (alternate hands).

- **Activities to develop catching** include catching various objects (balloons, beanbags, balls.). First the participants catch their own objects. Then they catch objects thrown by someone else, and finally they increase the distance between the catcher and the thrower.

- **Activities to develop trapping** include trapping slow and fast rolling balls; trapping balls or other objects such as beanbags that are lightly thrown at waist, chest, and stomach levels; trapping different size balls.

> **For more information about stages of motor development:**
>
> http://www.stan-co.k12.ca.us/calpe/Motor.html

Skill 6.19   Identify strategies, including technology, for presenting health, safety, and nutrition instruction, processes, and concepts

Teaching Styles[jmm33][v34]

Common teaching styles that teacher's can use to facilitate learning include command style, practice style, reciprocal style, and inclusion style.

In the **command style**, the teacher makes all the decisions and controls all activities. The command style is particularly useful in teaching students a skill in a short period of time. Because command style allows very little student-teacher and student-student interaction, instructors should limit its use to initial demonstrations and explanations.

Under the **Practice style**, students make decisions and move at their own skill level during the implementation phase of skill development. Practice style is particularly useful when students have achieved basic skill competency because they have self-paced practice and individualized feedback.

Reciprocal style involves the interaction of pairs of students. Reciprocal style provides needed social interaction, and students learn from each other through observation. The instructor is also free to interact with the students.

Inclusion style gives all students the chance to participate in the same task regardless of skill level. Students make decisions on how best to go about practicing and developing their skills. They learn their strengths and weaknesses through trial and error. For example, when learning to throw objects at a target, students can choose the size and type of target and the distance between themselves and the target that best suits their ability level.

Communication Delivery Systems

Three basic types of communication delivery systems relevant to physical education are written, verbal, and visual.

Written communication is particularly effective in communicating large amounts of information. In addition, instructors may give students written instructions for classroom activities to eliminate the need for extended and repeated explanation.

Verbal communication is traditionally the foundation of teacher-student interaction. Verbal communication is an effective method of explaining skills and concepts. Physical education instructors should, however, limit verbal instructions and explanations to provide maximum physical activity during class time.

Visual communication is an important, and often underused, method of communication. Visual demonstrations are often the most effective way to introduce athletic skills and activities.

Since motivation is essential to student learning, instructors should recognize and understand the important elements of student motivation. Important theories and concepts in student motivation include attribution theory, social learning theory, learned helplessness, and self-efficacy.

Attribution theory describes how people make causal explanations and how they answer questions beginning with *Why*. The theory focuses on the information people use to make causal inferences and the way they use this information to answer causal questions. For instance, a student's aggressively competitive behavior may reflect personality or be a response to situational pressures. Attribution theory describes the processes of explaining events and the behavioral and emotional consequences of those explanations. This theory also claims that students' perceptions of their educational experiences affect their motivation more than the experiences themselves.

Social learning theory focuses on the learning that occurs within a social context. It emphasizes that people learn from one another and includes such concepts as observational learning, imitation, and modeling. Social learning theory asserts that people can learn by observing the behavior of others and the outcomes of those behaviors. According to this theory, learning can occur without a permanent change in behavior. In addition, cognition plays an important role in learning. Awareness and expectations of future rewards or punishments can have a major effect on the behaviors that people exhibit. Thus, socialization and reward and punishment can motivate students to learn.

Learned helplessness occurs in situations where continued failure may inhibit a student's ability to try again and can lead to many forms of depression. Therefore, the way instructors respond to children's failures and successes is very important. Learned helplessness often occurs when students experience events over which they have, or feel as though they have, no control.

Self-efficacy describes the perceptions that students have about their abilities to perform at levels that influence the events that affect their lives. Self-efficacy perceptions determine how people feel, think, motivate themselves, and behave. Such beliefs produce these diverse effects through cognitive, motivational, affective, and selection processes. A strong sense of efficacy enhances human accomplishment and personal well-being in many ways. People with high confidence in their capabilities view difficult tasks as challenges rather than threats. A student with high self-efficacy will be highly motivated to participate in sports and game-related activities. To build efficacy, instructors must not only raise the students' perceptions of their capabilities, but also structure situations that breed success and limit repeated failure. Students with high self-efficacy measure success in terms of self-improvement rather than triumph over others.

Technology is the application of science to commercial, educational, health-related, military, or industrial objectives. Technology includes the use of computers; calculators; communication devices such as telephones and videoconference devices; or other entities and methodologies to achieve those objectives.

Technology has become vital in the instructional process because we record and exchange all grades, lesson plans, semester grades, descriptions of tests and test grades, absences, tardies, and behavior issues with computers.

Successful teachers integrate technology into the instructional process. Technology is not simply a practice tool or device without purpose. The use of a particular technological device or product of technology should be appropriate to the lesson content.

Instructors can use technology in a variety of ways to help students and athletes improve or learn. Some ways in which instructors can use technology include the following:

1. Actual use of technology—the teacher and the students use the technology in a hands-on setting. For example, students use a video or digital camera in physical education to analyze their skills.
2. Use of products of technology—Teachers and students may gather information or resources from the Internet or image results for analyzing a motor skill. In such a situation, the teacher can use the technology, or the products of technology, to present information, to provide examples and illustrations, and as the medium or object of intrusion.

Some of the offered examples currently available in technology-mediated instruction include audio technologies such as radio, telephone, voice mail, and audiocassettes; video technologies such as television, teleconferencing, compressed video, and prerecorded videocassettes; and information technologies such as stand-alone workstations, CD ROM prepackaged multimedia, e-mail, chat rooms, bulletin boards, and the World Wide Web.

Technology Resources

The best sources for identifying current technological resources for accessing information on physical activity and health are the Internet and local district technology workshops. District workshops are an extremely valuable resource for additional knowledge about using technology to get more information on specific subject matter including physical education.

Internet resources, including numerous web sites, form an important part of the current technology that helps teachers and students access information on physical activity and health. In addition, through these resources, educators, students, performers, parents, and athletes can stay current with programs and information about physical activity and health-related issues.

Some organizations such as the NASPE also provide information on physical fitness and health. For example, NASPE invites school districts nationwide to post their school wellness policy on the NASPE Forum.

Research also shows that athletes can use different devices to monitor physical activity and health. Such devices include health pyramids and diagrams, virtual bicycles, rowing machines, and treadmills. Such technology helps students and teachers plan and implement workouts and view workout results.

Teaching Strategies for Health, Nutrition & Safety

There is a wealth of resources in the community to help teachers with this area of the curriculum. Nurses, police officers, dentists and dieticians are just some of the experts that can come into the classroom to give presentations to students. For example, there are many community organizations that will supply provide a very interactive presentation about the importance of wearing a bicycle helmet and some of these organizations even provide the helmets to children whose families cannot afford them.

While teaching children about health, nutrition and safety, it is not enough to provide instruction in the class, and engage the students in activities. Both the instruction and the activities must be real life so that children can see how they are relative to their lives.

Some strategies to use include:

- showing videos

- establishing safety routines in the school

- have students give presentations to their classmates

- taking students on field trips to supermarkets to find nutritious food

- bringing nutritious foods into the classroom for students to sample,. Being aware of students who may have allergies

- set up a simulated restaurant in the classroom

- providing dental kits for the students

- role playing various scenarios involving safety

- participate in various events, such as the Buddy Walk to help children with Down Syndrome

- holding a health fair and invite other classes, parents and community representatives

Skill 6.20   Identify strategies, including technology, and processes for presenting visual arts, music, drama, and dance

Visual Arts

The components and strands of visual art encompass many areas. Students are expected to develop observation skills and be able to identify and recreate the experiences that teachers provide for them as learning tools. For example, students may walk as a group on a nature hike, observe the surrounding elements, and then discuss the repetition found in the leaves of trees or the bricks of the sidewalk or the size and shapes of the buildings and how they relate. They may also use such experiences to describe lines, colors, shapes, forms, and textures. Beginning elements of perspective are noticed at an early age. The question of why buildings look smaller when they are at a far distance and bigger when they are closer is sure to spark the imagination of early childhood students. Students can then take their inquiries to higher levels of learning with such hands-on activities as using paper and geometric shapes to construct three-dimensional buildings. Eventually students should acquire such higher level thinking skills as analysis, question artists and art work, and analyze many different aspects of visual art.

Having students create an *art sample book* is an excellent activity. Such books could include a variety of materials, such as sandpaper and cotton balls to represent texture elements that would serve as examples. Samples of square pieces of construction paper designed into various shapes could represent shape. String samples could represent the element of lines.

For the early childhood student, visual art should focus clearly on the colors necessary at this developmental level. To introduce more complex information about colors, teachers can discuss intensity, the strength of the color, and value, the lightness or darkness of the colors. Another valuable tool is the use color wheel and allowing students to experiment with mixing colors to create their own art experience is an excellent activity.

Students interpret works of art through a wide variety of rich art and literature experience. Students can react to art experiences by understanding the definitions of the basic principles such as line, color, value, space, texture, and shape and form. These experiences greatly affect early childhood students. The books of Eric Carle are an important resource. They are age appropriate for young children and include a wide variety of shape, color, line, and media for them to explore. Once teachers have introduced students to a wide range of materials, they can better relate and explain the elements they have observed through artwork and generously illustrated literature. Literature is the most common form of exposure for young students, but video and other types of media also provide rich art experiences.

Music

Students' daily routines can include exploration, interpretation, and understanding of musical sound. Immersing them in musical conversations as we sing, speak rhythmically, and walk in-step stimulates their awareness of the beauty and structure of musical sound. For example, students can explore creating moods with music by analyzing stories and creating musical compositions that reflect or enhance them.

In some schools, computer-assisted programs provide students with opportunities to evaluate music. These programs present two performances of one or more musical pieces so students can work with the teacher to compare and contrast the pieces. Using the Internet, students can collect musical information for evaluation and provide information about studied or performed compositions. With knowledge of these resources and tools, teachers can provide the richest education in music.

Drama

In theatre, students should learn to use all of their five senses to observe their environment and recreate experiences through drama and other theatre skills. Using role play and prior experiences, students should learn to react to a feeling or a situation and expand their ability to develop character. Using sight, smell, taste, touch, hearing and memory recall, students can retell stories, myths, and fables. Performances should be part of the drama experience so that students can learn to use costumes and props. Students can relate to familiar jobs that are relevant to their everyday experiences and should act out some of the following: firefighters, police officers, teachers, doctors, nurses, postal employees, clerks, and other service-related professions that students may have observed.

Dance

Begin with primitive patterns of rhythm. Rhythm is the basis of dance. Children can sit in a chair and clap or tap their hands on their legs to express thoughts of rhythm. Older children can use imagery to visualize and internalize the particular qualities of a specific movement.

Because the younger child is often unsteady, the initial emphasis is not on gracefulness but on developing body awareness. The uniqueness of dance is that it is self-expression that can be guided through instruction. We teach the elements that are available, such as time and space. The student uses listening skills to develop a sense of tempo.

Creative dance is most natural to a young child. Creative dance depicts feelings through movement and is the initial reaction to sound and movement. The older elementary student will incorporate mood and expressiveness. Stories can be told to release the dancer into imagination.

Isadora Duncan is called the mother of modern dance. Modern dance today refers to a concept of dance that develops such expressions of opposites as fast-slow, contract- release. Modern dancers often vary height and level to fall and recover. Modern dance is based on substance, dynamism, metakinesis, and form.

Students should be able to judge the effectiveness of a dance composition based on its intent, structure, meaning, and purpose. Dance is a way of expressing everything from feelings of mood to appreciation of cultures and historical time periods. Students express empathy for others as they take on various roles within the dance. Applying and participating in dances helps students develop self-confidence, body awareness, and communication skills and provides experiences in areas otherwise left undiscovered. School settings for dance have a feel of community. Therefore, the best way to evaluate dance in a school setting is as a group experience rather than as individual technical skill level, an assessment best left to dance schools. Dance is a way of expressing the connections and relationships among the dancers and the appreciation of dance as creative expression.

COMPETENCY 7.1 KNOWLEDGE OF THE DIVERSE NEEDS OF ALL CHILDREN AND THEIR FAMILIES

Skill 7.1 Identify strategies to adapt curriculum for children with diverse needs

No two students are alike. It follows, then, that no students *learn* alike. To apply a one-dimensional instructional approach and a strict tunnel vision perspective of testing imposes learning limits on students. All students have the right to an education, and no singular path to that education exists. A teacher must acknowledge the variety of learning styles and abilities among students within a class and the varieties from class to class and apply multiple instructional and assessment processes to ensure that every child has appropriate opportunities to master the subject matter, demonstrate such mastery, and improve and enhance learning skills with each lesson.

Students' attitudes and perceptions about learning are the most powerful factors influencing academic focus and success. When instructional objectives center on students' interests and are relevant to their lives, effective learning occurs. Learners must believe that the tasks that they are asked to perform have some value and that they have the ability and resources to perform them. A student who thinks a task is unimportant will not exert much effort.

If a student thinks he lacks the ability or resources to complete a task successfully, even attempting the task becomes too great a risk. Not only must teachers understand the students' abilities and interests, they must also help students develop positive attitudes and perceptions about tasks and learning.

Differentiated Instruction

The effective teacher tries to connect all students to the subject matter through multiple techniques so that students, through their own abilities, will relate to one or more techniques and excel in the learning process. Differentiated instruction encompasses several areas.

- Content—What is the teacher going to teach? Or, perhaps better put, what does the teacher want the students to learn? Differentiating content means that students have access to content that piques their interest about a topic and has a complexity that provides an appropriate challenge to their intellectual development.
- Process—A classroom management technique that maximizes instructional organization and delivery for the diverse student group. These techniques should include dynamic, flexible grouping activities, in which instruction and learning occur both as whole-class, teacher-led activities and as peer learning and teaching (while teacher observes and coaches) within small groups or pairs.

- Product—The expectations and requirements placed on students to demonstrate their knowledge or understanding. The type of product expected from each student should reflect each student's own capabilities.

> **Learn more about differentiated instruction:**
>
> http://www.frsd.k12.nj.us/rfmslibrarylab/di /differentiated_instruction.htm

Alternative Assessments

In alternative assessment, students create an answer or a response to a question or task. In traditional, inflexible assessments, students choose a prepared response from among a selection of responses such as matching, multiple-choice, and true or false.

When implemented effectively, an alternative assessment approach has the following characteristics, among others:

- Requires higher-order thinking and problem-solving
- Provides opportunities for student self-reflection and self-assessment
- Uses real world applications to connect students to the subject
- Provides opportunities for students to learn and examine subjects on their own and collaborate with their peers.
- Encourages students to continue learning beyond the requirements of the assignment
- Clearly defines objective and performance goals

Testing Modifications

Minimizing the effects of a student's disability or learning challenge and providing an equal opportunity for participation in assessments and demonstrate and express knowledge and ability are the goals of testing modifications.

Educators should identify testing modifications in the student's IEP, consistently implement the modifications, and use them to the least extent possible. Types of testing modifications include the following:

- Flexible scheduling—providing time extensions or altering testing duration (e.g., by inserting appropriate breaks).
- Flexible setting—Using special lighting or acoustics, minimizing distractions (e.g., testing the student in a separate location), using adaptive equipment.

- Alternate test format—Using large print or Braille, increasing the space allocated for student response, realigning the format of question and answer selections (e.g., vertically rather than horizontally).
- Mechanical aids—Using tape recorders, word processors, visual and auditory magnification devices, calculators, spell check and grammar check software (when spelling and grammar are not the focus of assessment).

Most classrooms have a mixture of the following:

- Differences among learners, classroom settings, and academic outcomes
- Biological, sociological, ethnicity, socioeconomic status, psychological needs, learning modalities, and styles among learners
- Differences in classroom settings that promote learning opportunities such as collaborative, participatory, and individualized learning groupings
- Expected learning outcomes that are theoretical, affective, and cognitive for students

Students generally do not realize their own abilities and frequently lack self-confidence. By providing certain types of feedback, teachers can instill positive self-concepts in children and, thereby, enhance their innate abilities. Such feedback includes attributing students' successes to their efforts and specifying what the student did that produced the success. Qualitative comments influence attitudes more than such quantitative feedback as grades.

Teachers must avoid teaching tasks that fit their own interests and goals and design activities that address the students' concerns. In order to meet this criterion, they must find out about students and have a sense of their interests and goals. Teachers can gain this sense by conducting student surveys and simply questioning and listening to students. Once they have this information, teachers can link students' interests with classroom tasks.

Teachers are learning the value of giving assignments that meet the individual abilities and needs of students. After teachers instruct, discuss, ask questions, and provide practice, they are asking students to generate tasks that will show their knowledge of the information presented rather than assigning one task to all students. Students are given choices and, therefore, have the opportunity to demonstrate more effectively the skills, concepts, or topics that they have learned as individuals. This student choice increases student originality, intrinsic motivation, and higher mental processes.

A diverse classroom should also address children who are learning English and those with disabilities and exceptionalities. The types of disabilities in children are numerous. Some disabilities are entirely physical, while others are entirely related to learning and the mind or background. Some involve a combination of both. It would be a disservice to say that all children should display the same characteristics to be considered normal. However, when teachers notice such abnormalities as a student's incredible ability to solve a math problem without working it out (a potential attribute of giftedness) or another student's extreme trouble with spelling (a potential attribute of dyslexia), they may assume that a disability or exceptional ability exists.

Common learning disabilities include attention deficit hyperactivity disorder (concentration can be very difficult), auditory processing disorders (listening comprehension is very difficult), visual processing disorders (reading can be problematic and visual memory may be impaired), dyslexia (reading can be confusing), and many others. Physical disabilities include Down's Syndrome (mental retardation may be a factor), cerebral palsy (physical movement is impaired), and many others. Developmental disabilities might include the absence of fine motor skills.

When giftedness is observed, teachers should also concern themselves with ensuring that such children get the attention they need and deserve so that they can continue to learn and grow.

Two of the more common approaches used in today's K-12 classrooms for children still acquiring English are Cognitive and Total Physical Response.

Cognitive approaches to language learning focus on concepts. While words and grammar are important in this approach, teachers use language for conceptual purposes rather than study words and grammar simply to learn new words and grammatical structures. This approach focuses heavily on students' learning styles, and it cannot necessarily be pinned down to specific techniques; it is. more of a philosophy of instruction.

Another very common motivational approach is Total Physical Response. This kinesthetic approach combines language learning and physical movement. In essence, students learn new vocabulary and grammar by responding with physical motion to verbal commands. Some claim it is effective because the physical actions create good brain connections with the words.

In general, the best methods do not treat students as if they have a language deficit. They build upon what students already know and instill the target language as a communicative process rather than a list of vocabulary words that have to be memorized.

To ensure maximum education for all learners, teachers must plan to meet the needs of all their students. The target of diversity offers teachers a variety of opportunities to expand their experiences with students, staff, community members and parents from culturally diverse backgrounds so that they can apply their experiences in promoting cultural diversity inclusion in the classroom. Teachers can engage and challenge students to develop and incorporate their own diversity skills in building character and relationships with cultures beyond their own. In changing the thinking patterns of students to become more inclusive in the twenty-first century, teachers are addressing the globalization of our world.

Skill 7.2 Identify the characteristics of children with diverse needs

Diversity in classroom makeup may not be as distinctive as race, ethnicity, and gender. Students who are physically or intellectually challenged may also add diversity to a general student population. A student population including members from varying socioeconomic situations also provides diversity. All students must be included in the learning process. Teachers must incorporate student acceptance of this and any specific requirements necessary to help individual students accomplish on a par with classmates in lesson planning, teacher presentations, and classroom activities.

For example, access to technology and media can vary greatly within the student population. In planning classroom work, homework assignments and other projects, the teacher must take this discrepancy into account. First, teachers must know the resources available to the students in the school, the library system, and the community. Then they must address any issues that might restrict a student's access, such as physical impediments, language difficulties, and expenses. Third, teachers must always plan work and give assignments so that every student has equal access to the information and technology required for the task. As in all aspects of education, each student must have an equal opportunity to succeed.

A positive self-concept is directly related to a student's ability to learn and become an integral member of society. If students think poorly of themselves or have sustained feelings of inferiority, they probably will not be able to realize their potential for learning. Pat of the teacher's task is ensuring that each student develops a positive self-concept.

A positive self-concept does not imply feelings of superiority, perfection, or competence and efficacy. Instead, a positive self-concept involves accepting ourselves, liking who we are, and having a proper respect for ourselves. The teacher who encourages these factors has contributed to the development of a positive self-concept in students.

Teachers can use a variety of approaches to enhancing self-concept among students. One such method is the process approach, which proposes a three-phase model for teaching. This model includes a sensing function, a transforming function, and an acting function. We can simplify these three factors into *reach*, *touch*, and *teach*. The sensing, or perceptual, function incorporates information or stimuli in an intuitive manner. The transforming function conceptualizes, abstracts, evaluates, and provides meaning and value to perceived information. The acting function chooses actions from several different alternatives. The process model may be applied to almost any curricular field.

An approach that aims directly at enhancing self-concept is Invitational Education. According to this approach, teachers and their behaviors may be inviting or they may be disinviting. Inviting behaviors enhance self-concept among students; disinviting behaviors diminish self-concept.

Disinviting behaviors include those that demean students and those that are chauvinistic, sexist, condescending, thoughtless, or insensitive to student feelings. Inviting behaviors are the opposite of these and characterize teachers who act with consistency and sensitivity. Inviting teacher behaviors reflect an attitude of *doing with* rather than *doing to*. Students are *invited* or *disinvited* depending on the teacher behaviors.

Invitational teachers exhibit the following skills (Biehler and Snowman, 394):

1. reaching each student—learning names, having one-to-one contact
2. listening with care—picking up subtle cues
3. being real with students—providing only realistic praise,
4. being real with oneself—honestly appraising your own feelings and disappointments
5. inviting good discipline— showing students you have respect in personal ways
6. handling rejection—not taking lack of student response in personal ways
7. inviting oneself—thinking positively about oneself

When educators promote diversity in learning environments and curriculum, both students and teachers benefit from increased academic success.

Using classrooms as vital resources for cultural and ethnic inclusion helps students by contributing cultural norms and artifacts to learning. Teachers can create global thinkers by helping students identify cultural assumptions and biases that may direct the type of social and academic groupings that occur in the classroom. For example, if a student is struggling in math, a teacher can examine the cultural aspect of learning math. For some students, math is insignificant when socioeconomic issues of poverty and survival are the daily reality of existence. When students see parents juggling finances, the only math that becomes important for them is that less is never enough to keep the lights on and mortgage paid.

Teachers can use a variety of instructional styles to facilitate diversity in cooperative learning and individualized instruction that will provide more opportunities for positive student experiences and academic success. Empowering the school culture and climate by establishing an anti-bias learning environment and promoting multicultural learning inclusion will discourage unfair labeling of certain students.

Teachers can use various toolkits to assess ethnic and cultural inclusion in the classroom. Looking at diverse or homogenous groupings in the classroom can provide teachers with opportunities to restructure cooperative learning groupings and increase diverse student interactions, which can provide increased improvements for school communities.

Culturegrams are representations that provide information about various cultures beyond just the basic facts that simpler graphs display[v36]. Culturegrams help students understand different cultures and research cultural diversity and are a useful tool teachers can use in profiling student learning styles and engagement in the classroom. Students can use technology to learn how students learn in other cultures and in other states. Observing students, as they communicate with other learners, is another way teachers can compile and categorize cultural profiles that may help identify learning styles and the ways students acquire learning. An interesting aspect of using culturegrams is the manner in which it helps students connect to other cultures and their perceptions of students who identify with different cultures[jmm37].

Skill 7.3   Identify ways to facilitate family support and involvement with children who have diverse needs

SEE Skill 5.2

Skill 7.4   Identify programs, curricula, and activities that provide for the language needs of children and their families who have limited English proficiency

Teaching students who are learning English as a second language poses some unique challenges, particularly in a standards-based environment. The key is realizing that no matter how little English a student knows, the teacher should teach with the student's developmental level in mind. Instruction should not be *dumbed-down* for ESOL students. Teachers should, however, use different approaches to ensure that these students have multiple opportunities to learn and practice English and still master content.

Many ESOL approaches are based on social learning methods. By being placed in mixed level groups or by being paired with a student of another ability level, students get a chance to practice English in a natural, non-threatening environment. In these groups, students should not be pushed to use complex language or experiment with words that are too difficult. They should simply get a chance to practice with simple words and phrases.

In teacher-directed instructional situations, visual aids, such as pictures, objects, and video are particularly effective in helping students make connections between words and familiar items.

ESOL students may need additional accommodations with assessments, assignments, and projects. For example, teachers may find that written tests provide little or no information about a student's understanding of the content. Therefore, an oral test may be more appropriate for ESOL students. When students are somewhat comfortable and capable with written tests, a shortened test may actually be preferable; teachers should note that they will need extra time to translate.

Skill 7.5   Identify characteristics of children at risk for school failure and select appropriate intervention strategies for these children

SEE Skill 7.1

Skill 7.6   Identify major trends in exceptional child education and their application in an early childhood setting

An exceptional child is one that is different in some way from the *normal* or *average* child. The term *exceptional child* includes those with special problems related to physical disabilities, sensory impairments, emotional disturbances, learning disabilities, and mental retardation. With developmental disabilities on the rise, the cause of and cure for these problems remain poorly understood. However, we do know that early and intensive intervention can have a profound impact on the quality of life for both children at risk and their families. The key is early detection. But recognizing the first signs of a developmental delay or disorder, such as autism, can be a challenge for parents and healthcare professionals alike.

Nearly 50 years of research, both quantitative (data-based) and qualitative (reports of parents and teachers), indicate that early intervention increases the developmental and educational gains for the child, improves the functioning of the family, and reaps long-term benefits for society.

Early intervention results in a child that

- Needs fewer special education and other rehabilitative services later in life
- Is retained in grade less often
- In some cases, is indistinguishable from non-handicapped classmates years after intervention

Most exceptional children require a lot of understanding and patience but profit from being included in regular classes. They benefit greatly from the varied teaching procedures and modified materials selected to meet the needs of each child. Isolating children with special needs or areas of delay has become less and less frequent.

It is never too early for the exceptional child to have opportunities to become friends and play with other children. All children learn give and to take, the rules of social interaction, and sharing from each other. The exceptional child should be treated as other children and should share in appropriate tasks with their peers. These children will also need special opportunities to practice and develop skills and have experiences adapted to their special needs and abilities.

Interventions should be understood as part of *caring* for a child rather than *curing* a child. Children have complex and variable developmental pathways; accordingly, any interventions should be based on the unique needs of an individual child. Teachers and families should consider the following actions:

- Adapt physical space and materials to promote active engagement with responsive toys and structured and clearly defined spaces.
- Structure the social environment to promote interaction and communication with peer models and responsive and imitative adults who expand the child's play and behavior.
- Structure routines and transitions and use a visual cue system.
- As much as possible, structure an environment that encourages the child's independence rather than dependence on the adult's presence.
- Use the child's current skills and behaviors to establish reasonable targets for growth and achievement and track these goals.
- Strive to accelerate learning by communicating goals, instructional activities, and progress across environments with all caregivers.

Skill 7.7   Identify strategies for working with foster, migrant, abandoned, and homeless children

Migrant, homeless, and abandoned children endure many educational challenges resulting from mobility and poverty. Particular challenges include moving from one school to another several times during the year and facing difficulties in enrollment or being placed in inappropriate classes because of missing school records. Poor attendance or non-attendance, language barriers, and social isolation are all conditions that can lead to poor school performance.

The unfortunate circumstances that can cause their high mobility comprise such conditions as abandonment, poverty, job relocation of caregivers, changes in family arrangements, lack of affordable accommodations, and other determining factors. Neglected or abandoned children or those whose placements have failed often have more medical problems and experience diet deficiencies. Teachers and school personnel should work to provide healthy school lunches and offer medical attention to these students while they are in their school jurisdictions.

The following organizations provide legal representation and strive to enforce the rights of foster, migrant, abandoned, and homeless children.

The National Association for the Education of Homeless Children and Youth (NAEHCY) http://www.naehcy.org/

Migrant Legal Action Program (MLAP) http://www.mlap.org/

National Alliance to END HOMELESSNESS
http://www.endhomelessness.org/

Skill 7.8   Identify strategies for accessing health information for monitoring children's medical needs, including medications for allergies and other health impairments

Some students experience a wide range of diverse medical needs that require little or no treatment; for others, treatment may be essential to life.

Successfully integrating a child with special health care needs safely into the school day requires excellent communication. Teachers, school professionals, and especially the school nurse should regularly communicate with the student's caregivers through such means as a log book, e-mail, or phone calls. Any new treatments, procedures, or medications must be carefully and full documented. The caregivers should give medical equipment, supplies, and medications to the school, and school authorities must store them in a secured place.

They should label the original container with the student's name, name of medication, directions for dosage, frequency to be administered, and the licensed prescriber's name.

In school districts where nurses are available on a daily basis, they should assume responsibility for administering medication to students. In schools where school nurses are not available on a daily basis, the principal should assume this responsibility.

In special circumstances, when time is of the essence in getting and using life-saving medication, such as asthma inhalers, students may be allowed to carry and self-administer such medication on school grounds. However a release form signed by the healthcare provider, the parent or guardian, and the student must be on file at the school.

If a student with a medical or health impairment or disability is entering school for the first time a specially designed instruction Individualized Educational Program (IEP) is required.

COMPETENCY 8.0   KNOWLEDGE OF DIAGNOSIS, ASSESSMENT, AND EVALUATION

Skill 8.1   Select developmentally appropriate, reliable, and valid formal and informal screening, progress monitoring, and diagnostic instruments and procedures that measure specific skills

The process of using multiple assessment information on student learning to collect, quantify, and qualify student performance data is called assessment. A comprehensive assessment system must include a diversity of such tools as norm-referenced, criterion-referenced, performance-based, or any student generated alternative assessments that can measure learning outcomes and goals for student achievement and success in school communities. The following are the four main kinds of assessment:

1. Observation—assessment by observing students and judging their actions.
2. Informal continuous assessment, less structured——assessment that, unlike a test or exam, is not formal but occurs on a daily or weekly basis. This is formative assessment and can consists of such things as teacher observations.
3. Informal continuous assessment, more structured—an assessment that occurs periodically such as a quiz or a group activity[jmm38]. This is summative assessment, which tests the student's knowledge and learning of a skill or concept.
4. Formal assessment—a structured, infrequent measure of learner achievement. It usually involves the use of tests and examinations to measure the learner's progress.

Informal assessment helps students learn better. The teacher has an ongoing view of how well the students are learning and progressing. We can apply informal assessment to homework assignments, field journals, and daily class work, which are good indicators of student progress and comprehension.

Formal assessment on the other hand is highly structured and appropriate for the student. It occurs at regular intervals and, if the progress is not satisfactory, parent involvement is absolutely essential. A test or examination is a good example of formal assessment. A science project is also is a formal assessment.

Informal Assessments

In recent years, the emphasis in assessments has shifted from *mastery testing* of isolated skills to authentic assessments of what children know. Using authentic assessments, teachers learn more precisely what each individual student knows, can do, and needs to do.

Conducting an entry survey is one of the simplest and most efficient ways for teachers to get to know their students. This record provides useful background information and valuable insights about the students' knowledge and experience as they enter a class or school. Teachers can customize entry surveys according to the type of information they consider valuable. Entry surveys often incorporate such information as student's name and age, family members, health factors, special interests, strengths, needs, fears, parental expectations, languages spoken in the home, and what the child likes about school.

At the beginning of each school term, teachers usually conduct some informal evaluations in order to obtain a general awareness of their students. These informal evaluations should be the result of a learning activity rather than a test and may include classroom observations and reading and writing samples. Teachers may also include notations about the students' cognitive abilities as demonstrated by classroom discussions and participation and the students' command of language. Teachers should not underestimate the value of these informal evaluations. These evaluations, if used effectively, will drive instruction and facilitate learning.

Structured Assessments

After conducting initial informal evaluations and following with appropriate instruction, teachers will need to fine tune individual evaluations in order to provide optimum learning experiences. They can use some of the same types of evaluations on an ongoing basis to determine individual learning needs as they used to determine initial general learning needs. Choosing an appropriate evaluation instrument for elementary-aged students is more difficult than choosing one for older students. Therefore, teachers must be knowledgeable about developmentally appropriate instruments. At the same time, teachers must identify the information that they want to gain from a specific evaluation instrument. Ultimately, these two factors—students' developmental stages and the information to be derived—determine which type of evaluation will be most appropriate and valuable. A few commercially designed assessment tools are available that are as effective as teacher-constructed tools.

A simple-to-administer, information-rich evaluation of a child's reading strengths and weaknesses is the running reading record. "This technique for recording reading behavior is the most insightful, informative, and instructionally useful assessment procedure you can use for monitoring a child's progress in learning to read;" (Traill, 1993) The teacher uses a simple coding system to record what a child does while reading text out loud. Later, the teacher can go back to the record and assess what the child knows about reading and what the teacher needs to address in an effort to help the student become a better reader.

When evaluating writing, teachers should discourage students from erasing errors and train them to cross out errors with a single line so that the teacher can actually see the process they use to complete writing assignments. This method is an important means of learning about students' writing and is an effective, valuable writing evaluation.

By observing students as they solve computation problems at their seats or perform at the board, teachers evaluate mathematics skills informally. They can observe the students' basic computation skills, their understanding of place value, and whether or not they transpose numbers. However, some teachers may prefer to administer some basic computation tests to determine a student's strengths and weaknesses. Although these tests are not as effective or thorough in assessing students, they are quick and easy to administer.

Formal Assessments

Norm-referenced Assessments
Educators use norm-referenced tests (NRT) to classify student learners for homogenous groupings based on ability levels or basic skills. In many school communities, NRTs are used to classify students into advanced placement (AP), honors, regular, or remedial classes. These classifications can have a significant impact on the student's future educational opportunities or success. Such national testing companies as Riverside (Iowa Test of Basic Skills), McGraw-Hill (Florida Achievement Test) and other major test publishers use NRTs to test a national sample of students to norm against standard test-takers. Stiggins (1994) states "Norm-referenced tests (NRT) are designed to highlight achievement differences between and among students to produce a dependable rank order of students across a continuum of achievement from high achievers to low achievers."

Educators may select NRTs to focus on student learners with lower basic skills that could limit developing curriculum content that can accelerate student skills from basic to higher skill application. Teachers often make this selection to address state assessment and core subject expectations. NRT ranking ranges from 1-99 with 25 percent of students scoring in the lower ranking of 1-25 and 25 percent of students scoring in the higher ranking of 76-99. Florida uses a variety of NRTs that range from Iowa Basic Skills Testing to California Battery Achievement testing to measure student learning in reading and math.

Criterion-referenced Assessments

Criterion-referenced assessment focuses on specific student learning goals and performance compared to a norm group of student learners. According to Bond (1996) "Educators or policy makers may choose to use a Criterion-referenced test (CRT) when they wish to see how well students have learned the knowledge and skills which they are expected to have mastered." Many school districts and state legislatures use CRTs to ascertain whether schools are meeting national and state learning standards. The latest national educational mandates of No Child Left Behind (NCLB) and Adequate Yearly Progress (AYP) use CRTs to measure student learning, school performance, and school improvement goals as structured accountability expectations in school communities. CRTs are generally used in learning environments to reflect the effectiveness of curriculum implementation and learning outcomes.

Performance-based Assessments

A number of state testing programs currently use performance-based assessments to measure the learning outcomes of individual students in subject content areas. Washington State uses performance-based assessments for the Washington Assessment of Student Learning (WASL) in Reading, Writing, Math, and Science to measure student-learning performance. Attaching passing the WASL to the graduation requirements for the class of 2008 has created a high-stakes testing and educational accountability for both students and teachers in meeting the expected skill-based requirements for tenth grade students taking the test.

In today's classrooms, performance-based assessments in core subject areas must have established and specific performance criteria that start with pre-testing in a subject area and maintain daily or weekly testing to gauge student learning goals and objectives. To understand a student's learning is to understand how a student processes information. Effective performance assessments show the gaps or holes in student learning so that teachers can concentrate on providing fillers to bridge non-sequential learning gaps. Typical performance assessments include oral and written student work in the form of research papers, oral presentations, class projects, journals, student portfolio collections of work, and community service projects.

Tests

Tests and similar direct assessment methods represent the most easily identified types of assessment. Thorndike (1997) identifies three types of assessment instruments:

1. Standardized achievement tests
2. Assessment material packaged with curricular materials
3. Teacher-made assessment instruments
   > Pencil and paper test
   > Oral tests
   > Product evaluations
   > Performance tests
   > Effective measures (p.199)

Kellough and Roberts (1991) take a slightly different perspective. They describe the following "three avenues for assessing student achievement":

1. what the learner says
2. what the learner does, and
3. what the learner writes..." (p.343)

SEE also Skill 8.2

Learn more about formative and summative assessment:

http://www.provost.cmich.edu/assessment/toolkit/formativesummative.htm

http://jan.ucc.nau.edu/edtech/etc667/proposal/evaluation/summative_vs._formative.htm

---

Skill 8.2   Identify procedures for accurately establishing, maintaining, and using formal and informal student records

Student Records

The information found in student records, teacher observations, and diagnostic tests are only as valuable as the teacher's ability to understand it. Although the student's cumulative record contains this information, each teacher must read and interpret it. Diagnostic test results are somewhat uniform and easy to interpret. They usually include a scoring guide that tells the teacher what the numbers actually mean. Teachers also need to realize that these number scores leave room for uncontrollable factors and are not the ultimate indicator of a child's ability or learning needs. Many factors influence these scores including the rapport the child had with the tester, how the child was feeling when the test was administered, and how the child regarded the value or importance of the test. Therefore, the teacher should regard these scores as *ball park* figures.

When teachers read other teachers' observations, they should remember that each person brings certain biases to an observation. Readers may also influence the information in observations with their own interpretations. When using teacher observations as a basis for designing learning programs, educators must be aware of these shortcomings.

Student records may provide the most assistance in guiding instruction. These records contain information gathered over a period of time and may show student growth and progress. They also contain information provided by several people including teachers, parents, and other educational professionals. By reading this compilation of information, the teacher may get a more accurate feel for a student's needs. All of this information is only a stepping-stone in determining how a child learns, what a child knows, and what a child needs to know to progress.

Other Assessments

The following types of assessment represent the more common types now available to the classroom teacher, but the list is not comprehensive.

Anecdotal Records

The teacher records notes concerning an area of interest or concern with a particular student. These records should focus on observable behaviors and should be descriptive in nature. They should not include assumptions or speculations regarding effective areas such as motivation or interest. These records are usually compiled over a period of several days to several weeks.

Rating Scales & Checklists

These assessments are generally self-appraisal instruments completed by the students or observations-based instruments completed by the teacher. The focus of these assessments is frequently on behavior or effective areas such as interest and motivation.

Portfolio Assessment

The use of student portfolios for some aspect of assessment has become quite common. The purpose, nature, and policies of portfolio assessment vary greatly from one setting to another. In general, a student's portfolio contains samples of work collected over an extended period. The nature of the subject, age of the student, and scope of the portfolio all contribute to the specific mechanics of analyzing, synthesizing, and otherwise evaluating the portfolio contents.

In most cases, the student and teacher make joint decisions about which work samples go into the student's portfolios. A collection of work compiled over an extended time allows teacher, student, and parents to view the student's progress from a unique perspective. Qualitative changes over time can be readily apparent from work samples. Such changes are difficult to establish with strictly quantitative records typical of the scores recorded in the teacher's grade book.

Questioning

Oral questioning by the teacher is one of the most frequently occurring forms of assessment in the classroom. As teachers question students, they collect a great deal of information about the degree of learning and potential sources of confusion for the students. While questioning is often viewed as a component of instructional methodology, it is also a powerful assessment tool.

SEE also Skill 8.1

Skill 8.3 **Interpret formal and informal assessment data to make instructional decisions about the educational needs of children**

SEE Skill 8.2

Skill 8.4   Identify procedures for appropriately using portfolio assessment to plan instruction that better extends the child's level of learning and interest

Portfolios are a focused collection of student work that exhibits the student's efforts, progress, and achievements in one or more areas of the curriculum and represents a variety of work assignments. It should include a collection of the student's best work or best efforts, student-selected samples of work experiences related to outcomes being assessed, and charts of growth toward achieving expected outcomes. The portfolio may also contain one or more works-in-progress that demonstrate the formation of a project, such as a story that is developing through different stages of origin, drafting, and revision.

Procedures for Planning Instruction

- Portfolio assessment is continuous and ongoing, providing both formative (ongoing) and summative (culminating) opportunities for monitoring students' progress toward achieving essential outcomes.

- Portfolio assessment is multidimensional. It includes a varied collection of student work and works-in-progress that reflect various aspects of students' learning processes.

- Portfolio assessment provides for collaborative reflection, including ways for students to explore their own thinking processes as they monitor their own comprehension and reflect upon their approaches to problem-solving and decision-making.

In today's classrooms, teachers appreciate portfolios as an assessment tool because they are representative of classroom-based performance. Students greatly benefit from portfolio instruction, which encourages self-directed learning.

For further reading about portfolio assessment:

http://www.pgcps.org/%7Eelc/portfolio.html

Skill 8.5 **Identify procedures and legal requirements that provide for appropriate and effective family conferences and/or home visits (in accordance with due process and confidentiality) regarding the assessment, education, growth, and development of children**

Parent Conferences

The parent-teacher conference is generally for one of three purposes. First, the teacher may wish to share information with the parents concerning the performance and behavior of the child. Second, the teacher may be interested in obtaining information from the parents about the child. Such information may help answer the teacher's questions or concerns. A third purpose may be to request parental support or involvement in specific activities or requirements. In many situations, more than one of the purposes may be involved.

Planning the Conference

When a conference is scheduled, whether at the request of the teacher or parent, the teacher should allow sufficient time to prepare thoroughly. Collect all relevant information, samples of student work, records of behavior, and other items needed to help the parent understand the circumstances. It is also a good idea to compile a list of questions or concerns you wish to address. Arrange the time and location of the conference to provide privacy and to avoid interruptions.

Conducting the Conference

Begin the conference by putting the parents as ease. Take the time to establish a comfortable mood, but do not waste time with unnecessary small talk. Begin your discussion with positive comments about the student. Identify strengths and desirable attributes, but do not exaggerate.

As you address issues or areas of concern, focus on observable behaviors and concrete results or information. Do not make judgmental statements about parent or child. Share specific work samples, anecdotal records of behavior, and other information that demonstrates clearly the concerns you have. Be a good listener and hear the parent's comments and explanations. Such background information can be invaluable in understanding the needs and motivations of the child.

Finally, end the conference with a plan of action agreed on by parents and teacher and, when appropriate, the child. Bring the conference to a close politely but firmly and thank the parents for their involvement.

After the Conference

A day or two after the conference, send a follow-up note to the parents. In this note, briefly and concisely reiterate the plan or step agreed to in the conference. Be polite and professional; avoid the temptation to be too informal or chatty. If the issue is a long term one such as the behavior or on-going work performance of the student, make periodic follow-up contacts to keep the parents informed of the progress.

Due Process

SEE Skill 2.3

Confidentiality

Information about a student's performance in school should be given only to a parent or guardian. This information is confidential and comes under the Privacy Act. During the conference, teachers should not discuss the performance or behavior of other students, even if these students have a direct impact on the student being discussed. If it becomes necessary to do so, the parents of this other student must be invited to participate in the conference as well.

COMPETENCY 9.0   KNOWLEDGE OF CHILD GUIDANCE AND CLASSROOM BEHAVIORAL MANAGEMENT

Skill 9.1   Identify developmentally appropriate components of a positive and effective classroom behavioral management plan

Behavior management techniques should focus on positive procedures that can be used at home and at school. When an intervention is needed, the least restrictive method should be used first, except in severe situations such as fighting and dangerous behaviors. For example, a child who begins talking instead of working in class would not be immediately placed into time out because the teacher can use less intrusive techniques to prompt the child to return to task. The teacher could use a signal or verbal prompt to gain the child's attention, then praise him when he is back on task.

Classroom management plans should be in place when the school year begins. When developing a management plan, teachers should decide what behaviors will be expected of the class as a whole, anticipate possible problems, and teach the behaviors early in the school year. Involving the students in the development of the rules lets them know the rationale for the rules and lets them assume responsibility because they had a part in developing them.

Procedures that use social humiliation such as withholding of basic needs and causing pain or extreme discomfort should never be used in a behavior management plan. Emergency intervention procedures used when the student is a danger to himself or others are not considered behavior management procedures. Throughout the year, the teacher should periodically review the types of interventions being used, assess the effectiveness of the interventions used in the management plan, and make revisions as needed for the best interests of the child.

Behavior Management Plan Strategies for Increasing Desired Behaviors

- **Prompt**
  A prompt is a visual or verbal cue that assists the child through the behavior shaping process. In some cases, the teacher may use a physical prompt such as guiding a child's hand. Visual cues include signs or other visual aids. Verbal cues include talking a child through the steps of a task. The gradual removal of the prompt as the child masters the target behavior is called fading.

- **Modeling**

  In order for modeling to be effective, the child must be at the cognitive and developmental level that enables model imitation. Teachers are behavior models in the classroom, but peers are powerful models as well, especially in adolescence. A child who does not perceive a model as acceptable will not likely copy the model's behavior, so teachers should be careful to reinforce appropriate behavior and not fall into the trap of attending to inappropriate behaviors. Children who see that the students who misbehave get the teacher's constant attention will most likely begin to model those students' behaviors.

- **Token Economy**

  A token economy mirrors our money system in that the students earn tokens that are of little value in themselves but that can be traded for tangible or activity rewards, just as currency can be spent for merchandise. Using stamps, stickers, stars, or point cards instead of items such as poker chips decreases the likelihood of theft, loss, and noise in the classroom.

Tips for a token economy:

1. Keep the system simple to understand and administer.
2. Develop a reward menu that is deliverable and varied.
3. Decide on the target behaviors.
4. Explain the system completely and in positive terms before beginning the economy.
5. Periodically review the rules.
6. Price the rewards and costs fairly and post the menu where it will be easily read.
7. Gradually fade to a variable schedule of reinforcement.

Learn about other behavior management strategies:

http://www.bbbautism.com/behavior_management_strategies.htm

Skill 9.2 **Identify developmentally appropriate positive strategies for guiding children's behavior and responding to challenging behaviors**

Teaching social skills can be rather difficult because social competence requires a repertoire of skills in a number of areas. The socially competent person must be able to get along with family and friends, function in a work environment, take care of personal needs, solve problems in daily living, and identify sources of help. A class of emotionally handicapped students may present several deficits in a few areas or a few deficits in many areas. Therefore, the teacher must begin with an assessment of the skill deficits and prioritize the ones to teach first.

Type of Assessment	Description
Direct Observation	Teacher observes student in various settings with a checklist
Role Play	Teacher observes students in structured scenarios
Teacher Ratings	Teacher rates student with a checklist or formal assessment instrument
Sociometric Measures: Peer Nomination	Student names specific classmates who meet a stated criterion (i.e., playmate). Score is the number of times a child is nominated.
Peer Rating	Students rank all their classmates on a Likert-type scale (e.g., 1-3 or 1-5 scale) on stated criterion. Individual score is the average of the total ratings of their classmates.
Paired-Comparison	Student is presented with paired classmate combinations and asked to choose who is most or least liked in the pair.
Context Observation	Student is observed to determine if the skill deficit is present in one setting but not others.

Type of Assessment	Description
Comparison with other student	Student's social skill behavior is compared to two other students in the same situation to determine if there is a deficit or if the behavior is not really a problem.

Social skills instruction can include teaching for conversation skills, assertiveness, play and peer interaction, problem solving and coping skills, self-help, task-related behaviors, self-concept related skills such as expressing feelings and accepting consequences, and job related skills.

Methods for Guiding Behavior

Punishment should not be the first strategy in behavior management plans because it tends to suppress behavior, not eliminate it. Punishment focuses on the negative rather than positive behaviors. Also, the child might comply out of fear, stress, or tension rather than a genuine behavior change. Furthermore, punishment can be misused to the point that it is no longer effective. Forms of punishment include the following:

1. **Subtracting something the child likes such as recess**

2. **Response Cost**
   In token economies, response cost results in loss of points or token. Response-cost or loss of privileges is preferred to adding aversives, but for long-term changes in behavior, punishment is less effective than other forms of decreasing misbehavior, such as extinction and ignoring.

3. **Time Out**
   Time-out means removing a child from the reinforcing situation to a setting that is not reinforcing. Time out may be **observational**—sitting at the end of the basketball court for five minutes or putting one's head down at the desk. The point is to have the child observe the others engaging in the appropriate behavior. **Exclusion time-out** involves placing a visual barrier between the student and the rest of the class. This barrier could be a divider between the desks and the time-out area, or the teacher could remove the child to another room.

4. Seclusion time-out

This method necessitates a special time-out room that adheres to mandated standards and a log of the children who are taken to time out, the reasons, and the time spent there.

To be effective, time-out must be consistently applied, and students must know why they are being sent to the time out area and for how long. The teacher briefly explains the reason for time-out, directs the child to the area, and refrains from long explanations, arguments, or debates. The time-out area should be as neutral as possible, away from busy areas, and easily observed by the monitor, but not by the rest of the class. The duration of time-out should vary with the age of the child and be timed so the child knows when the end of time-out has arrived.

Time-out as part of a behavior management plan needs to be periodically evaluated for its effectiveness. By analyzing records of time-out (as required and directed by the school district), the teacher can see if the technique is working. If a student regularly goes to time-out at a certain time, the student may be avoiding a frustrating situation or a difficult academic subject. Seclusion time out may be effective for children who tend to be group-oriented, acting-out, or aggressive. Isolation from the group is not rewarding for them. Shy, solitary, or withdrawn children may actually prefer to be in time-out and increase the target behavior in order to go to time-out.

5. Overcorrection

Overcorrection is more effective with severe and profoundly handicapped students. The student is required to repeat an appropriate behavior for a specified number of times when the inappropriate behavior is exhibited.

6. Suspension

Suspension is the punishment of last resort. In addition to restrictions on suspension for students with disabilities, suspension translates into a vacation from school for many students with behavioral problems. Furthermore, suspension does not relieve the teacher from the responsibility of exploring alternatives that may be effective with the child. An alternative to out-of-school suspension is in-school suspension. The student is placed in a special area to do his or her class work for a specified time and with minimal privileges.

Other Strategies for Behavior Management

1. Counseling Techniques
These techniques include life-space interview, reality therapy, and active listening.

2. Consequences
Consequences should be as close as possible to consequences in the outside world, especially for adolescents.

3. Student Participation
Students, especially older students, should participate as much as possible in the planning, goal setting, and evaluation of their behavior management plans.

4. Contingency Plans
Because adolescents frequently have a number of reinforcers outside of school, the teacher should try to incorporate contingencies for school behavior at home, since parents can control important reinforcers such as movies, going out with friends, and car privileges.

5. Consistency
Consistency, especially with adolescents, reduces the occurrence of power struggles and teaches them that predictable consequences follow for their choice of actions.

Initially, the target behavior may increase or worsen when the student realizes that the behavior is no longer reinforced. However, if the behavior management plan is properly administered, the teacher should begin to see results. Behavior management plan evaluation is a continuous process, since changes in behavior require changes in the target behavior, knowledge of outside variables that may account for behavior change, or changes in reinforcement schedules and menus.

It has already been established that appropriate verbal techniques include a soft non-threatening voice, void of undue roughness, anger, or impatience regardless of whether the teacher is instructing, providing student alert, or giving a behavior reprimand.

Verbal techniques that may be effective in modifying student behavior include stating the student's name and explaining briefly and succinctly what the student is doing that is inappropriate and what the student should be doing. Verbal techniques for reinforcing behavior include both encouragement and praise delivered by the teacher.

In addition, for verbal techniques to effect student behavior and learning positively, the teacher must give clear, concise directives while implying warmth toward the students.

Other factors that contribute to enhanced student learning concern body language. The teacher needs to make eye contact with individual students; smile and nod approvingly; move closer to the students; give gentle pats on the shoulder, arm, or head; and bend over so that the teacher is face to face with the children. Some of these same techniques can be applied as a means of desisting student misbehaviors. Rather than smiling, the teacher may need to make eye contact first and then nod disapprovingly. Again the teacher can use a gentle tap on the shoulder or arm to get a student's attention in an attempt to stop deviancy.

It is also helpful for the teacher to display the classroom rules prominently to serve as a visual reminder of the students' expected behaviors. In a study of classroom management procedures, the combination of conspicuously displayed rules, frequent verbal references to the rules, and appropriate consequences for appropriate behaviors led to increased levels of on-task behavior.

Skill 9.3 Identify learning opportunities for promoting positive self-concept, self-esteem, and prosocial and social-emotional development through interaction with others

SEE Skill 9.2

Skill 9.4 Identify developmentally appropriate conflict resolution strategies and guidelines for their implementation

Instructors can foster critical-thinking and evaluative skills by making children active partners in the entire learning and training process. Instructors should encourage students to employ self-assessment and self-monitoring techniques and skills.

Problem Solving

Problem solving is a higher-order cognitive process that requires the modulation and control of more routine or fundamental skills. It is the ability to solve a problem. For example, students could use their problem-solving skills during a game of chess. Alternatively, they could strategize during a timeout in the last few seconds of a basketball game when their team is down by two points. Developing adequate problem solving skills also promotes self-confidence and a sense of accomplishment.

Goal Setting, Problem Solving & Decision Making

Three key elements are necessary for promoting students' goal-setting analysis, problem-solving, and decision-making skills[jmm39]. First, instructors must give students a clear understanding of the goals they need to attain, problems they need to solve, and decisions they need to make. Second, instructors must give students the requisite information needed to attain the goals, solve the problems, and make the decisions. Third, instructors need to give students the opportunity to assume active responsibility for these matters and create opportunities for them to act on those responsibilities.

Finally, instructors should emphasize to students that taking action is their responsibility. The more they get accustomed to making decisions and following through, the better equipped they will be to act similarly in future situations.

Conflict Management

Interpersonal conflict is a major source of stress and worry. Common sources of interpersonal conflict include problems with family relationships, competition, and disagreement over values or decisions. Teaching students to manage conflict successfully will help them reduce stress levels throughout their lives, and, thereby, mitigate the adverse health effects of stress. The following is a list of conflict resolution principles and techniques.

1. Think before reacting—In a conflict situation, resisting temptation to react immediately is important. You should step back, consider the situation, and plan an appropriate response. In addition, you should not react to petty situations with anger.

2. Listen—Be sure to listen carefully to the opposing party. Try to understand the other person's point of view.

3. Find common ground—Try to find some common ground as soon as possible. Early compromise can help ease the tension.

4. Accept responsibility—Every conflict has plenty of blame to go around. Admitting when you are wrong shows you are committed to resolving the conflict.

5. Attack the problem, not the person—Personal attacks are never beneficial and usually lead to greater conflict and hard feelings.

6. Focus on the future—Instead of trying to assign blame for past events, focus on what we need to do differently to avoid future conflict.

Skill 9.5   Identify appropriate strategies to teach character development to young children

Many individual schools, school districts, and even states are now requiring that character education be taught in the classroom. Teachers can build a caring atmosphere that supports character building by implementing character development examples. The most identifiable and common character development traits are *Responsibility, Caring, Self-discipline, Citizenship, Honesty, Respect, and Patriotism.*

Strategies for Teaching Character Development

- Hold class meetings in which students can establish group goals.
- Allow students to decide on rules of conduct.
- Teach conflict resolution so that students can become skilled at settling conflicts peacefully.
- Concentrate on problem-solving rather than rewards and punishments.

Teachers can incorporate daily lessons, current events, movies, and television programs to engage students in thinking about characters and their value systems.

For example; when reading a book, have the students analyze the characters of the story. What were their strengths and weaknesses?

Teachers can ask such classic hypothetical questions as *What would you do if you found a wallet with money in it? What would you do if your best friend begged you to help him or her cheat on a test?*

The best strategies of a character development education always involve students in honest, thoughtful discussions concerning the moral implications of every day life.

Skill 9.6   Identify the roles of early childhood professionals in collaboration with other professionals in helping children and their families cope with stressors

Although the definition of normal or acceptable behavior can vary a great deal depending upon a student's age and level of maturity, the following are common signs that a student is experiencing stress.

Stress Factors

- behavioral problems such as excessive anger, bullying, or eating disorders
- a significant drop in grades
- episodes of sadness
- nightmares
- decreased interest in previously enjoyed activities
- overly aggressive behavior such as biting, kicking, or hitting
- an increase in physical complaints such as headaches and stomach aches

Parents need to spend time with their children; sometimes just listening to them is enough. Letting children talk about their days gives them peace of mind and reassures them that everything is all right. Often children do not have time to play creatively or relax after school. Time should be allotted for children to be children with no responsibilities. Parents can ensure that children get plenty of sleep at night. Children also need to eat a healthy diet of each of the food groups. Adequate preventive health care is also crucial to the mental and physical well-being of a child.

Teachers and other professionals can also identify when a student is displaying symptoms of stress and then take preventive steps to alleviate the stress. Many times just asking the students what is bothering them will alleviate the stress. Children need to feel that teachers care about them and their daily lives. Let the student know that it's ok to feel angry, scared, lonely, or anxious.

Teachers can also read books to young students. Books are a creative method that lets children identify with characters in stressful situations. The following books address the problems of stress:

Alexander and the Terrible, Horrible No Good, Very Bad Day by Judith Viorst

Tear Soup by Pat Schweibert, Chuck DeKlyen, and Taylor Bills

Dinosaurs Divorce by Marc Brown and Laurene Krasny Brown.

Pre-Test

Child Growth and Development

1. **Which of the following is a sign of child abuse? (Skill 1.1; Average rigor)**

    A. Awkward social behavior around other children

    B. Bruises

    C. Withdrawn

    D. All of the above

2. **Who should you talk to if you suspect child abuse? (Skill 1.1; Average rigor)**

    A. The child

    B. The child's parent

    C. Your supervisor

    D. Another teacher

3. **Which of the following might cause a child to become easily agitated in class? (Skill 1.1; Average rigor)**

    A. Lack of sleep

    B. Lack of training in manners

    C. Being raised in a single parent home

    D. Watching too much TV

4. **What developmental patterns should a professional teacher assess to meet the needs of the student? (Skill 1.1; Average rigor)**

    A. Academic, regional, and family background

    B. Social, physical, academic

    C. Academic, physical, and family background

    D. Physical, family, ethnic background

5. A preschool teacher is concerned because the three year olds in her class do not play with each other. Each student plays without interacting with others in the class. What advice would you give her? (Skill 1.2; Rigorous)

   A. Contact the parents immediately so they can talk to their doctors about medications that might help.

   B. Plan more activities that require interactions between the children.

   C. Tell the children that you expect them to share and play together. If they don't, then punish them.

   D. Don't worry. It is typical for young children engage in "parallel" activities playing alongside their peers without directly interacting with one another.

6. During a conference about reading difficulties, a parent asks a first grade teacher for advice on how to make sure the three year old sibling doesn't end up having trouble learning to read like his brother. Based on research, what should the teacher recommend? (Skill 1.4; Rigorous)

   A. Intense practice on alphabet

   B. Exposure to numerous books

   C. Work on rhyming words and sounds

   D. All of the above

7. A teacher notices that a student is sullen, and has several bruises on his head, arms and legs. When asked, the student responds that he hit his arm getting out of bed that morning. The teacher should: (Skill 1.5; Average rigor)

   A. Attempt to get more information from the student

   B. Report suspected abuse to the school counselor

   C. Consult a colleague and see what they would do

   D. Wait and see if other signs of abuse become evident

8. **Which of the following is a TRUE statement? (Skill 1.6; Rigorous)**

   A. Younger children tend to process information at a slower rate than older children (age eight and older).

   B. Older children tend to process information at a slower rate than younger children (younger than age 8).

   C. Children process information at the same rate as adults.

   D. All children process information at the exact same rate.

9. **A child exhibits the following symptoms: a lack of emotional responsiveness, indifference to physical contact, abnormal social play, and abnormal speech. What is the likely diagnosis for this child? (Skill 1.6; Average rigor)**

   A. Separation anxiety

   B. Mental retardation

   C. Autism

   D. Hypochondria

10. **How many stages of intellectual development does Piaget define? (Skill 1.7; Easy)**

    A. Two

    B. Four

    C. Six

    D. Eight

11. **Which of the following is NOT one of Gardner's Multiple Intelligences? (Skill 1.7; Average rigor)**

    A. Intrapersonal

    B. Musical

    C. Technological

    D. Logical/mathematical

12. **Research over several decades has shown that student performance is directly impacted by: (Skill 1.8; Average rigor)**

    A. The teacher's high expectations

    B. The IQ of the parents

    C. The IQ of the student

    D. Whether the child lives in an apartment or in a house

13. How can student misconduct be redirected at times? (Skill 1.8; Average rigor)

   A. State expectations about behavior

   B. Let students discipline their peers

   C. Let minor infractions of the rules go unnoticed

   D. Increase disapproving remarks

Foundations of Learning

14. According to Piaget, what stage is characterized by the ability to think abstractly and to use logic? (Skill 2.1; Rigorous)

   A. Concrete operations

   B. Pre-operational

   C. Formal operations

   D. Conservative operational

15. According to Piaget's theory of cognitive development, what is the process of incorporating new objects, information or experiences into the existing cognitive structures? (Skill 2.1; Rigorous)

   A. Attachment

   B. Conservation

   C. Identification

   D. Assimilation

16. At approximately what age is the average child able to define abstract terms such as honesty and justice? (Skill 2.1; Rigorous)

   A. 10-12 years old

   B. 4-6 years old

   C. 14-16 years old

   D. 6-8 years old

17. **The NCLB (No Child Left Behind) Act mandates that early childhood programs: (Skill 2.1; Rigorous)**

    A. Provide Headstart for every child in our country

    B. Construct curriculum models specific to the development of early childhood and elementary programs for academic enhancement

    C. Protect the privacy of student education records

    D. Have a seatbelt for every student riding a school bus

18. **Which of the following is a widely known curriculum model for early childhood programs? (Skill 2.2; Easy)**

    A. Montessori method

    B. DISTAR method

    C. Success for All

    D. Voyager

19. **Head Start Programs were created in what decade? (Skill 2.2; Easy)**

    A. 2000's

    B. 1990's

    C. 1980's

    D. 1960's

20. **What is the most important factor in raising academic outcomes for all students as required in the NCLB law? (Skill 2.2; Rigorous)**

    A. The curriculum model used

    B. The quality of instruction in the classroom

    C. The location of the school

    D. The number of years of experience the teacher has

21. **Effective curriculum models for early childhood programs should include which of the following: (Skill 2.2; Rigorous)**

    A. Differentiated instruction for group/individual academic needs

    B. Best practices and instructional approaches

    C. A and B

    D. None of the above

22. To determine if a child has a disability that may qualify the child for services under IDEA, the school should collect which of the following pieces of information: (Skill 2.3; Average rigor)

    A. The present levels of academic achievement

    B. Vision and hearing screening information

    C. A complete psychological evaluation

    D. All of the above

23. Failure to make a report when abuse or neglect is suspected is punishable by which of the following? (Skill 2.3; Average rigor)

    A. revocation of certification and license

    B. a monetary fine

    C. criminal charges

    D. All of the above

24. IDEA is a federal law passed in 1990 that has a direct impact on classrooms. The acronym IDEA stands for: (Skill 2.3; Average rigor)

    A. Individuals with Disabilities Education Act

    B. Individualized Differentiation for Education Always

    C. Idealistic Dedicated Educational Access

    D. Instructional Differentiation Education Act

25. In your classroom, there is a student who has been exhibiting difficulty in the area of reading. The child has a learning disability and already receives special education services. According to IDEA, who must be involved in developing the child's IEP (individual educational plan) to address these concerns? (Skill 2.3; Rigorous)

    A. A medical doctor

    B. The school psychologist

    C. The parent or guardian

    D. The principal

Research standards and trends

26. **Educators seeking quality strategies to improve early childhood education for students could gain information from which of the following: (Skill 3.1; Easy)**

    A. Websites

    B. Professional organizations

    C. Journal articles

    D. All of the above

27. **What is the world's largest educational organization that works on behalf on the education of young children? (Skill 3.2; Easy)**

    A. NAEYC

    B. SPCA

    C. NAACP

    D. IRA

28. **Which international organization is devoted to studying the research and data from national organizations and school communities on effective reading instruction and strategies that promote reading acquisition? (Skill 3.2; Rigorous)**

    A. FCRR

    B. AECI

    C. IRA

    D. AERA

29. **The NCLB Act requires schools to establish AYP. What does the acronym AYP stand for? (Skill 3.3; Easy)**

    A. Advocates for Youth Programs

    B. Adequate Yearly Progress

    C. All Young People

    D. None of the above

30. **Which of the following is considered a current trend in education? (Skill 3.3; Easy)**

    A. Differentiated instruction so that no child is left behind

    B. Innovations in technology

    C. Instruction in the 3 Rs (reading, writing and arithmetic)

    D. A and B

31. **The annual cost of teacher turnover in school communities has been estimated to be in the range of: (Skill 3.3; Rigorous)**

    A. 5-7 billion dollars

    B. 5-7 hundred dollars

    C. 5-7 thousand dollars

    D. 5-7 million dollars

32. **When students engage in this type of learning in order to understand the world around them, the learning process involves the formulation of questions that convert new information into an active application of knowledge. (Skill 3.3; Rigorous)**

    A. Hands-on learning

    B. Guided reading

    C. Inquiry-based learning

    D. Teacher directed model

33. **What can be done to decrease violent behavior that even young children are exhibiting at school? (Skill 3.3; Rigorous)**

    A. Build more alternative schools

    B. Provide teachers with classroom management training

    C. Increase parent training

    D. Provide students with social strategies to improve cooperative learning and communication

34. **Assessment where students create an answer or a response to a question or task is known as: (Skill 3.3; Average rigor)**

    A. Traditional assessment

    B. Alternative assessment

    C. Multiple choice

    D. True assessment

35. When implemented effectively, an alternative assessment approach will: (Skill 3.3; Rigorous)

   A. Require higher-order thinking and problem-solving

   B. Provide opportunities for student self-reflection and self-assessment

   C. Use real world applications to connect students to the subject

   D. All of the above

Effective Practices

36. What are critical elements of the instructional process? (Skill 4.1; Rigorous)

   A. Content, goals, teacher needs

   B. Means of getting money to regulate instruction

   C. Content, materials, activities, goals, learner needs

   D. Materials, definitions, assignments

37. What would improve planning for instruction? (Skill 4.1; Average rigor)

   A. Describe the role of the teacher and student

   B. Evaluate the outcomes of instruction

   C. Rearrange the order of activities

   D. Give outside assignments

38. When are students more likely to understand complex ideas? (Skill 4.1; Rigorous)

   A. If they do outside research before coming to class

   B. Later when they write out the definitions of complex words

   C. When they attend a lecture on the subject

   D. When they are clearly defined by the teacher and are given examples and non-examples of the concept

39. **What should a teacher do when students have not responded well to an instructional activity? (Skill 4.1; Average rigor)**

    A. Reevaluate learner needs

    B. Request administrative help

    C. Continue with the activity another day

    D. Assign homework on the concept

40. **If teachers attend to content, instructional materials, activities, learner needs, and goals in instructional planning, what could be an outcome? (Skill 4.1; Rigorous)**

    A. Planning for the next year

    B. Effective classroom performance

    C. Elevated test scores on standardized tests

    D. More student involvement

41. **Reducing off task time and maximizing the amount of time students spend attending to academic tasks is closely related to which of the following? (Skill 4.2; Rigorous)**

    A. Using whole class instruction only

    B. Business-like behaviors of the teacher

    C. Dealing only with major teaching functions

    D. Giving students a maximum of two minutes to come to order

42. **The concept of efficient use of time includes which of the following? (Skill 4.2; Easy)**

    A. Daily review, seatwork, and recitation of concepts

    B. Lesson initiation, transition, and comprehension check

    C. Review, test, review

    D. Punctuality, management transition, and wait time avoidance

43. **What is an example of an academic transition signal? (Skill 4.2; Average rigor)**

   A. "How do clouds form?"

   B. "Today we are going to study clouds."

   C. "We have completed today's lesson."

   D. "That completes the description of cumulus clouds. Now we will look at the description of cirrus clouds."

44. **What environmental element can cause some students to become restless and hyperactive? (Skill 4.3; Average rigor)**

   A. Bright lights

   B. The arrangement of student desks

   C. The proximity of the classroom to the playground

   D. All of the above

45. **A print-rich environment would have which of the following components: (Skill 4.4; Easy)**

   A. A word wall

   B. Classroom libraries

   C. Labels for objects in the room

   D. All of the above

46. **Strong and effective lesson plans always answer 3 questions, sometimes referred to as the 3 W's. The 3 W questions for a lesson are: (Skill 4.6; Rigorous)**

   A. What? How? Why?

   B. Who? What? When?

   C. When? Where? Why?

   D. None of the above

47. **A teacher has just received her class roster and knows that must determine the abilities of the incoming students assigned to her class as she begins planning to meet the state requirements for that grade and subject area. What is the best way to determine a student's current ability level? (Skill 4.7; Easy)**

   A. Administer a pre-test before each lesson

   B. Talk to the child's teacher from the previous school year

   C. Look at standardized test results

   D. Consult the child's cumulative academic record

48. **Which of the following is a true statement? (Skill 4.11; Rigorous)**

    A. Recess is not important to a child's development

    B. Playtime is only provided in schools to help children get "their energy out"

    C. Play is very important to human development and teaches children many things

    D. None of the above

49. **Playing team sports at young ages should be done for the following purpose: (Skill 4.11; Rigorous)**

    A. To develop the child's motor skills

    B. To prepare children for competition in high school

    C. To develop the child's interests

    D. Both A and C

50. **Why is repetition an important part of child's play? (Skill 4.12; Rigorous)**

    A. It allows the child to master the skill and then move into creativity

    B. It allows the child to stress the caregiver who is bored with playing the same thing over and over

    C. It is a creative outlet for the child

    D. None of the above

Family and Community Involvement

51. **If a child is falling behind in school, which of the following might make a difference to the child's academic progress? (Skill 5.1; Average rigor)**

    A. Assign the child to a special education class

    B. Assign an adult mentor

    C. Assign the child additional homework

    D. Ask the parents to review lessons each night

52. **Which of the following is a technological strategy that keeps students and teachers interactively communicating about issues in the classroom and beyond? (Skill 5.1; Easy)**

    A. Myspace.com

    B. Distance learning

    C. Email

    D. None of the above

53. **The commitment that a community shows to its educational communities is: (Skill 5.1; Average rigor)**

    A. Judged by how much money is contributed

    B. Something that doesn't matter much to the school

    C. A valuable investment in the future

    D. Something that will cause immediate gains in the school's AYP results

54. **Because teachers today will deal with an increasingly diverse group of cultures in their classrooms, they must: (Skill 5.2; Rigorous)**

    A. Ignore the cultures represented and continue to teach to the majority

    B. Learn to deal with a variety of family expectations for school and teachers

    C. Provide a special celebration for each culture represented

    D. Both A and C

55. **You receive a phone call from a parent who is angry about the grade their child receives on the report card. As the conversation continues, the parent becomes verbally abusive and uses curse words. What should you do? (Skill 5.2; Rigorous)**

    A. Raise your voice to establish your authority

    B. Hang up and get assistance from your administrator

    C. Blame the parent for the poor grade

    D. Apologize over and over and hope that the parent will calm down and stop cursing.

56. How should a teacher respond to criticism about her teaching strategies from a parent? (Skill 5.2; Rigorous)

A. Explain to the parent that negative feedback is hurtful and mean-spirited

B. Dismiss the criticism as an attempt to undermine her performance

C. Think about the criticism objectively and consider that it might be true

D. Change her teaching strategies to eliminate the aspect being criticized

57. When communicating with parents for whom English is not the primary language you should: (Skill 5.2; Average rigor)

A. Provide materials whenever possible in their native language

B. Use an interpreter

C. Provide the same communication as you would to native English speaking parents

D. All of the above

58. Which of the following could be a purpose of a parent-teacher conference? (Skill 5.2; Average rigor)

A. To involve the parent in their child's education

B. To resolve a concern about the child's performance

C. To inform parents of positive behaviors by the child

D. All of the above

59. Which of the following is NOT a right of parents? (Skill 5.2; Average rigor)

A. To be informed of the teacher's concerns about their child

B. To require the teacher to use the teaching method that works for the child

C. To administer discipline to their child in the classroom

D. Both B and C

60. Which of the following is a true statement? (Skill 5.2; Rigorous)

   A. Various cultures have different views of how children should be educated

   B. Various cultures share the same views of how children should be educated

   C. Parent's views about how children should be educated are always correct

   D. Teacher's views about how children should be educated are always correct

Curriculum

61. Which of the following is **not** a motivation behind providing reading activities, including reading aloud, to young children? (Skill 6.1; Rigorous)

   A. Developing Word Consciousness Skills

   B. Developing Functions of Print Skills

   C. Developing Phonics Skills

   D. Developing Language Skills

62. Which of the following strategies encourages print awareness in classrooms? (Skill 6.2; Easy)

   A. Word walls

   B. Using big books to read to students

   C. Using highlighters to locate upper case letters

   D. All of the above

63. Ms. Smith hands each child in the classroom a letter of the alphabet. She then challenges each child to go around the classroom and find at least five things in the classroom which begin with that letter. Ms. Smith is teaching the students which of the following skills? (Skill 6.2; Rigorous)

   A. Phonemic Awareness

   B. Vocabulary

   C. Meaning of Print

   D. Letter Identification

64. **Which of the following explains a significant difference between phonics and phonemic awareness? (Skill 6.3; Average rigor)**

   A. Phonics involves print, phonemic awareness involves language

   B. Phonics is harder than phonemic awareness

   C. Phonics involves sounds, phonemic awareness involves letters

   D. Phonics is the application of sounds to print, phonemic awareness is oral

65. **Ms. Walker's lesson objective is to teach her first graders the concept of morphology in order to improve their reading skills. Which group of words would be most appropriate for her to use in this lesson? (Skill 6.4; Rigorous)**

   A. far   farm   farmer

   B. far   feather   fever

   C. far   fear   fare

   D. far   fare   farce

66. **Academically, appropriate literature primarily helps students to _____. (Skill 6.5; Rigorous)**

   A. become better readers

   B. see how the skills they learned are applied to writing

   C. enjoy library time

   D. increase academic skills in other content areas

67. **According to Marilyn Jager Adams, which skill would a typically developing student demonstrate after he is able to separate the onset and rhyme of words (i.e. /c/ /at/)? (Skill 6.6; Rigorous)**

   A. Recognize the odd member in a group

   B. Replace sounds in words

   C. Count the sounds in a word

   D. Count syllables in a word

68. **All of the following are true about phonological awareness EXCEPT: (Skill 6.7; Average rigor)**

   A. It may involve print

   B. It is a prerequisite for spelling and phonics

   C. Activities can be done by the children with their eyes closed

   D. Starts before letter recognition is taught

69. Standing in line at the grocery store, Megan, age three, turns to her mother and asks in a regular tone of voice, "Mom, why is that woman so fat?" Megan's mother is mortified when sharing this story with Megan's preschool teacher. Which concept of language can the teacher explain to Megan's mother to help her better understand the situation? (Skill 6.8; Rigorous)

A. Syntax

B. Semantics

C. Morphology

D. Pragmatics

70. Which of the following is NOT a component of reading fluency? (Skill 6.9; Easy)

A. Phoneme knowledge

B. Accuracy

C. Rate

D. Automacity

71. Repeated readings of the same text are beneficial to developing readers because _____. (Skill 6.10; Rigorous)

A. repeated reading helps students memorize the text

B. repeated reading helps in pairing students

C. repeated reading ensures students recognize the words readily and can read at an improved pace

D. repeated reading helps teachers determine students' level of reading

72. When introducing new vocabulary to students, the number of new words being taught at one time should be _____. (Skill 6.11; Rigorous)

A. one to two

B. two to three

C. three to four

D. four to five

73. Which of the following is NOT a common method of teaching comprehension? (Skill 6.12; Easy)

A. Summarizing

B. Question asking

C. Graphic organizers

D. Phonics drills

74. When students know that letters stand for a message, they are said to be in the_____ stage of spelling. (Skill 6.13; Rigorous)

A. non-phonemic

B. pre-phonemic

C. early phonemic

D. letter-name sounding

75. The _____ level of learning of Bloom's taxonomy requires students to take the analyzed parts from the previous level and converge them into creative new wholes. (Skill 6.14; Average rigor)

A. Comprehension

B. Analysis

C. Synthesis

D. Evaluation

76. Mrs. Baker's class has 22 students. Mrs. Smith's class has 16 students. How many more students are in Mrs. Baker's class? (Skill 6.15; Easy)

A. 22 more students

B. 14 more students

C. 6 more students

D. 38 more students

77. Kindergarten students are exploring fractions with fraction-pie puzzles. One puzzle has the pie divided into fourths. It has four equal pieces. Which puzzle will have twice as many pieces? (Skill 6.15; Average Rigor)

A. The puzzle divided into eighths (eight equal pieces)

B. The puzzle divided into halves (two equal pieces)

C. The puzzle divided into sixths (six equal pieces)

D. The puzzles divided into twelfths (twelve equal pieces)

78. PreK students are using snap-together cubes to measure objects in the classroom. They want to know which is longer, the doll bed or the red truck. After snapping together enough cubes to "measure" each they determine that the doll bed is longer. Which math principles are demonstrated in this activity? (Skill 6.15; Rigorous)

A. Measurement, rote counting

B. Addition, measurement

C. Rote counting, using a model

D. Measurement, using a model

79. **What are the three primary types of illustrations used in teaching social studies to young children? (Skill 6.16; Average rigor)**

    A. maps, charts, and contour lines

    B. graphs, maps, and distortion diagrams

    C. maps, charts and graphs

    D. bar charts, pie charts and graphs

80. **Which of the following is not a basic type of map projection? (Skill 6.16; Rigorous)**

    A. Flat-Plane

    B. Cylindrical

    C. Conical

    D. Conformational

81. **An appropriate method for graphically representing data to the scientific community would be _____. (Skill 6.17; Easy)**

    A. charts

    B. spreadsheets

    C. Power Point presentations

    D. all of the above

82. **When creating a model, what is the most important aspect of the possibilities listed below? (Skill 6.17; Rigorous)**

    A. Scale

    B. Color

    C. Details

    D. Intended audience

83. **Which type of communication is most effective for introducing athletic skills? (Skill 6.18; Easy)**

    A. written

    B. verbal

    C. visual

    D. all of the above

84. **Which style of teaching would be best to use when there is only a small amount of time to teach students a physical skill? (Skill 6.19; Rigorous)**

    A. command style

    B. practice style

    C. reciprocal style

    D. inclusion style

85. Which subject would be most likely to develop a student's body awareness and listening skills? (Skill 6.20; Average rigor)

A. visual arts

B. dance

C. drama

D. music

Diversity

86. Flexible scheduling and use of mechanical aids are examples of _____. (Skill 7.1; Easy)

A. alternative assessments

B. testing modifications

C. differentiated instruction

D. multiple intelligences

87. What would a teacher wanting to improve a student's self-esteem be best to tell the student? (Skill 7.1; Rigorous)

A. what they did that helped produce a successful result

B. the high grade they achieved

C. how they performed compared to other students

D. the actions they can take to perform better in the future

88. What are the three functions of the three-phase model for teaching? (Skill 7.2; Average rigor)

A. planning, implementing, assessing

B. content, process, and product

C. sensing, transforming, and acting

D. thinking, behaving, revising

89. Which of the following is a disinviting behavior? (Skill 7.2; Average rigor)

A. learning student's names

B. being real with students

C. inviting oneself

D. reacting to rejection

90. A teacher can help instill confidence in the parents of diverse children by talking about the child _____. (Skill 7.3; Rigorous)

A. unemotionally

B. indirectly

C. personally

D. logically

91. Which of the following would be most useful for an ESOL student? (Skill 7.4; Average rigor)

A. placing the student in a mixed learning group

B. making content two grades below the student's level

C. encouraging the student to use complex language

D. having the student complete activities independently

92. What type of learning disability does a student that has difficulty concentrating most likely have? (Skill 7.5; Easy)

A. attention deficit hyperactivity disorder

B. auditory processing disorder

C. visual processing disorder

D. dyslexia

93. An exceptional child is one who has _____. (Skill 7.6; Average rigor)

A. sensory impairments

B. emotional disturbances

C. mental retardation

D. any of the above

94. What is the most important factor in improving the developmental and educational gains for an exceptional child? (Skill 7.6; Average rigor)

A. varied teaching procedures

B. the social environment

C. early intervention

D. encouraging independence

95. Which of the following problems are likely to be faced by migrant, homeless, and abandoned children? (Skill 7.7; Easy)

A. poor attendance

B. language barriers

C. social isolation

D. all of the above

96. Which child would be most likely to have medical and health problems that the school could address? (Skill 7.7; Average rigor)

A. a migrant child

B. an abandoned child

C. a foster child

D. an adopted child

97. For a student to be allowed to carry and self-administer asthma medication, what must be on file with the school? (Skill 7.8; Rigorous)

A. medical certificate

B. Individualized Educational Program

C. release form

D. medication log book

Diagnosis, Assessment and Evaluation

98. Which type of assessment is the least structured? (Skill 8.1; Easy)

A. observation

B. informal continuous assessment

C. formal assessment

D. standardized testing

99. Which type of assessment has the main purpose of helping learners learn better? (Skill 8.1; Rigorous)

A. formal assessment

B. observation

C. informal assessment

D. exam

100. What are entry surveys, collections of reading and writing samples, and classroom observations examples of? (Skill 8.1; Average rigor)

A. informal assessments

B. structured assessments

C. formal assessments

D. criterion-references assessments

101. Which factor is it most important to consider when choosing structured assessment methods? (Skill 8.1; Rigorous)

A. the authenticity of the methods

B. the results of informal evaluations

C. the formal assessments required

D. the developmental stage of students

102. Which type of assessment would be used to place students into honors, regular, and remedial classes? (Skill 8.1; Rigorous)

A. norm-referenced assessments

B. criterion-referenced assessments

C. performance-based assessments

D. observation-based assessments

103. Teachers should regard a student's test results as _____. (Skill 8.2; Average rigor)

 A. exact indications of the student's ability

 B. ball park figures indicating the student's ability

 C. possible indicators of a student's ability

 D. unlikely to be a true indication of a student's ability

104. What is it most important for a teacher to consider when reading another teacher's observations of a student? (Skill 8.2; Average rigor)

 A. mood

 B. discrimination

 C. dishonesty

 D. bias

105. What should a teacher record in anecdotal records of a student? (Skill 8.2; Average rigor)

 A. assumptions about the student's interest

 B. theories explaining the student's attitude

 C. speculations about the student's motivation

 D. observed behaviors

106. Which of the following is a common self-appraisal instrument? (Skill 8.2; Average rigor)

 A. rating scales

 B. questioning

 C. portfolio assessment

 D. anecdotal records

107. Portfolio assessment is especially useful for identifying _____. (Skill 8.3; Easy)

 A. quantitative changes

 B. qualitative changes

 C. behavioral changes

 D. attitude changes

108. A teacher wishes to identify the sources of confusion that are resulting in students performing poorly on standardized tests. What would be the best method to use for this purpose? (Skill 8.3; Rigorous)

 A. rating scales

 B. questioning

 C. portfolio assessment

 D. anecdotal records

109. **What type of opportunities does portfolio assessment provide for monitoring student progress? (Skill 8.4; Average rigor)**

   A. formative

   B. summative

   C. alternative assessment

   D. both formative and summative

110. **What is one of the main advantages of portfolio assessment for students? (Skill 8.4; Average rigor)**

   A. It promotes creativity

   B. It generates opportunities to use diverse skills

   C. It encourages students to reflect on their own work

   D. It develops communication skills

111. **What is the purpose of a parent-teacher conference? (Skill 8.5; Average rigor)**

   A. sharing information with the parents

   B. obtaining information from the parents

   C. requesting parent support

   D. any or all of the above

112. **What is it best to begin a parent-teacher conference with? (Skill 8.5; Easy)**

   A. student weaknesses

   B. positive comments

   C. entertaining anecdotes

   D. issues of concern

113. **Information about a student's school performance can be given to _____. (Skill 8.5; Average rigor)**

   A. the student's parents or guardians

   B. the student's parents or guardians and those of other parents

   C. any interested party

   D. any or all of the above

Guidance and Classroom Behavioral Management

114. **What type of procedures should be used as the basis for behavior management techniques? (Skill 9.1; Average rigor)**

   A. positive

   B. negative

   C. restrictive

   D. combative

115. When should a classroom management plan be implemented? (Skill 9.1; Easy)

    A. when a parent requests one

    B. when behavioral issues are impacting students

    C. at the start of the school year

    D. on the first instance that undesired behaviors are observed

116. Which type of social skills assessment involves the teacher observing students in structured scenarios? (Skill 9.2; Average rigor)

    A. role play

    B. teacher ratings

    C. peer nomination

    D. peer rating

117. What is the main reason that punishment should not be the first method used to guide behavior? (Skill 9.2; Rigorous)

    A. It can isolate students

    B. It can create strained relationships

    C. It can result in behavior suppression

    D. It can produce feelings of anger and resentment

118. What is the most severe form of punishment? (Skill 9.3; Easy)

    A. time-out

    B. suspension

    C. overcorrection

    D. response cost

119. When reprimanding students, what type of voice is most effective? (Skill 9.3; Average rigor)

    A. impatient

    B. angry

    C. non-threatening

    D. unemotional

120. What should a physical education instructor emphasize to encourage students to make decisions? (Skill 9.4; Rigorous)

    A. there is sometimes more than one right decision

    B. decision-making and problem-solving are related

    C. taking action is the student's responsibility

    D. asking others for assistance can be helpful

121. What is a conflict resolution principle? (Skill 9.4; Average rigor)

A. attack the person

B. react immediately

C. find common ground

D. focus on the past

122. Which of the following is NOT a common character development trait? (Skill 9.5; Average rigor)

A. responsibility

B. intelligence

C. caring

D. honesty

123. The best strategies for teaching character development focus on the moral implications of _____. (Skill 9.5; Average rigor)

A. historical events

B. everyday life

C. major issues

D. hypothetical situations

124. A student's normal behavior is highly dependent on the student's _____. (Skill 9.6; Average rigor)

A. number of friends

B. academic performance

C. maturity level

D. health status

125. Which of the following is an effective method for helping young children cope with stress? (Skill 9.6; Average rigor)

A. reading them books

B. encouraging them to play sports

C. helping them make friends

D. persuading them not to focus on their feelings

Pre-Test Answer Key

1.	D	43.	D	85.	B
2.	C	44.	A	86.	B
3.	A	45.	D	87.	A
4.	B	46.	A	88.	C
5.	D	47.	D	89.	D
6.	D	48.	C	90.	C
7.	B	49.	D	91.	A
8.	A	50.	A	92.	A
9.	C	51.	B	93.	D
10.	B	52.	B	94.	C
11.	C	53.	C	95.	D
12.	A	54.	B	96.	B
13.	A	55.	B	97.	C
14.	C	56.	C	98.	A
15.	D	57.	D	99.	C
16.	A	58.	D	100.	A
17.	B	59.	D	101.	D
18.	A	60.	A	102.	A
19.	D	61.	C	103.	B
20.	B	62.	D	104.	D
21.	C	63.	C	105.	D
22.	D	64.	D	106.	A
23.	D	65.	A	107.	B
24.	A	66.	B	108.	B
25.	C	67.	C	109.	D
26.	D	68.	A	110.	C
27.	A	69.	D	111.	D
28.	C	70.	A	112.	B
29.	B	71.	C	113.	A
30.	D	72.	B	114.	A
31.	A	73.	D	115.	C
32.	C	74.	B	116.	A
33.	D	75.	C	117.	C
34.	B	76.	C	118.	B
35.	D	77.	A	119.	C
36.	C	78.	D	120.	C
37.	B	79.	C	121.	C
38.	D	80.	D	122.	B
39.	A	81.	D	123.	B
40.	B	82.	A	124.	C
41.	B	83.	C	125.	A
42.	D	84.	A		

Pre-Test Rigor Table

	Easy %20	Average Rigor %40	Rigorous %40
Question #	10, 18, 19, 26, 27, 29, 30, 42, 45, 47, 52, 62, 70, 73, 76, 81, 83, 86, 92, 95, 98, 107, 112, 115, 118	1, 2, 3, 4, 7, 9, 11, 12, 13, 22, 23, 24, 34, 37, 39, 43, 44, 51, 53, 57, 58, 59, 64, 68, 78,77, 79, 85, 88, 89, 91, 93, 94, 96, 100, 103, 104, 105, 106, 109, 110, 111, 113, 114, 116, 119, 121, 122, 123, 124, 125	5, 6, 8, 14, 15, 16, 17, 20, 21, 25, 28, 31, 32, 33, 35, 36, 38, 40, 41, 46, 48, 49, 50, 54, 55, 56, 60, 61, 63, 65, 66, 67, 69, 71, 72, 74, 78, 80, 82, 84, 87, 90, 97, 99, 101, 102, 108, 117, 120

Pre-Test Rationales with Sample Questions

Child Growth and Development

1. **Which of the following is a sign of child abuse? (Skill 1.1; Average rigor)**

    A. Awkward social behavior around other children
    B. Bruises
    C. Withdrawn
    D. All of the above

Answer D: All of the above

Awkward social behavior around other children, bruises, and withdrawn behavior are all signs of child abuse.

2. **Who should you talk to if you suspect child abuse? (Skill 1.1; Average rigor)**

    A.   The child
    B.   The child's parent
    C.   Your supervisor
    D.   Another teacher

Answer C: Your supervisor

The child who is undergoing the abuse is the one whose needs must be served first. A suspected case gone unreported may destroy a child's life, and their subsequent life as a functional adult. It is the duty of any citizen who suspects abuse and neglect to make a report, and it is especially important and required for State licensed and certified persons to make a report. If you contact the parent first and the parent is the abuser, then the child's life may be endangered.

3. **Which of the following might cause a child to become easily agitated in class? (Skill 1.1; Average rigor)**

    A.   Lack of sleep
    B.   Lack of training in manners
    C.   Being raised in a single parent home
    D.   Watching too much TV

Answer A: Lack of sleep

Symptoms of lack of sleep include a lack of concentration, particularly in the classroom. Children who lack sufficient sleep or nutrition may become agitated more easily than other children. The lack of training in manners or how many parents in the home is not the cause of agitation. Watching too much TV could be the cause if it disrupts the appropriate amount of sleep. It is always a good idea for teachers to pay attention to the abnormalities in behavior of children, or even sudden drop-offs in achievement or attention, and notify parents or the superiors at the school with concerns.

4. **What developmental patterns should a professional teacher assess to meet the needs of the student? (Skill 1.1; Average rigor)**

    A.   Academic, regional, and family background
    B.   Social, physical, academic
    C.   Academic, physical, and family background
    D.   Physical, family, ethnic background

Answer B: Social, physical, academic

The effective teacher applies knowledge of physical, social, and academic developmental patterns and of individual differences, to meet the instructional needs of all students in the classroom and. The most important premise of child development is that all domains of development (physical, social, and academic) are integrated. The teacher has a broad knowledge and thorough understanding of the development that typically occurs during the students' current period of life. More importantly, the teacher understands how children learn best during each period of development. An examination of the student's file coupled with ongoing evaluation assures a successful educational experience for both teacher and students.

5. **A preschool teacher is concerned because the three year olds in her class do not play with each other. Each student plays without interacting with others in the class. What advice would you give her? (Skill 1.2; Rigorous)**

    A. Contact the parents immediately so they can talk to their doctors about medications that might help.
    B. Plan more activities that require interactions between the children.
    C. Tell the children that you expect them to share and play together. If they don't, then punish them.
    D. Don't worry. It is typical for young children engage in "parallel" activities playing alongside their peers without directly interacting with one another.

Answer D: Don't worry. It is typical for young children engage in "parallel" activities playing alongside their peers without directly interacting with one another.

At age 3, children are happier in the presence of a few other children their own age, but seldom play together with them. This type of play is known as parallel play and is typical social development for this age.

6. **During a conference about reading difficulties, a parent asks a first grade teacher for advice on how to make sure the three year old sibling doesn't end up having trouble learning to read like his brother. Based on research, what should the teacher recommend? (Skill 1.4; Rigorous)**

    A. Intense practice on alphabet
    B. Exposure to numerous books
    C. Work on rhyming words and sounds
    D. All of the above

Answer D: All of the above

Best practices and strategies that teach young children how to read and write are controversial among educators and childhood development researchers. There is not one method that guarantees success for each child but all authorities agree that early childhood literacy programs should include intensive instruction in phonics awareness, including alphabet and sound correlations and direct immersion in a variety of books for young readers. If a parent provides experiences in those areas before formal schooling then the child will certainly have advantages when formal reading instruction begins.

7. **A teacher notices that a student is sullen, and has several bruises on his head, arms and legs. When asked, the student responds that he hit his arm getting out of bed that morning. The teacher should: (Skill 1.5; Average rigor)**

    A. Attempt to get more information from the student
    B. Report suspected abuse to the school counselor
    C. Consult a colleague and see what they would do
    D. Wait and see if other signs of abuse become evident

Answer B: Report suspected abuse to the school counselor.

The most important concern is for the safety and well being of the student. Teachers should not promise students that they won't tell because they are required by law to err on the side of caution and report suspected abuse. Failure or delay in reporting suspected abuse may be a cause for further abuse to the student. In some cases, a teacher's decision to overlook suspected abuse may result in revoking the teacher's license. Teachers are not required to investigate abuse for themselves or verify their suspicions.

8. **Which of the following is a TRUE statement? (Skill 1.6; Rigorous)**

    A. Younger children tend to process information at a slower rate than older children (age eight and older).
    B. Older children tend to process information at a slower rate than younger children (younger than age 8).
    C. Children process information at the same rate as adults.
    D. All children process information at the exact same rate.

Answer A: Younger children tend to process information at a slower rate than older children (age eight and older).

Younger children tend to process information at a slower rate than older children (age eight and older). Because of this, the learning activities selected for younger students (below age eight) should focus on short time frames in highly simplified form. The nature of the activity and the content in which the activity is presented affects the approach that the students will take in processing the information.

9. **A child exhibits the following symptoms: a lack of emotional responsivity, indifference to physical contact, abnormal social play, and abnormal speech. What is the likely diagnosis for this child? (Skill 1.6; Average rigor)**

    A. Separation anxiety
    B. Mental retardation
    C. Autism
    D. Hypochondria

Answer C: Autism

According to many psychologists who have been involved with treating autistic children, it seems that these children have built a wall between themselves and everyone else, including their families and even their parents. They do not make eye contact with others and do not even appear to hear the voices of those who speak to them. They cannot empathize with others and have no ability to appreciate humor. The prognosis for autistic children is painfully discouraging. Only about five percent of autistic children become socially well adjusted in adulthood. Another twenty percent make fair social adjustments. The remaining seventy-five percent are socially incapacitated and must be supervised for the duration of their lives. Treatment may include outpatient psychotherapy, drugs, or long-term treatment in a residential center, but neither the form of treatment nor even the lack of treatment seems to make a difference in the long run.

10. **How many stages of intellectual development does Piaget define? (Skill 1.7; Easy)**

    A. Two
    B. Four
    C. Six
    D. Eight

Answer B: Four

The stages are:
1. Sensorimotor stage: from birth to age 2 years (children experience the world through movement and senses).
2. Preoperational stage: from ages 2 to 7(acquisition of motor skills).
3. Concrete operational stage: from ages 7 to 11 (children begin to think logically about concrete events).
4. Formal Operational stage: after age 11 (development of abstract reasoning).

11. Which of the following is NOT one of Gardner's Multiple Intelligences? (Skill 1.7; Average rigor)

    A. Intrapersonal
    B. Musical
    C. Technological
    D. Logical/mathematical

Answer C: Technological

Gardner's Multiple Intelligences Theory suggests that students learn in (at least) seven different ways. These include visually/spatially, musically, verbally, logically/mathematically, interpersonally, intrapersonally, and bodily/kinesthetically. Since the publication of *Frames of Mind*, Gardner has additionally identified the 8th dimension of intelligence: Naturalist Intelligence, and is still considering a possible ninth—Existentialist Intelligence.

12. Research over several decades has shown that student performance is directly impacted by: (Skill 1.8; Average rigor)

    A. The teacher's high expectations
    B. The IQ of the parents
    C. The IQ of the student
    D. Whether the child lives in an apartment or in a house

Answer A: The teacher's high expectations

The teacher must be cognizant of the profound effect which he or she will have as an authority figure, instructor and behavior model for students in the early formative years. The most directed, purposeful and productive time in the average child's day is the time spent in the classroom and the school environment, generally. Considerable research has been done, over several decades, regarding student performance. Time and again, a direct correlation has been demonstrated between the teacher's expectations for a particular student and that student's academic performance.

13. How can student misconduct be redirected at times? (Skill 1.8; Average rigor)

    A. State expectations about behavior
    B. Let students discipline their peers
    C. Let minor infractions of the rules go unnoticed
    D. Increase disapproving remarks

Answer A: State expectations about behavior.

The effective teacher demonstrates awareness of what the entire class is doing and is in control of the behavior of all students even when the teacher is working with only a small group of the children. In an attempt to prevent student misbehaviors the teacher makes clear, concise statements about what is happening in the classroom directing attention to content and the students' accountability for their work rather than focusing the class on the misbehavior. It is also effective for the teacher to make a positive statement about the appropriate behavior that is observed. If deviant behavior does occur, the effective teacher will specify who the deviant is, what he or she is doing wrong, and why this is unacceptable conduct or what the proper conduct would be. This can be a difficult task to accomplish as the teacher must maintain academic focus and flow while addressing and desisting misbehavior. The teacher must make clear, brief statements about the expectations without raising his/her voice and without disrupting instruction.

Foundations of Learning

14. According to Piaget, what stage is characterized by the ability to think abstractly and to use logic? (Skill 2.1; Rigorous)

    A. Concrete operations
    B. Pre-operational
    C. Formal operations
    D. Conservative operational

Answer C: Formal operations.

The four development stages are described in Piaget's theory as follows:
1. Sensorimotor stage: from birth to age 2 years (children experience the world through movement and senses).
2. Preoperational stage: from ages 2 to 7 (acquisition of motor skills).
3. Concrete operational stage: from ages 7 to 11 (children begin to think logically about concrete events).
4. Formal operational stage: after age 11 (development of abstract reasoning).

These chronological periods are approximate and, in light of the fact that studies have demonstrated great variation between children, cannot be seen as rigid norms. Furthermore, these stages occur at different ages, depending upon the domain of knowledge under consideration. The ages normally given for the stages reflect when each stage tends to predominate even though one might elicit examples of two, three, or even all four stages of thinking at the same time from one individual, depending upon the domain of knowledge and the means used to elicit it.

15. According to Piaget's theory of cognitive development, what is the process of incorporating new objects, information or experiences into the existing cognitive structures? (Skill 2.1; Rigorous)

    A. Attachment
    B. Conservation
    C. Identification
    D. Assimilation

Answer D: Assimilation.

Piaget felt that development from one stage to the next is caused by the accumulation of errors in the child's understanding of the environment; this accumulation eventually causes such a degree of cognitive disequilibrium that thought structures require reorganizing. Once knowledge is constructed internally, it is then tested against reality the same way a scientist tests the validity of hypotheses. Like a scientist, the individual learner may discard, modify, or reconstruct knowledge based on its utility in the real world. Much of this construction (and later reconstruction) is, in fact, done subconsciously; however, once reconstruction has occurred, the conclusion is assimilated and becomes a feature of the child's personality.

16. **At approximately what age is the average child able to define abstract terms such as honesty and justice? (Skill 2.1; Rigorous)**

    A. 10-12 years old
    B. 4-6 years old
    C. 14-16 years old
    D. 6-8 years old

Answer A: 10-12 years old.

The usual age for the fourth stage (the formal operational stage) as described by Piaget is from 10 to 12 years old. It is in this stage that children begin to be able to define abstract terms.

17. **The NCLB (No Child Left Behind) Act mandates that early childhood programs: (Skill 2.1; Rigorous)**

    A. Provide Headstart for every child in our country
    B. Construct curriculum models specific to the development of early childhood and elementary programs for academic enhancement
    C. Protect the privacy of student education records
    D. Have a seatbelt for every student riding a school bus

Answer B: Construct curriculum models specific to the development of early childhood and elementary programs for academic enhancement.

Head Start is a national program that promotes school readiness by enhancing the social and cognitive development of children, but it is not provided for every child. The Family Educational Rights and Privacy Act (FERPA) (20 U.S.C. § 1232g; 34 CFR Part 99) is a Federal law that protects the privacy of student education records. While adding seatbelts for every student in every bus would enhance safety, it is not yet a federal mandate.

18. Which of the following is a widely known curriculum model for early childhood programs? (Skill 2.2; Easy)

    A. Montessori method
    B. DISTAR method
    C. Success for All
    D. Voyager

Answer A: Montessori method

The philosophy and curriculum of the Montessori method is based on the work and writings of the Italian physician Maria Montessori. Her method appears to be the first curriculum model for children of preschool age that was widely disseminated and replicated. It is based on the idea that children teach themselves through their own experiences. Materials used proceed from the simple to the complex and from the concrete to the abstract and sixty-three percent of class time is spent in independent activity.

19. Head Start Programs were created in what decade? (Skill 2.2; Easy)

    A. 2000's
    B. 1990's
    C. 1980's
    D. 1960's

Answer D: 1960's

Head Start Programs were created in the early 60s to provide a comprehensive curriculum model for preparation of low-income students for success in school communities.

20. **What is the most important factor in raising academic outcomes for all students as required in the NCLB law? (Skill 2.2; Rigorous)**

   A. The curriculum model used
   B. The quality of instruction in the classroom
   C. The location of the school
   D. The number of years of experience the teacher has

Answer B: The quality of instruction in the classroom

The NCLB (No Child Left Behind) Act requires states to develop curriculum models demonstrating excellent academic outcomes for all children. The goal of any curriculum model is to provide consistency in instruction and create evaluation criteria for uniformity in programming.

Researchers continue to show that most curriculum models produce effective academic outcomes when implemented as designed. However, there are limitations to how effectively the curriculum model is implemented in each classroom. Therefore, **the quality of instruction for students by experienced educators** will ultimately be what improves the academic outcomes for all students.

21. **Effective curriculum models for early childhood programs should include which of the following: (Skill 2.2; Rigorous)**

   A. Differentiated instruction for group/individual academic needs
   B. Best practices and instructional approaches
   C. A and B
   D. None of the above

Answer C: A and B

Curriculum models should include both (A) differentiated instruction for group/individual academic needs, and references to (B) best practices and instructional approaches for children. In addition strong models also include a portfolio of evaluation assessments and world wide applications.

22. **To determine if a child has a disability that may qualify the child for services under IDEA, the school may collect which of the following pieces of information: (Skill 2.3; Average rigor)**

    A. The present levels of academic achievement
    B. Vision and hearing screening information
    C. A complete psychological evaluation
    D. All of the above

Answer D: All of the above

To begin the process of determining if a child has a disability the teacher will take information about the child's present levels of academic achievement to the appropriate school committee for discussion and consideration. The committee will recommend the next step to be taken. Often subsequent steps may include a complete psychological evaluation along with certain physical examinations such as vision and hearing screening and a complete medical examination by a doctor.

23. **Failure to make a report when abuse or neglect is suspected is punishable by which of the following? (Skill 2.3; Average rigor)**

    A. revocation of certification and license
    B. a monetary fine
    C. criminal charges
    D. All of the above

Answer D: All of the above

Failure to make a report when abuse or neglect is suspected is punishable by (A) revocation of certification and license, (B) a fine, and (C) criminal charges. It is the duty of any citizen who suspects abuse and neglect to make a report, and it is especially important and required for State licensed and certified persons (like teachers) to make a report. All reports can be kept confidential if required. Do not wait once your suspicion is firm. All you need to have is a reasonable suspicion, not actual proof, which is the job for the investigators.

24. IDEA is a federal law passed in 1990 that has a direct impact on classrooms. The acronym IDEA stands for: (Skill 2.3; Average rigor)

    A. Individuals with Disabilities Education Act
    B. Individualized Differentiation for Education Always
    C. Idealistic Dedicated Educational Access
    D. Instructional Differentiation Education Act

Answer A: Individuals with Disabilities Education Act

IDEA (Individuals with Disabilities Education Act) passed in 1990, has a direct impact on classroom. This law ensures that all children with disabilities and their families receive the help and support they need. It governs how states and public agencies can provide intervention services and how schools can provide special education services for these children.

25. In your classroom, there is a student who has been exhibiting difficulty in the area of reading. The child has a learning disability and already receives special education services. According to IDEA, who must be involved in developing the child's IEP (individual educational plan) to address these concerns? (Skill 2.3; Rigorous)

    A. A medical doctor
    B. The school psychologist
    C. The parent or guardian
    D. The principal

Answer C: The parent or guardian

Under the IDEA, parent/guardian involvement in the development of the student's IEP is **required** and absolutely essential for the advocacy of the disabled student's educational needs. IEPs must be tailored to meet the student's needs, and no one knows those needs better than the parent/guardian and other significant family members. Optimal conditions for a disabled student's education exist when teachers, school administrators, special education professionals and parents/guardians work together to design and execute the IEP.

Research, standards and trends

26. **Educators seeking quality strategies to improve early childhood education for students could gain information from which of the following: (Skill 3.1; Easy)**

    A. Websites
    B. Professional organizations
    C. Journal articles
    D. All of the above

Answer D: All of the above

It is important to stay current with the latest research and teaching strategies to meet the needs of all children. The best information can be found in a variety of books, websites, or journal articles provided by professional organizations devoted to the education of young children.

27. **What is the world's largest educational organization that works on behalf on the education of young children? (Skill 3.2; Easy)**

    A. NAEYC
    B. SPCA
    C. NAACP
    D. IRA

Answer A: NAEYC

The focus of the National Association for the Education of Young Children (NAEYC) is on improving and developing programs and services for children from birth through the age of 8 years old. The SPCA is the Society for Prevention of Cruelty to Animals. The National Association for the Advancement of Colored People (NAACP), is a civil rights organization for ethnic minorities in the United States. The International Reading Association (IRA) provides a comprehensive professional organization for effectively preparing teachers and educators for reading instruction.

28. **Which international organization is devoted to studying the research and data from national organizations and school communities on effective reading instruction and strategies that promote reading acquisition? (Skill 3.2; Rigorous)**

   A. FCRR
   B. AECI
   C. IRA
   D. AERA

Answer C: IRA (International Reading Association)

Of these choices, only the **IRA** (International Reading Association) has an **international** focus and a focus entirely on **reading instruction**.

The Florida Center for Reading Research (FCRR) provides information about research-based practices related to literacy instruction and assessment for children in pre-school through 12th grade, and conducts applied research that will have an immediate impact on policy and practices related to literacy instruction in Florida.

The Association for Childhood Education International (ACEI) focuses on the educational development for students throughout the world, but does not exist solely for reading instruction.

The American Educational Research Association (AERA) is the country's largest professional organization identified as devoted to improvement in the "scientific study of education," for example, to promotion of "credible scientific research" as to how students best learn to read.

29. **The NCLB Act requires schools to establish AYP. What does the acronym AYP stand for? (Skill 3.3; Easy)**

   A. Advocates for Youth Programs
   B. Adequate Yearly Progress
   C. All Young People
   D. None of the above

Answer B: Adequate Yearly Progress

Under the accountability provisions in the No Child Left Behind (NCLB) Act, all public school campuses, school districts, and the state are evaluated for Adequate Yearly Progress (**AYP**). Districts, campuses, and the state are required to meet AYP criteria on three measures: Reading/Language Arts, Mathematics, and either Graduation Rate (for high schools and districts) or Attendance Rate (for elementary and middle/junior high schools).

30. **Which of the following is considered a current trend in education? (Skill 3.3; Easy)**

    A. Differentiated instruction so that no child is left behind
    B. Innovations in technology
    C. Instruction in the 3 Rs (reading, writing and arithmetic)
    D. A and B

Answer D: A and B

Differentiated instruction (A) so that no child is left behind is an important trend that will allow schools to address the needs of all learners as required by the NCLB law. In the global economy, skills in technology (B) have become increasingly important and teachers must stay current in the use of technology for instruction.

31. **The annual cost of teacher turnover in school communities has been estimated to be in the range of: (Skill 3.3; Rigorous)**

    A. 5-7 billion dollars
    B. 5-7 hundred dollars
    C. 5-7 thousand dollars
    D. 5-7 million dollars

Answer A: 5-7 billion dollars

There is much attention to teacher salaries throughout the nation but not much consideration of other factors that impact school budgets and legislative educational initiatives. The cost of teacher turnover in school communities has been estimated to be in the range of 5-7 billion dollars which further impacts the legislature's ability to provide enough funding for all educational communities. When considering the comprehensive cost of educating students, more attention may need to be given to retaining current teachers through ongoing professional development training and support.

32. **When students engage in this type of learning in order to understand the world around them, the learning process involves the formulation of questions that convert new information into an active application of knowledge. (Skill 3.3; Rigorous)**

    A. Hands-on learning
    B. Guided reading
    C. Inquiry-based learning
    D. Teacher directed model

Answer C: Inquiry-based learning

A current trend in education, inquiry-based learning requires students to be actively involved in the learning process and in the construction of new knowledge. When students engage in inquiry-based learning in order to understand the world around them, the learning process involves the formulation of questions that convert new information into an active application of knowledge.

33. **What can be done to decrease violent behavior that even young children are exhibiting at school?(Skill 3.3; Rigorous)**

    A. Build more alternative schools
    B. Provide teachers with classroom management training
    C. Increase parent training
    D. Provide students with social strategies to improve cooperative learning and communication

Answer D: Provide students with social strategies to improve cooperative learning and communication

Early violence in elementary school communities coupled with classroom management issues have contributed to a reduction in teaching and instructional time for young learners. While increasing training for parents and teachers may help, a better solution is to provide young learners with ethical and social strategies to improve cooperative learning and communication. Once students internalize these skills and become "self-managed" learners the time spent on conflict will be reduced while increasing the time spent on learning acquisition.

34. Assessment where students create an answer or a response to a question or task is known as: (Skill 3.3; Average rigor)

A. Traditional assessment
B. Alternative assessment
C. Multiple choice
D. True assessment

Answer B: Alternative assessment

Alternative assessment is an assessment where students create an answer or a response to a question or task, as opposed to traditional, inflexible assessments where students choose a prepared response from among a selection of responses, such as matching, multiple-choice or true/false.

35. When implemented effectively, an alternative assessment approach will: (Skill 3.3; Rigorous)

A. Require higher-order thinking and problem-solving
B. Provide opportunities for student self-reflection and self-assessment
C. Use real world applications to connect students to the subject
D. All of the above

Answer D: All of the above

When implemented effectively, an alternative assessment approach will exhibit these characteristics, among others:
- Requires higher-order thinking and problem-solving
- Provides opportunities for student self-reflection and self-assessment
- Uses real world applications to connect students to the subject
- Provides opportunities for students to learn and examine subjects on their own, as well as to collaborate with their peers.
- Encourages students to continuing learning beyond the requirements of the assignment
- Clearly defines objective and performance goals

Effective practices

36. What are critical elements of instructional process? (Skill 4.1; Rigorous)

A. Content, goals, teacher needs
B. Means of getting money to regulate instruction
C. Content, materials, activities, goals, learner needs
D. Materials, definitions, assignments

Answer C: Content, materials, activities, goals, learner needs.

Goal-setting is a vital component of the instructional process. The teacher will, of course, have overall goals for her class, both short-term and long-term. However, perhaps even more important than that is the setting of goals that take into account the individual learner's needs, background, and stage of development. Making an educational program child-centered involves building on the natural curiosity children bring to school, and asking children what they want to learn. Student-centered classrooms contain not only textbooks, workbooks, and literature but also rely heavily on a variety of audiovisual equipment and computers. There are tape recorders, language masters, filmstrip projectors, and laser disc players to help meet the learning styles of the students. Planning for instructional activities entails identification or selection of the activities the teacher and students will engage in during a period of instruction.

37. What would improve planning for instruction? (Skill 4.1; Average rigor)

A. Describe the role of the teacher and student
B. Evaluate the outcomes of instruction
C. Rearrange the order of activities
D. Give outside assignments

Answer B: Evaluate the outcomes of instruction.

Important as it is to plan content, materials, activities, goals taking into account learner needs and to base what goes on in the classroom on the results of that planning, it makes no difference if students are not able to demonstrate improvement in the skills being taught. An important part of the planning process is for the teacher to constantly adapt all aspects of the curriculum to what is actually happening in the classroom. Planning frequently misses the mark or fails to allow for unexpected factors. Evaluating the outcomes of instruction regularly and making adjustments accordingly will have a positive impact on the overall success of a teaching methodology.

38. When are students more likely to understand complex ideas? (Skill 4.1; Rigorous)

    A. If they do outside research before coming to class
    B. Later when they write out the definitions of complex words
    C. When they attend a lecture on the subject
    D. When they are clearly defined by the teacher and are given examples and non-examples of the concept

Answer D: When they are clearly defined by the teacher and are given examples and non-examples of the concept.

Several studies have been carried out to determine the effectiveness of giving examples as well as the difference in effectiveness of various types of examples. It was found conclusively that the most effective method of concept presentation included giving a definition along with examples and non-examples and also providing an explanation of them. These same studies indicate that boring examples were just as effective as interesting examples in promoting learning. Additional studies have been conducted to determine the most effective number of examples that will result in maximum student learning. These studies concluded that a few thoughtfully selected examples are just as effective as many examples. It was determined that the actual number of examples necessary to promote student learning was relative to the learning characteristics of the learners. It was again ascertained that learning is facilitated when examples are provided along with the definition.

39. **What should a teacher do when students have not responded well to an instructional activity? (Skill 4.1; Average rigor)**

    A. Reevaluate learner needs
    B. Request administrative help
    C. Continue with the activity another day
    D. Assign homework on the concept

Answer A: Reevaluate learner needs.

The value of teacher observations cannot be underestimated. It is through the use of observations that the teacher is able to informally assess the needs of the students during instruction. These observations will drive the lesson and determine the direction that the lesson will take based on student activity and behavior. After a lesson is carefully planned, teacher observation is the single most important component of an instructional presentation. If the teacher observes that a particular student is not on-task, she will change the method of instruction accordingly. She may change from a teacher-directed approach to a more interactive approach. Questioning will increase in order to increase the participation of the students. If appropriate, the teacher will introduce manipulative materials to the lesson. In addition, teachers may switch to a cooperative group activity, thereby removing the responsibility of instruction from the teacher and putting it on the students.

40. **If teachers attend to content, instructional materials, activities, learner needs, and goals in instructional planning, what could be an outcome?) (Skill 4.1; Rigorous)**

    A. Planning for the next year
    B. Effective classroom performance
    C. Elevated test scores on standardized tests
    D. More student involvement

Answer B: Effective classroom performance.

Another outcome will be teacher satisfaction in a job well-done and in the performance of her students. Her days will have far fewer disruptions and her classroom will be easy to manage.

41. **Reducing off task time and maximizing the amount of time students spend attending to academic tasks is closely related to which of the following? (Skill 4.2; Rigorous)**

   A. Using whole class instruction only
   B. Business-like behaviors of the teacher
   C. Dealing only with major teaching functions
   D. Giving students a maximum of two minutes to come to order

Answer B: Business-like behaviors of the teacher

The effective teacher continually evaluates his/her own physical/mental/social/emotional well-being with regard to the students in his/her classroom. There is always the tendency to satisfy social and emotional needs through relationships with the students. A good teacher genuinely likes his/her students, and that's a positive thing. However, if students are not convinced that the teacher's purpose for being there is to get a job done, the atmosphere in the classroom becomes difficult to control. This is the job of the teacher. Maintaining a business-like approach in the classroom yields many positive results. It's a little like a benevolent boss.

42. **The concept of efficient use of time includes which of the following? (Skill 4.2; Easy)**

   A. Daily review, seatwork, and recitation of concepts
   B. Lesson initiation, transition, and comprehension check
   C. Review, test, review
   D. Punctuality, management transition, and wait time avoidance

Answer D: Punctuality, management transition, and wait time avoidance

The "benevolent boss" described in the rationale for question 34 applies here. One who succeeds in managing a business follows these rules; so does the successful teacher.

43. **What is an example of an academic transition signal? (Skill 4.2; Average rigor)**

A. "How do clouds form?"
B. "Today we are going to study clouds."
C. "We have completed today's lesson."
D. "That completes the description of cumulus clouds. Now we will look at the description of cirrus clouds."

Answer D: "That completes the description of cumulus clouds. Now we will look at the description of cirrus clouds."

Transitions are language bridges between one topic and another. The teacher should thoughtfully plan transitions when several topics are going to be presented in one lesson to be sure that students are carried along. Without transitions, sometimes students are still focused on a previous topic and are lost in the discussion.

44. **What environmental element can cause some students to become restless and hyperactive? (Skill 4.3; Average rigor)**

A. Bright lights
B. The arrangement of student desks
C. The proximity of the classroom to the playground
D. All of the above

Answer A: Bright lights

Environmental preferences such as lighting, noise level, and room temperature are factors that can affect students in various ways and are often directly related to individual learning styles. A number of students learn best in bright light, but others learn considerably better in low-lighted areas. Bright light can actually cause some students to become restless and hyperactive.

45. A print-rich environment would have which of the following components: (Skill 4.4; Easy)

    A. A word wall
    B. Classroom libraries
    C. Labels for objects in the room
    D. All of the above

Answer D: All of above

Components of a print-rich environment include classroom libraries, word walls, and labels for classroom objects.

46. Strong and effective lesson plans always answer 3 questions, sometimes referred to as the 3 W's. The 3 W questions for a lesson are: (Skill 4.6; Rigorous)

    A. What? How? Why?
    B. Who? What? When?
    C. When? Where? Why?
    D. None of the above

Answer A: What? How? Why?

Each lesson plan should include the 3 W's, WHAT are we learning today? HOW will we learn the objective? WHY is it important to learn this?

47. **A teacher has just received her class roster and knows that must determine the abilities of the incoming students assigned to her class as she begins planning to meet the state requirements for that grade and subject area. What is the best way to determine a student's current ability level? (Skill 4.7; Easy)**

    A. Administer a pre-test before each lesson
    B. Talk to the child's teacher from the previous school year
    C. Look at standardized test results
    D. Consult the child's cumulative academic record

Answer D: Consult the child's cumulative academic record

The most complete source of information about a child's current ability level would be found in their cumulative school records. This is also the most time efficient place to look because it will contain the previous year's academic and behavioral grades, as well as all standardized test results and special programming requirements. Administering a pre-test before a lesson will give the teacher valuable information, but it is not possible to do this for each lesson. After reviewing the cumulative record, a conversation with the previous year's teacher may provide some helpful insights about an individual student.

48. **Which of the following is a true statement? (Skill 4.11; Rigorous)**

    A. Recess is not important to a child's development.
    B. Playtime is only provided in schools to help children get "their energy out."
    C. Play is very important to human development and teaches children many things.
    D. None of the above

Answer C: Play is very important to human development and teaches children many things.

Too often, recess and play is considered peripheral or unimportant to a child's development. It's sometimes seen as a way to allow kids to just get physical energy out or a "tradition" of childhood. The truth is, though, that play is very important to human development. Play is an activity that helps teach basic values such as sharing and cooperation. It also teaches that taking care of oneself (as opposed to constantly working) is good for human beings and further creates a more enjoyable society.

49. **Playing team sports at young ages should be done for the following purpose: (Skill 4.11; Rigorous)**

    A. To develop the child's motor skills
    B. To prepare children for competition in high school
    C. To develop the child's interests
    D. Both A and C

Answer D: Both (A) To develop the child's motor skills **and (C)** To develop the child's interests

Sports, for both boys and girls, can be equally valuable. Parents and teachers, though, need to remember that sports at young ages should only be for the purpose of development of interests and motor skills—not competition. Many children will learn that they do not enjoy sports, and parents and teachers should be respectful of these decisions.

50. **Why is repetition an important part of child's play? (Skill 4.12; Rigorous)**

    A. It allows the child to master the skill and then move into creativity.
    B. It allows the child to stress the caregiver who is bored with playing the same thing over and over.
    C. It is a creative outlet for the child.
    D. None of the above

Answer A: It allows the child to master the skill and then move into creativity.

Repetition is an important aspect of children's play. Doing the same thing over and over may be boring to the adult caregiver, but the repetition allows the child to master the new skill and then move on to experimentation and creativity.

Family and Community Involvement

51. If a child is falling behind in school, which of the following might make a difference to the child's academic progress? (Skill 5.1; Average rigor)

    A. Assign the child to a special education class
    B. Assign an adult mentor
    C. Assign the child additional homework
    D. Ask the parents to review lessons each night

Answer B: Assign an adult mentor

Mentoring has become an instrumental tool in addressing student achievement and access to learning. Adult mentors work individually with identified students on specific subject areas to reinforce the learning through tutorial instruction and application of knowledge. Providing students with adult role models to reinforce the learning has become a crucial instructional strategy for teachers seeking to maximize student learning beyond the classroom. Students who work with adult mentors from culturally diverse backgrounds are given a multicultural aspect of learning that is cooperative and multi-modal in personalized instruction.

52. Which of the following is a technological strategy that keeps students and teachers interactively communicating about issues in the classroom and beyond? (Skill 5.1; Easy)

    A. Myspace.com
    B. Distance learning
    C. Email
    D. None of the above

Answer B: Distance learning

The interpersonal use of technology provides a mentoring tutorial support system and different conceptual learning modalities for students seeking to understand classroom material. Technology provides a networking opportunity for students to find study buddies and peer study groups, along with free academic support to problem-solve and develop critical thinking skills that are imperative in acquiring knowledge and conceptual learning. Distance Learning is a technological strategy that keeps students and teachers interactively communicating about issues in the classroom and beyond.

53. The commitment that a community shows to its educational communities is: (Skill 5.1; Average rigor)

    A. Judged by how much money is contributed.
    B. Something that doesn't matter much to the school
    C. A valuable investment in the future.
    D. Something that will cause immediate gains in the school's AYP results

Answer C: A valuable investment in the future.

The commitment that a community shows to its educational communities is a valuable investment in the future. While monetary gifts are valued, there are many ways for the community to invest in the school. As mentioned in this section, adult mentors can make a tremendous difference for many students. Having an involved community will create a better school for all children and will eventually lead to improved academic results.

54. Because teachers today will deal with an increasingly diverse group of cultures in their classrooms, they must: (Skill 5.2; Rigorous)

    A. Ignore the cultures represented and continue to teach to the majority
    B. Learn to deal with a variety of family expectations for school and teachers
    C. Provide a special celebration for each culture represented.
    D. Both A and C

Answer B: Learn to deal with a variety of family expectations for school and teachers

First, teachers must show respect to all parents and families. They need to set the tone that suggests that their mission is to develop students into the best people they can be. And then they need to realize that various cultures have different views of how children should be educated.

55. You receive a phone call from a parent who is angry about the grade their child receives on the report card. As the conversation continues, the parent becomes verbally abusive and uses curse words. What should you do? (Skill 5.2; Rigorous)

    A. Raise your voice to establish your authority.
    B. Hang up and get assistance from your administrator.
    C. Blame the parent for the poor grade.
    D. Apologize over and over and hope that the parent will calm down and stop cursing.

Answer B: Hang up and get assistance from your administrator.

Teachers will need to be patient with difficult families, but should help them realize that certain methods of criticism (including verbal attacks, etc.) are unacceptable. In the described circumstance, it would be appropriate for the teacher to hang up so they could get assistance from an administrator. This situation, however, is very unusual, and most teachers will find that when they really attempt to be friendly and personal with parents, the parents will reciprocate and assist in the educational program.

56. How should a teacher respond to criticism about her teaching strategies from a parent? (Skill 5.2; Rigorous)

    A. Explain to the parent that negative feedback is hurtful and mean-spirited
    B. Dismiss the criticism as an attempt to undermine her performance
    C. Think about the criticism objectively and consider that it might be true
    D. Change her teaching strategies to eliminate the aspect being criticized

Answer C: Think about the criticism objectively and consider that it might be true.

Any time a teacher receives negative feedback, her reaction should be to think about its validity. This approach would benefit the teacher's skills of self-assessment and awareness of her teaching, as well as being the appropriate professional response to negative feedback. Negative feedback and experiences should always be viewed as opportunities to better one's performance.

57. When communicating with parents for whom English is not the primary language you should: (Skill 5.2; Average rigor)

   A. Provide materials whenever possible in their native language
   B. Use an interpreter
   C. Provide the same communication as you would to native English speaking parents
   D. All of the above

Answer D: All of the above.

When communicating with non English speaking parents it is important to treat them as you would any other parent and utilize any means necessary to ensure they have the ability to participate in their child's educational process.

58. Which of the following could be a purpose of a parent-teacher conference? (Skill 5.2; Average rigor)

   A. To involve the parent in their child's education
   B. To resolve a concern about the child's performance
   C. To inform parents of positive behaviors by the child
   D. All of the above

Answer D: All of the above

The purpose of a parent teacher conference is to involve parents in their child's education, address concerns about the child's performance and share positive aspects of the student's learning with the parents.

59. Which of the following is NOT a right of parents? (Skill 5.2; Average rigor)

    A. To be informed of the teacher's concerns about their child
    B. To require the teacher to use the teaching method that works for the child
    C. To administer discipline to their child in the classroom
    D. Both B and C

Answer D: Both B and C

It is a parent's right to be involved in their child's education and to be informed of the teacher's reports on his/her progress as well as the teacher's concerns about their child's learning or behavior. Since parents are entrusting the child to the teacher's professional care, they are entitled to know what concerns the teacher about their child during their absence. Parents do not have the right to mandate the teaching method used (B) or to disrupt class by administering disciplinary consequences (C).

60. Which of the following is a true statement? (Skill 5.2; Rigorous)

    A. Various cultures have different views of how children should be educated.
    B. Various cultures share the same views of how children should be educated.
    C. Parent's views about how children should be educated are always correct.
    D. Teacher's views about how children should be educated are always correct.

Answer A: Various cultures have different views of how children should be educated.

Teachers must show respect to all parents and families. They need to set the tone that suggests that their mission is to develop students into the best people they can be. And then they need to realize that various cultures have different views of how children should be educated. It is important that teachers act like they are partners in the children's education and development. Parents know their children best, and it is important to get feedback, information, and advice from them.

Curriculum

61. Which of the following is <u>not</u> a motivation behind providing reading activities, including reading aloud, to young children? (Skill 6.1; Rigorous)

    A. Developing Word Consciousness Skills
    B. Developing Functions of Print Skills
    C. Developing Phonics Skills
    D. Developing Language Skills

Answer C: Developing Phonics Skills

There are almost unlimited positive reasons for encouraging adults to provide reading activities for young children. While it can be true that reading aloud may improve the phonics skills for some students, it is not a motivation for providing such activities to students.

62. Which of the following strategies encourages print awareness in classrooms? (Skill 6.2; Easy)

    A. Word walls
    B. Using big books to read to students
    C. Using highlighters to locate upper case letters
    D. All of the above

Answer D: All of the above

Classrooms rich in print provide many opportunities to students to see, use, and experience text in various forms. Word walls, big books, and highlighting certain textual features are all ways to expose students to various forms of text.

63. **Ms. Smith hands each child in the classroom a letter of the alphabet. She then challenges each child to go around the classroom and find at least five things in the classroom which begin with that letter. Ms. Smith is teaching the students which of the following skills? (Skill 6.2; Rigorous)**

   A. Phonemic Awareness
   B. Vocabulary
   C. Meaning of Print
   D. Letter Identification

Answer C: Meaning of Print

Connecting letters to objects or sounds helps the students begin to recognize that print has meaning. This is an essential foundation skill for students to develop before phonics instruction is begun.

64. **Which of the following explains a significant difference between phonics and phonemic awareness? (Skill 6.3; Average rigor)**

   A. Phonics involves print, phonemic awareness involves language
   B. Phonics is harder than phonemic awareness
   C. Phonics involves sounds, phonemic awareness involves letters
   D. Phonics is the application of sounds to print, phonemic awareness is oral

Answer D: Phonics is the application of sounds to print, phonemic awareness is oral

Both phonics and phonemic awareness activities involve sounds, but it is with phonics that the application of these sounds is applied to print. Phonemic awareness is an oral activity.

65. **Ms. Walker's lesson objective is to teach her first graders the concept of morphology in order to improve their reading skills. Which group of words would be most appropriate for her to use in this lesson? (Skill 6.4; Rigorous)**

   A. far farm farmer
   B. far feather fever
   C. far fear fare
   D. far fare farce

Answer A: far farm farmer

The concept of morphology is to understand how words relate to each other and can be built upon to increase reading skills. In the correct answer, the student can utilize the information they learned from learning to read far to help them decode the other words; this is morphology.

66. **Academically, appropriate literature primarily helps students to _____. (Skill 6.5; Rigorous)**

   A. become better readers
   B. see how the skills they learned are applied to writing
   C. enjoy library time
   D. increase academic skills in other content areas

Answer B: see how the skills they learned are applied to writing.

When students are exposed to appropriate literature selections, as well as are taught to select appropriate texts for themselves, they are able to observe how the reading and writing skills they learn in classroom mini-lessons are applied to published writing. Published works are an excellent place for students to see not only proper conventions of grammar, but "real-life" examples of imagery and figurative language.

67. **According to Marilyn Jager Adams, which skill would a typically developing student demonstrate after he is able to separate the onset and rhyme of words (i.e. /c/ /at/)? (Skill 6.3; Rigorous)**

    A. Recognize the odd member in a group
    B. Replace sounds in words
    C. Count the sounds in a word
    D. Count syllables in a word

Answer C: Count the sounds in a word

Ms. Adams breaks phonemic awareness tasks into five stages. The third stage is the ability to blend words and split words into chunks such as the example. After this stage, students will typically be able to orally segment all parts of a words into the correct number of phonemes. They may have difficulty counting the number due to other reasons, but should be able to orally separate each sound in a word.

68. **All of the following are true about phonological awareness EXCEPT: (Skill 6.3; Easy)**

    A.   It may involve print.
    B.   It is a prerequisite for spelling and phonics.
    C.   Activities can be done by the children with their eyes closed.
    D.   Starts before letter recognition is taught.

Answer A: It may involve print.

The key word here is EXCEPT which will be highlighted in upper case on the test as well. All of the options are correct aspects of phonological awareness except the first one, A, because phonological awareness DOES NOT involve print.

69. **Standing in line at the grocery store, Megan, age three, turns to her mother and asks in a regular tone of voice, "Mom, why is that woman so fat?" Megan's mother is mortified when sharing this story with Megan's preschool teacher. Which concept of language can the teacher explain to Megan's mother to help her better understand the situation? (Skill 6.4; Rigorous)**

   A. Syntax
   B. Semantics
   C. Morphology
   D. Pragmatics

Answer D: Pragmatics

Pragmatics is the development and understanding of social relevance to conversations and topics. It develops as children age. In this situation, Megan simply does not understand to the same level of an adult how that question could be viewed as offensive to certain members of society.

70. **Which of the following is NOT a component of reading fluency? (Skill 6.9; Easy)**

   A. Phoneme knowledge
   B. Accuracy
   C. Rate
   D. Automacity

Answer A: Phoneme knowledge

Accuracy, rate, prosody, and automacity are the main components of reading fluency. Phoneme knowledge allows students to better decode and read basic words – this will eventually help with reading fluency, but is more of a subcomponent of a students accuracy in reading.

71. **Repeated readings of the same text are beneficial to developing readers because _____. (Skill 6.10; Rigorous)**

    A. repeated reading helps students memorize the text
    B. repeated reading helps in pairing students
    C. repeated reading ensures students recognize the words readily and can read at an improved pace
    D. repeated reading helps teachers determine students' level of reading

Answer C: repeated reading ensures students recognize the words readily and can read at an improved pace

Repeated readings allow students to have repeated exposure to the same vocabulary, sentences, and punctuation. This repeated exposure allows students to learn the right way to read something the first time while then providing ample opportunities (the repeated reading sessions) to internalize the elements of the text. Some argue that repeated reading helps students to simply memorize the text, however this can be checked by the teacher by having the student start at different points in the text (i.e., a new page).

72. **When introducing new vocabulary to students, the number of new words being taught at one time should be _____. (Skill 6.11; Rigorous)**

    A. one to two
    B. two to three
    C. three to four
    D. four to five

Answer B: two to three

The number of words that require explicit teaching should only be two or three. If the number is higher than that, the children need guided reading and the text needs to be broken down into smaller sections for teaching. When broken down into smaller sections, each text section should only have two to three words which need explicit teaching.

73. **Which of the following is NOT a common method of teaching comprehension? (Skill 6.12; Easy)**

    A. Summarizing
    B. Question asking
    C. Graphic organizers
    D. Phonics drills

Answer D: Phonics drills

Summarizing, question asking, and graphic organizers are just a few of the strategies for teaching comprehension. Others include studying text structure, question answering, monitoring comprehension, textual marking, and discussion. Phonics drills may help students to decode and identify words better, but they do not directly help students to comprehend what they are reading.

74. **When students know that letters stand for a message, they are said to be in the_____ stage of spelling. (Skill 6.13; Rigorous)**

    A. non-phonemic
    B. pre-phonemic
    C. early phonemic
    D. letter-name sounding

Answer B: pre-phonemic

The pre-phonemic stage of spelling is the first stage of spelling where the students know that letters stand for a message, but they cannot link the spelling to meaningful pronunciation yet. In the early phonemic stage, students are beginning to understand spelling and can start to write letters. Finally, letter-name spelling is when students spell some words correctly, and they are developing a sight vocabulary. There is no non-phonemic stage of spelling.

75.   The _____ level of learning of Bloom's taxonomy requires students to take the analyzed parts from the previous level and converge them into creative new wholes. (Skill 6.14; Average rigor)

A. Comprehension
B. Analysis
C. Synthesis
D. Evaluation

Answer C: Synthesis

Synthesis requires students to take the analyzed parts from the previous level and converge them into creative new wholes; tasks at this level ask students to collect, compose, design, manage, plan, organize, and formulate

76.   Mrs. Baker's class has 22 students. Mrs. Smith's class has 16 students. How many more students are in Mrs. Baker's class? (Skill 6.15; Easy)

A.   22 more students
B.   14 more students
C.   6 more students
D.   38 more students

Answer C: 6 more students

The words *how many more* indicate that this is a subtraction problem. It is necessary to regroup the numbers to complete the subtraction. Students are expected to add a label (*more students*) for a complete answer.

77.   Kindergarten students are exploring fractions with fraction-pie puzzles. One puzzle has the pie divided into fourths. It has four equal pieces. Which puzzle will have twice as many pieces? (Skill 6.15; Average Rigor)

A.   The puzzle divided into eighths (eight equal pieces)
B.   The puzzle divided into halves (two equal pieces)
C.   The puzzle divided into sixths (six equal pieces)
D.   The puzzles divided into twelfths (twelve equal pieces)

Answer A: The puzzle divided into eighths (eight equal pieces)

The puzzle with eight pieces has twice as many pieces as the puzzle with four pieces. 4 X 2 = 8

78. **PreK students are using snap-together cubes to measure objects in the classroom. They want to know which is longer, the doll bed or the red truck. After snapping together enough cubes to "measure" each they determine that the doll bed is longer. Which math principles are demonstrated in this activity? (Skill 6.15; Rigorous)**

    A. Measurement, rote counting
    B. Addition, measurement
    C. Rote counting, using a model
    D. Measurement, using a model

Answer D: Measurement, using a model

The students are using a nonstandard unit of measurement (snap-together cube) to measure and create models that represent the length of the doll bed and of the red truck.

79. **What are the three primary types of illustrations used in teaching social studies to young children? (Skill 6.16; Average Rigor)**

    A. maps, charts, and contour lines
    B. graphs, maps, and distortion diagrams
    C. maps, charts and graphs
    D. bar charts, pie charts and graphs

Answer C: maps, charts and graphs

We use **illustrations** of various sorts because it is often easier to demonstrate a given idea visually instead of orally. Sometimes it is even easier to do so with an illustration than a description. This is especially true in the areas of education and research because humans are visually stimulated. It is a fact that any idea presented visually in some manner is always easier to understand and to comprehend than simply getting an idea across verbally, by hearing it or reading it. Throughout this document, there are several illustrations that have been presented to explain an idea in a more precise way. Sometimes these will demonstrate some of the types of illustrations available for use in the arena of political science. Among the more common illustrations used in political science are various types of **maps, graphs and charts**.

80. **Which of the following is not a basic type of map projection? (Skill 6.16; Rigorous)**

    A.   Flat-Plane
    B.   Cylindrical
    C.   Conical
    D.   Conformational

Answer D: Conformational

However, the basic ideas behind map projections can be understood by looking at the three most common types:

(1) **Cylindrical Projections** - These are done by taking a cylinder of paper and wrapping it around a globe. A light is used to project the globe's features onto the paper. Distortion is least where the paper touches the globe. For example, suppose that the paper was wrapped so that it touched the globe at the equator, the map from this projection would have just a little distortion near the equator. However, in moving north or south of the equator, the distortion would increase as you moved further away from the equator. The best known and most widely used cylindrical projection is the **Mercator Projection.** It was first developed in 1569 by Gerardus Mercator, a Flemish mapmaker.

(2) **Conical Projections** - The name for these maps come from the fact that the projection is made onto a cone of paper. The cone is made so that it touches a globe at the base of the cone only. It can also be made so that it cuts through part of the globe in two different places. Again, there is the least distortion where the paper touches the globe. If the cone touches at two different points, there is some distortion at both of them. Conical projections are most often used to map areas in the **middle latitudes**. Maps of the United States are most often conical projections. This is because most of the country lies within these latitudes.

(3) **Flat-Plane Projections** - These are made with a flat piece of paper. It touches the globe at one point only. Areas near this point show little distortion. Flat-plane projections are often used to show the areas of the north and south poles. One such flat projection is called a **Gnomonic Projection**. On this kind of map all meridians appear as straight lines, Gnomonic projections are useful because any straight line drawn between points on it forms a **Great-Circle Route**.

Great-Circle Routes can best be described by thinking of a globe and when using the globe the shortest route between two points on it can be found by simply stretching a string from one point to the other. However, if the string was extended in reality, so that it took into effect the globe's curvature, it would then make a great-circle. A great-circle is any circle that cuts a sphere, such as the globe, into two equal parts. Because of distortion, most maps do not show great-circle routes as straight lines, Gnomonic projections, however, do show the shortest distance between the two places as a straight line, because of this they are valuable for navigation. They are called Great-Circle Sailing Maps.

81. **An appropriate method for graphically representing data to the scientific community would be _____. (Skill 6.17; Easy)**

   A. charts
   B. spreadsheets
   C. Power Point presentations
   D. all of the above

Answer D: all of the above

Scientific information and/or experimental results must be communicated by clearly describing the information using accurate data, visual presentations (including bar/line/pie graphs), tables/charts, diagrams, artwork, power point presentation, and other appropriate media. Modern technology must be used whenever it is necessary. The method of communication must be suitable to the audience. Written communication is as important as oral communication. This is essential for submitting research papers to scientific journals, newspapers, other magazines etc.

82. **When creating a model, what is the most important aspect of the possibilities listed below? (Skill 6.17; Rigorous)**

   A. Scale
   B. Color
   C. Details
   D. Intended audience

Answer A: Scale

Physical models are created by first determining what aspects of a concept are to be represented, and at what scale. A physical model of something large is usually smaller and relative size may be a very important concept in generating the model. For example, while a physical model of the Solar System is clearly smaller than the actual Solar System, planet sizes and distances will be scaled down relative to each other.

83. **Which type of communication is most effective for introducing athletic skills? (Skill 6.19; Easy)**

A. written
B. verbal
C. visual
D. all of the above

Answer C: visual

Visual communication is usually the most effective method for introducing athletic skills and athletic activities. It involves providing students with a visual demonstration of the skill or activity.

84. **Which style of teaching would be best to use when there is only a small amount of time to teach students a physical skill? (Skill 6.19; Rigorous)**

A. command style
B. practice style
C. reciprocal style
D. inclusion style

Answer A: command style

The command style involves the teacher making all the decisions and controlling all activities. It is useful for teaching students a skill in a small amount of time, but should be limited to initial demonstrations and explanations.

85. **Which subject would be most likely to develop a student's body awareness and listening skills? (Skill 6.20; Average rigor)**

A. visual arts
B. dance
C. drama
D. music

Answer B: dance

Younger children learn to develop body awareness through dance. Listening skills are also developed as the students listen to the rhythm of the music and develop a sense of tempo.

Diversity

86. **Flexible scheduling and use of mechanical aids are examples of _____. (Skill 7.1; Easy)**

    A. alternative assessments
    B. testing modifications
    C. differentiated instruction
    D. multiple intelligences

Answer B: testing modifications

Testing modifications are changes made to minimize the effect of a student's disability or learning challenge on completing assessments. Testing modifications include flexible scheduling, flexible setting, alternate test format, and use of mechanical aids.

87. **What would a teacher wanting to improve a student's self-esteem be best to tell the student? (Skill 7.1; Rigorous)**

    A. what they did that helped produce a successful result
    B. the high grade they achieved
    C. how they performed compared to other students
    D. the actions they can take to perform better in the future

Answer: A. what they did that helped produce a successful result

Teachers can instill positive self-concepts and help create self-confidence by providing positive feedback. The most effective feedback for enhancing self-confidence is qualitative comments, where the student's success is attributed to their effort and where the teacher focuses on what the student did that attributed to their success.

88. **What are the three functions of the three-phase model for teaching? (Skill 7.2; Average rigor)**

    A. planning, implementing, assessing
    B. content, process, and product
    C. sensing, transforming, and acting
    D. thinking, behaving, revising

Answer C: sensing, transforming, and acting

The three-phase model for teaching is part of the process approach to enhancing self-concept among students. The model includes a sensing function, a transforming function, and an acting function.

89. **Which of the following is a disinviting behavior? (Skill 7.2; Average rigor)**

A. learning student's names
B. being real with students
C. inviting oneself
D. reacting to rejection

Answer D: reacting to rejection

The approach known as designated Invitational Education considers that teachers and their behaviors may be either inviting or disinviting. Inviting behaviors enhance self-concept, while disinviting behaviors reduce self-concept. Inviting behaviors include reaching each student, listening with care, being real with students, being real with oneself, inviting good discipline, handling rejection, and inviting oneself. The behaviors that are the opposite of these are disinviting.

90. **A teacher can help instill confidence in the parents of diverse children by talking about the child _____. (Skill 7.3; Rigorous)**

A. unemotionally
B. indirectly
C. personally
D. logically

Answer C: personally

When speaking to the parents of children, teachers often have greater success when they speak about the child personally, rather than talking about the group of students as a whole. Speaking about the child personally helps instill confidence in the parents and makes it more likely they will believe that the child is in good hands.

91. **Which of the following would be most useful for an ESOL student? (Skill 7.4; Average rigor)**

    A. placing the student in a mixed learning group
    B. making content two grades below the student's level
    C. encouraging the student to use complex language
    D. having the student complete activities independently

Answer A: placing the student in a mixed learning group

ESOL approaches are often based on social learning methods. One common method is to place the student in a mixed learning group. This allows the student the chance to practice English in a non-threatening environment. Activities such as making the content lower than the grade, encouraging the student to use complex language, or having the student complete activities independently would be likely to isolate the student.

92. **What type of learning disability does a student that has difficulty concentrating most likely have? (Skill 7.5; Easy)**

    A. attention deficit hyperactivity disorder
    B. auditory processing disorder
    C. visual processing disorder
    D. dyslexia

Answer A: attention deficit hyperactivity disorder

Attention deficit hyperactivity disorder is one type of common learning disability. Students who have this learning disability are likely to have difficulty concentrating.

93. **An exceptional child is one who has _____. (Skill 7.6; Average rigor)**

    A. sensory impairments
    B. emotional disturbances
    C. mental retardation
    D. any of the above

Answer D: any of the above

An exceptional child is one who is different in some way from the "normal" or "average" child. This can be due to physical disabilities, sensory impairments, emotional disturbances, learning disturbances, or mental retardation.

94. **What is the most important factor in improving the developmental and educational gains for an exceptional child? (Skill 7.6; Average rigor)**

   A. varied teaching procedures
   B. the social environment
   C. early intervention
   D. encouraging independence

Answer C: early intervention

The most important factor in improving the developmental and educational gains for an exceptional child is early intervention. Research has shown that early intervention reduces the need for special education and other rehabilitative services later in life, makes it less likely that the child will be retained in grade, and can result in the child being indistinguishable from non-handicapped classmates.

95. **Which of the following problems are likely to be faced by migrant, homeless, and abandoned children? (Skill 7.7; Easy)**

   A. poor attendance
   B. language barriers
   C. social isolation
   D. all of the above

Answer D: all of the above

Migrant, homeless, and abandoned children face a number of educational problems. Common problems faced include poor attendance, language barriers, and social isolation. These can lead to poor school performance.

96. **Which child would be most likely to have medical and health problems that the school could address? (Skill 7.7; Average rigor)**

   A. a migrant child
   B. an abandoned child
   C. a foster child
   D. an adopted child

Answer B: an abandoned child

Children who have been neglected or abandoned often have medical problems and may experience problems due to poor nutrition. Teachers and schools can help address these problems by providing healthy school lunches and by offering medical attention to students of high mobility.

97. **For a student to be allowed to carry and self-administer asthma medication, what must be on file with the school? (Skill 7.8; Rigorous)**

    A. medical certificate
    B. Individualized Educational Program
    C. release form
    D. medication log book

Answer C: release form

Life-saving medication where time is of the essence may be carried by students and self-administered. The most common example is an asthma inhaler. For this to occur, a release form must be on file with the school. The release form must be signed by the healthcare provider, the parent or guardian, and the student.

Diagnosis, Assessment and Evaluation

98. **Which type of assessment is the least structured? (Skill 8.1; Easy)**

    A. observation
    B. informal continuous assessment
    C. formal assessment
    D. standardized testing

Answer A: observation

Observation is an assessment activity that involves noticing someone and judging their action. It is the least structured type of assessment.

99. **Which type of assessment has the main purpose of helping learners learn better? (Skill 8.1; Rigorous)**

    A. formal assessment
    B. observation
    C. informal assessment
    D. exam

Answer C: informal assessment

The main purpose of informal assessment is to help learners learn better. It aims to help the teacher understand how the student is learning and progressing.

100. **What are entry surveys, collections of reading and writing samples, and classroom observations examples of? (Skill 8.1; Rigorous)**

    A. informal assessments
    B. structured assessments
    C. formal assessments
    D. criterion-references assessments

Answer A: informal assessments

There are many types of informal assessments used. These include entry surveys, collections of reading and writing samples, classroom observations, and notations about students cognitive abilities as seen in classroom activities.

101. **Which factor is it most important to consider when choosing structured assessment methods? (Skill 8.1; Rigorous)**

    A. the authenticity of the methods
    B. the results of informal evaluations
    C. the formal assessments required
    D. the developmental stage of students

Answer D: the developmental stage of students

The structured assessment methods used in class take into account two major factors. The first is the developmental stage of students, where teachers must choose assessment methods that are appropriate for the developmental level of students. The second consideration is the purpose of the assessment.

102. **Which type of assessment would be used to place students into honors, regular, and remedial classes? (Skill 8.1; Rigorous)**

    A. norm-referenced assessments
    B. criterion-referenced assessments
    C. performance-based assessments
    D. observation-based assessments

Answer A: norm-referenced assessments

Norm-references assessments are used to classify students into a ranking category. Norm-references assessments are used to place students into honors, remedial, and regular classes.

103. **Teachers should regard a student's test results as _____. (Skill 8.2; Average rigor)**

    A. exact indications of the student's ability
    B. ball park figures indicating the student's ability
    C. possible indicators of a student's ability
    D. unlikely to be a true indication of a student's ability

Answer B: ball park figures indicating the student's ability

The test results achieved by students should be regarded as indications of the student's ability, but ball park figures rather than exact indications. This occurs because other factors can influence the test results, such as the students mood on the day of the test or other factors.

104. **What is it most important for a teacher to consider when reading another teacher's observations of a student? (Skill 8.2; Average rigor)**

    A. mood
    B. discrimination
    C. dishonesty
    D. bias

Answer D: bias

When reading another teacher's observations of a student, teachers must be aware that the teacher may be biased. This could result in either a more positive or a more negative assessment.

105. **What should a teacher record in anecdotal records of a student? (Skill 8.2; Average rigor)**

    A. assumptions about the student's interest
    B. theories explaining the student's attitude
    C. speculations about the student's motivation
    D. observed behaviors

Answer D: observed behaviors

Anecdotal records of a student should include observable behaviors. Anecdotal records should not include assumptions or speculations about the student's motivation or interest.

106. **Which of the following is a common self-appraisal instrument? (Skill 8.2; Average rigor)**

A. rating scales
B. questioning
C. portfolio assessment
D. anecdotal records

Answer A: rating scales

Rating scales and checklists can be self-appraisal instruments completed by the student. They can also be completed by the teacher.

107. **Portfolio assessment is especially useful for identifying _____. (Skill 8.2; Average rigor)**

A. quantitative changes
B. qualitative changes
C. behavioral changes
D. attitude changes

Answer B: qualitative changes

One of the major benefits of portfolio assessments is that they can help identify qualitative changes that have occurred over time. These changes are often not as easily able to be identified using methods such as quizzes and exams.

108. **A teacher wishes to identify the sources of confusion that are resulting in students performing poorly on standardized tests. What would be the best method to use for this purpose? (Skill 8.3; Rigorous)**

A. rating scales
B. questioning
C. portfolio assessment
D. anecdotal records

Answer B: questioning

Oral questioning is an assessment method often used by teachers. While asking questions, the teacher can identify the degree of student knowledge as well as the areas where students may by experiencing confusion or misunderstandings.

109. What type of opportunities does portfolio assessment provide for monitoring student progress? (Skill 8.4; Average rigor)

    A. formative
    B. summative
    C. alternative assessment
    D. both formative and summative

Answer D: both formative and summative

Portfolio assessment provides the opportunity for formative, or ongoing, assessment. It also provides the opportunity for summative, or culminating, assessment.

110. What is one of the main advantages of portfolio assessment for students? (Skill 8.4; Average rigor)

    A. It promotes creativity.
    B. It generates opportunities to use diverse skills.
    C. It encourages students to reflect on their own work.
    D. It develops communication skills.

Answer C: It encourages students to reflect on their own work.

One of the main advantages of portfolio assessment for students is that it provides them with the opportunity to assess and reflect on their own work. This also encourages self-directed learning.

111. What is the purpose of a parent-teacher conference? (Skill 8.5; Average rigor)

    A. sharing information with the parents
    B. obtaining information from the parents
    C. requesting parent support
    D. any or all of the above

Answer D: any or all of the above

A parent t-teacher conference can be held for a number of reasons. These include allowing the teacher to provide parents with information, allowing the teacher to obtain information from the parents, and asking the parents for involvement in the student's learning activities.

112. **What is it best to begin a parent-teacher conference with? (Skill 8.5; Easy)**

   A. student weaknesses
   B. positive comments
   C. entertaining anecdotes
   D. issues of concern

Answer B: positive comments

A parent-teacher conference should begin with positive comments about the students. However, these should be accurate statements and not exaggerate the student's good points.

113. **Information about a student's school performance can be given to _____. (Skill 8.5; Average rigor)**

   A. the student's parents or guardians
   B. the student's parents or guardians and those of other parents
   C. any interested party
   D. any or all of the above

Answer A: the student's parents or guardians

Information about a student's school performance is confidential and comes under the Privacy Act. Information can be given only to the student's parents or guardians.

Guidance and Classroom Behavioral Management

114. **What type of procedures should be used as the basis for behavior management techniques? (Skill 9.1; Average rigor)**

   A. positive
   B. negative
   C. restrictive
   D. combative

Answer A: positive

Behavior management techniques should always focus on positive procedures. The procedures used should also be ones that can be used at home as well as at school.

115. When should a classroom management plan be implemented? (Skill 9.1; Easy)

A. when a parent requests one
B. when behavioral issues are impacting students
C. at the start of the school year
D. on the first instance that undesired behaviors are observed

Answer C: at the start of the school year

A classroom management plan should be implemented at the beginning of the school year. It can then be analyzed and monitored for effectiveness throughout the year, and changes made if they are necessary.

116. Which type of social skills assessment involves the teacher observing students in structured scenarios? (Skill 9.2; Average rigor)

A. role play
B. teacher ratings
C. peer nomination
D. peer rating

Answer A: role play

There are many ways to assess student's social skills. Role play is a method that involves the teacher observing students as they take part in structured scenarios.

117. What is the main reason that punishment should not be the first method used to guide behavior? (Skill 9.2; Rigorous)

A. It can isolate students.
B. It can create strained relationships.
C. It can result in behavior suppression.
D. It can produce feelings of anger and resentment.

Answer C: It can result in behavior suppression.

Punishment is not the first choice as the method used to guide behavior, as it can suppress behavior, rather than eliminate it. When this occurs, a genuine behavior change does not occur and it is less likely that the change will be permanent.

118. **What is the most severe form of punishment? (Skill 9.3; Easy)**

    A. time-out
    B. suspension
    C. overcorrection
    D. response cost

Answer B: suspension

There are various methods of punishment. From the least severe to the most severe, they include: subtracting something that the child does not like; response cost; time-out; seclusion time-out; overcorrection; and suspension.

119. **When reprimanding students, what type of voice is most effective? (Skill 9.3; Average rigor)**

    A. impatient
    B. angry
    C. non-threatening
    D. unemotional

Answer C: non-threatening

Verbal techniques are important in promoting positive behavior. It has been found that when reprimanding students, it is best that a non-threatening voice is used. The tone should be free from roughness, anger, and impatience.

120. **What should a physical education instructor emphasize to encourage students to make decisions? (Skill 9.4; Rigorous)**

    A. there is sometimes more than one right decision
    B. decision-making and problem-solving are related
    C. taking action is the student's responsibility
    D. asking others for assistance can be helpful

Answer C: taking action is the student's responsibility

It has been found that it is important for instructors to emphasize to students that taking action is their responsibility. This makes it more likely that students will take responsibility for making their own decisions.

121. **What is a conflict resolution principle? (Skill 9.4; Average rigor)**

   A. attack the person
   B. react immediately
   C. find common ground
   D. focus on the past

Answer C: find common ground

One of the conflict resolution principles is "find common ground." This means that people should try to find something they do agree on as soon as possible. If an early compromise can be reached, the tension can often be resolved more quickly.

122. **Which of the following is NOT a common character development trait? (Skill 9.5; Average rigor)**

   A. responsibilty
   B. intelligence
   C. caring
   D. honesty

Answer B: intelligence

There are various common character development traits that are developed in children. These include responsibility, caring, self-discipline, citizenship, honesty, respect, and patriotism.

123. **The best strategies for teaching character development focus on the moral implications of _____. (Skill 9.5; Average rigor)**

   A. historical events
   B. everyday life
   C. major issues
   D. hypothetical situations

Answer B: everyday life

Teaching character development has been found to be most effective when students take part in discussions focused on the moral implications of their everyday life. Examples include discussions about problems that might be encountered such as finding out a friend has cheated on a test or finding a wallet full of money.

124. A student's normal behavior is highly dependent on the student's _____. (Skill 9.6; Average rigor)

A. number of friends
B. academic performance
C. maturity level
D. health status

Answer C: maturity level

A student's normal behavior depends on their maturity level. It is important to consider this when determining if a person is showing signs of stress.

125. Which of the following is an effective method for helping young children cope with stress? (Skill 9.6; Average rigor)

A. reading them books
B. encouraging them to play sports
C. helping them make friends
D. persuading them not to focus on their feelings

Answer A: reading them books

For younger children, reading them books is an effective method for helping them deal with stress. By seeing how other characters deal with stress, students can learn how to cope with stress and understand that feeling stressed is normal.

Post-Test

Child Growth and Development

1. **Which of the following is NOT a sign of child abuse? (Skill 1.1; Easy)**

   A. Awkward social behavior around other children

   B. Participation in class discussions

   C. Awkward social behavior around adults

   D. Bruises

2. **If child abuse is suspected what action should the teacher take? (Skill 1.1; Average rigor)**

   A. Wait to see if the child talks about it again

   B. Talk to your supervisor about your concerns

   C. Call the child's parent

   D. Talk to another teacher about your suspicions

3. **While children develop at different rates, which of the following can cause learning difficulties? (Skill 1.1; Average rigor)**

   A. Lack of sleep

   B. Poor nutrition

   C. Prenatal exposure to nicotine

   D. All of the above

4. **Which of the following is a true statement? (Skill 1.2; Rigorous)**

   A. Physical development does not influence social development

   B. Social development does not influence physical development

   C. Cognitive development does not influence social development

   D. All domains of development (physical, social and cognitive) are integrated and influence other domains.

5. Researchers and practitioners agree that the best method to teach young children to read and write is: (Skill 1.4; Rigorous)

    A. Intense phonics instruction

    B. Exposure to numerous books

    C. Wait until child exhibits "readiness" and then the method won't matter

    D. Unknown

6. A teacher notices that a student is quiet, and has several bruises on his head, arms and legs. When asked, the student tells the teacher that his dad hit him, but then begs her not to tell. The teacher should: (Skill 1.5; Rigorous)

    A. Report suspected abuse to the school counselor

    B. Attempt to get more information from the student and agree not to tell anyone

    C. Consult a colleague and see what they would do

    D. Wait and see if other signs of abuse become evident

7. Bobby, a nine year-old, has been caught stealing frequently in the classroom. What might be a factor contributing to this behavior? (Skill 1.5; Rigorous)

    A. Need for the items stolen

    B. Serious emotional disturbance

    C. Desire to experiment

    D. A normal stage of development

8. Marcus is a first grade boy of good developmental attainment. His learning progress is good the first half of the year. He shows no indicators of emotional distress. After the holiday break, he returns much changed. He is quieter, sullen even, tending to play alone. He has moments of tearfulness, sometimes almost without cause. He avoids contact with adults as often as he can. Even play with his friends has become limited. He has episodes of wetting not seen before, and often wants to sleep in school. What approach is appropriate for this sudden change in behavior? (Skill 1.5; Rigorous)

A. Give him some time to adjust. The holiday break was probably too much fun to come back to school from

B. Report this change immediately to administration. Do not call the parents until administration decides a course of action

C. Document his daily behavior carefully as soon as you notice such a change, report to administration the next month or so in a meeting

D. Make a courtesy call to the parents to let them know he is not acting like himself, being sure to tell them he is not making trouble for others

9. Learning activities for younger students (below age eight) should focus on short time frames because: (Skill 1.6; Average rigor)

A. Younger children tend to process information at a slower rate than older children (age eight and older)

B. Young children have long attention spans

C. Young children can understand complex instructional activities

D. Young children need to sit quietly and listen to learn

10. Who developed the theory of multiple intelligences? (Skill 1.7; Easy)

A. Bruner

B. Gardner

C. Kagan

D. Cooper

11. **What is one way of effectively managing student conduct? (Skill 1.8; Average rigor)**

   A. State expectations about behavior

   B. Let students discipline their peers

   C. Let minor infractions of the rules go unnoticed

   D. Increase disapproving remarks

12. **What was the result of studies done in low SES primary classrooms taught by effective teachers? (Skill 1.8; Rigorous)**

   A. More teacher-student interactions and less time in which a child is unoccupied

   B. No pauses between academic tasks

   C. More tasks chosen by the student

   D. More time spent in small group work

13. **Research has shown that high teacher's expectations are likely to directly impact _____. (Skill 1.8; Easy)**

   A. co-worker morale

   B. student performance

   C. the district's overall rating

   D. student's enjoyment of school

Foundations of Learning

14. **According to Piaget, when does the development of symbolic functioning and language take place? (Skill 2.1; Rigorous)**

   A. Concrete operations stage

   B. Formal operations stage

   C. Sensorimotor stage

   D. Preoperational stage

15. **According to Piaget, what is a child born with? (Skill 2.1; Rigorous)**

   A. The tendency to actively relate pieces of information acquired

   B. The ability to adapt

   C. Primary emotions

   D. Desire

16. **Which of the following are widely known curriculum models for early childhood programming? (Skill 2.2; Rigorous)**

    A. Montessori, Highscope, DISTAR

    B. Montessori, Creative curriculum, High/Scope

    C. Montessori, DISTAR, Junior Great Books

    D. Montessori, High/Scope, Success for All

17. **Which federal law directed states to construct curriculum models specific to the development of early childhood and elementary programs for academic enhancement? (Skill 2.2; Rigorous)**

    A. IDEA

    B. Head Start

    C. FERPA

    D. NCLB

18. **Head Start Programs were created in the early 60s to provide: (Skill 2.2; Average rigor)**

    A. A comprehensive curriculum model for preparation of low-income students for success in school communities

    B. A national curriculum that ensures that "no child is left behind"

    C. A parent involvement program in every school

    D. Prekindergarten for every 4 year old

19. **Which of the following is a true statement? (Skill 2.2; Rigorous)**

    A. The quality of instruction doesn't matter if the correct curriculum is followed

    B. The NCLB Act mandates which curriculum schools should use to guarantee student academic success

    C. The quality of instruction is important for student academic success

    D. The quality of instruction doesn't matter as long as parents are involved in their children's education

20. Effective curriculum models for early childhood programs should include which of the following: (Skill 2.2; Average rigor)

    A. Cognitive development

    B. Social development

    C. Both cognitive and social development

    D. None of the above

21. What would be appropriate information to consider if a school was trying to determine if a child has a disability that may qualify the child for services under IDEA? (Skill 2.3; Rigorous)

    A. The present levels of academic achievement and the child's current vision and hearing screening information

    B. A complete psychological evaluation

    C. Both A and B

    D. None of the above

22. Which school group meets to review information about children with exceptional learning needs? (Skill 2.3; Easy)

    A. The Child Study team

    B. The Site Based decision-making committee

    C. The special education teachers

    D. None of the above

23. It is important to make a report when abuse or neglect is suspected because: (Skill 2.3; Average rigor)

    A. Failure to do so could result in revocation of certification and license

    B. Failure to do so could result in a monetary fine

    C. Both A and B

    D. None of the above

24. IDEA sets policies that provide for inclusion of students with disabilities. What does inclusion mean? (Skill 2.3; Rigorous)

    A. Inclusion is the name of the curriculum that must followed in special education classes

    B. Inclusion is the right of students with disabilities to be placed in the regular classroom

    C. Inclusion refers to the quality of instruction is important for student academic success

    D. Inclusion means that students with disabilities should always be placed in classes for gifted and talented students.

25. Under the IDEA, Congress provides safeguards for students against schools' actions, including the right to sue in court, and encourages states to develop hearing and mediation systems to resolve disputes. This is known as: (Skill 2.3; Rigorous)

    A. Due process

    B. Mediation

    C. Safe Schools Initiative

    D. Parent involvement

Research, standards and trends

26. Why should teachers view the websites of professional organizations like the IRA? (Skill 3.1; Average rigor)

    A. To find new video games for teaching children

    B. To chat with other early childhood educators

    C. To find quality strategies to improve early childhood education for students

    D. To post student work for parent viewing

27. Which of the following organizations target improvement of education specifically for young children? (Skill 3.2; Rigorous)

    A. SPCA, NCTM, and NAACP

    B. NAEYC, SECA, and ACEI

    C. NAACP, IRA, and NCTM

    D. None of the above

28. You've received a job offer to teach pre-kindergarten, but you've never taught children this young. What professional organization might publish journal articles that would be useful to you? (Skill 3.2; Rigorous)

    A. FCRR

    B. IRA

    C. NAEYC

    D. AERA

29. Teacher turnover is a problem in today's schools. What factors are contributing to this problem? (Skill 3.3; Rigorous)

    A. Violence in schools

    B. Increasing federal mandates

    C. Diversity of student needs

    D. All of the above

30. Which current trend in education is creating conflicting issues which impact educational development and implementation of effective curriculum for young learners? (Skill 3.3; Rigorous)

    A. The NCLB law

    B. Innovations in technology

    C. The Whole Language movement

    D. Parent involvement

31. When considering the comprehensive cost of educating students, what is a hidden cost that may not be often considered? (Skill 3.3; Rigorous)

    A. The increase in students speaking who do not speak English

    B. Federal mandates

    C. The cost of technology

    D. Teacher turnover rate

32. In traditional classrooms, what is the mode of learning for students seeking to understand new content? (Skill 3.3; Average rigor)

A. Inquiry based learning

B. Lecture

C. Hands on learning

D. None of the above

33. What two things have contributed to a reduction in teaching and instructional time for young learners? (Skill 3.3; Rigorous)

A. Increased expectations for learning coupled with increased teachers who are alternatively certified

B. Increased early violence in communities coupled with classroom management issues

C. Increased expectations for learning coupled with a decrease in parent involvement

D. Increasing numbers of alternatively certified teachers coupled with a decrease in parent involvement

34. Traditional assessment methods include the following: (Skill 3.3; Easy)

A. Multiple choice questions

B. Questions that require self-reflection

C. True/false questions

D. Both A and C

35. Effective teachers use differentiated instruction to connect all students to the subject matter by using the following classroom management strategies: (Skill 3.3; Average rigor)

A. Peer teaching

B. Flexible groups

C. Whole class, teacher-led activities

D. All of the above

Effective Practices

36. **What is one component of the instructional planning model that must be given careful evaluation? (Skill 4.1; Average rigor)**

    A. Students' prior knowledge and skills

    B. The script the teacher will use in instruction

    C. Future lesson plans

    D. Parent participation

37. **When is utilization of instructional materials most effective? (Skill 4.1; Average rigor)**

    A. When the activities are sequenced

    B. When the materials are prepared ahead of time

    C. When the students choose the pages to work on

    D. When the students create the instructional materials

38. **What is evaluation of the instructional activity based on? (Skill 4.1; Average rigor)**

    A. Student grades

    B. Teacher evaluation

    C. Student participation

    D. Specified criteria

39. **What should a teacher do when students have not responded well to an instructional activity? (Skill 4.1; Rigorous)**

    A. Revaluate learner needs.

    B. Skill-building and analysis of outcomes

    C. Interaction with students and manipulation of subject matter

    D. Management techniques and levels of questioning

40. **The teacher states, "We will work on the first page of vocabulary words. On the second page we will work on the structure and meaning of the words. We will go over these together and then you will write out the answers to the exercises on your own. I will be circulating to give help if needed". What is this an example of? (Skill 4.1; Rigorous)**

    A. Evaluation of instructional activity

    B. Analysis of instructional activity

    C. Identification of expected outcomes

    D. Pacing of instructional activity

41. The teacher states that the lesson the students will be engaged in will consist of a review of the material from the previous day, demonstration of the scientific of an electronic circuit, and small group work on setting up an electronic circuit. What has the teacher demonstrated? (Skill 4.2; Rigorous)

    A. The importance of reviewing

    B. Giving the general framework for the lesson to facilitate learning

    C. Giving students the opportunity to leave if they are not interested in the lesson

    D. Providing momentum for the lesson

42. Which of the following words would be included on the classroom word wall? (Skill 4.4; Average rigor)

    A. High frequency words

    B. Words students encounter in their daily reading and writing

    C. Words that students misspell

    D. All of the above

43. As teachers select instructional materials it is important that teachers remember: (Skill 4.7; Average rigor)

    A. It is unlawful for students to study from textbooks or materials that are brought from home

    B. It is unlawful for students to study from textbooks or materials that are more than 10 years old

    C. It is unlawful to require students to study from textbooks or materials other than those approved by the state Department of Education

    D. None of the above

44. Prior experiences influence the individual's cognitive style, or method of accepting, processing, and retaining information. According to Marshall Rosenberg, students can be categorized as: (Skill 4.7; Rigorous)

    A. rigid-inhibited, undisciplined, acceptance-anxious, or creative

    B. hyperactive, well-behaved, disinterested or cognitively delayed

    C. Visual, auditory, kinesthetic or multi-modality learners

    D. None of the above

45. An early warning sign of emergent literacy difficulties is: (Skill 4.9; Average rigor)

   A. Failure to identify the letters in their own name

   B. Inability to count to 10

   C. Trouble singing the ABC song correctly

   D. Difficulty tying their shoes

46. Intervention and prevention of emergent literacy difficulties is most advantageous when it is diagnosed: (Skill 4.9; Average rigor)

   A. Before the child finishes first grade

   B. Before the child takes the first required state reading assessment

   C. Early in the middle school years

   D. Early in the preschool years

47. When teachers plan lessons around broad themes that students can identify with, such as "The Environment", this is known as: (Skill 4.10; Average rigor)

   A. Environmental curriculum

   B. Integrated curriculum

   C. Practical curriculum

   D. Child-centered curriculum

48. A child learns the following skills from playing: (Skill 4.11; Easy)

   A. Basic values and fine motor skills

   B. How to compete in today's world

   C. How to boss others around

   D. How to read and do math

49. When a young child says "I'm bored," this may be a signal to do what? (Skill 4.12; Rigorous)

   A. Schedule an art class after school

   B. Provide more unstructured play time

   C. Increase the child's television watching time

   D. Ask the teacher to test the child for gifted characteristics

50. The classroom should be like a little "community" where children get opportunities to: (Skill 4.12; Easy)

   A. Do whatever they want to do

   B. Be in charge of the class

   C. Earn income for work that is completed

   D. Help with chores and maintain responsibility for certain things as practice for citizenship skills

Family and Community Involvement

51. Assigning a student an adult mentor is an effective tool for addressing student achievement because: (Skill 5.1; Average rigor)

   A. The mentor can reinforce learning through tutorial instruction

   B. It provides the student with an appropriate adult role model

   C. The mentor can help the student with the practical application of the lesson

   D. All of the above

52. With state and federal educational funding becoming increasingly subject to legislative budget cuts, what can the school community provide to support the school? (Skill 5.1; Average rigor)

   A. Money to supplement teacher salaries

   B. Free notebooks, backpacks and student supplies for low income students who may have difficulty obtaining the basic supplies for school

   C. Advice on how to save money when running a school

   D. All of the above

53. Researchers have shown that school involvement and connections with community institutions yield greater retention rates of students graduating and seeking higher education experiences. What is a current barrier to community involvement? (Skill 5.1; Rigorous)

    A. The current disconnect and autonomy that has become commonplace in today's society

    B. The amount of gang activity in many communities

    C. The tough economic times we are facing

    D. None of the above

54. You've recently taken a job in a new school and you notice that there is a more diverse group of cultures represented in the student body. Since you've never taught in a similar school you ask your colleagues for advice. You learned that: (Skill 5.2; Rigorous)

    A. You must treat all parents alike

    B. Share personal things about each child so parents will feel more confident that their child will be "in the right hands."

    C. Establish that you are the expert and they are "just the parent."

    D. Criticize the parent for not being involved enough if the child is failing

55. A parent has left an angry message on the teacher's voicemail. The message relates to a concern about a student and is directed at the teacher. The teacher should: (Skill 5.2; Rigorous)

    A. Call back immediately and confront the parent

    B. Cool off, plan what to discuss with the parent, then call back

    C. Question the child to find out what set off the parent

    D. Ignore the message, since feelings of anger usually subside after a while

56. Which of the following should NOT be a purpose of a parent-teacher conference? (Skill 5.2; Average rigor)

    A. To involve the parent in their child's education

    B. To establish a friendship with the child's parents

    C. To resolve a concern about the child's performance

    D. To inform parents of positive behaviors by the child

57. Teachers and parents should be: (Skill 5.2; Easy)

    A. Enemies

    B. Friends

    C. Partners

    D. None of the above

58. Tommy is a student in your class, his parents are deaf. Tommy is struggling with math and you want to contact the parents to discuss the issues. How should you proceed? (Skill 5.2; Rigorous)

    A. Limit contact due to the parents inability to hear

    B. Use a TTY phone to communicate with the parents

    C. Talk to your administrator to find an appropriate interpreter to help you communicate with the parents personally

    D. Both B and C but not A

59. Which of the following is a right of parents? (Skill 5.2; Easy)

    A. To be informed of the teacher's concerns about their child

    B. To require the teacher to use the teaching method that works for the child

    C. To administer discipline to their child in the classroom

    D. To attend all classes to support their child

60. Which of the following is NOT a true statement? (Skill 5.2; Rigorous)

    A. Various cultures have different views of how children should be educated

    B. Parent's views about how children should be educated are always correct

    C. Various cultures share the same views of how children should be educated

    D. Both B and C

Curriculum

61. Which of the following is the most commonly practiced strategy to encourage literacy growth? (Skill 6.1; Average rigor)

    A. Storybook reading

    B. Teaching phonics

    C. Teaching fluency

    D. Letter identification

62. In the early childhood classroom, it is important to limit language that is considered teacher talk. This is because…(Skill 6.2; Rigorous)

    A. Typically it does not require a response

    B. The vocabulary is too difficult for the children

    C. Students need time to talk

    D. It only creates gains in receptive language

63. Which of the following demonstrates the difference between phonemic awareness and phonological awareness? (Skill 6.3; Rigorous)

A. Phonemic awareness is the understanding that words are made up of sounds while phonological awareness is the understanding that letters are the representation of sounds

B. Phonemic awareness is the ability to rhyme and identify beginning sounds while phonological awareness is the understanding that letters are the representation of sounds

C. Phonemic awareness is the understanding ability to distinguish sounds while phonological awareness is the understanding that letters are the representation of sounds

D. Phonemic awareness is the understanding that words are made up of sounds while phonological awareness is the ability to distinguish sounds

64. Michael keeps using phrases such as "she go to the store." Which of the following areas should Michael's teacher work with to improve Michael's skills? (Skill 6.4; Average rigor)

A. Morphology

B. Syntax

C. Phonics

D. Semantics

65. Which of the following is NOT a type of common nonfiction? (Skill 6.5; Easy)

A. Essay

B. Biography

C. Textbook

D. Novel

66. The smallest unit of sound is… (Skill 6.6; Easy)

A. Phoneme

B. Morpheme

C. Syllable

D. Letter

67. Research into students who are learning English as a second language has found that they have difficulty manipulating the sound system of English. This difficulty is in which area of reading development? (Skill 6.6; Rigorous)

A. Comprehension

B. Fluency

C. Phonics

D. Phonemic Awareness

68. Which of the following is not a core part of phonics instruction? (Skill 6.7; Rigorous)

A. Alphabetic principle

B. Vowel Patterns

C. Letter names

D. Consonant Patterns

69. Alex is in a small reading group with his teacher. She is teaching Alex about the word families –art and –at. Which of the following is Alex's teachers working on with his reading group? (Skill 6.8; Average rigor)

A. Syntax

B. Morphology

C. Semantics

D. Phonics

70. Children who are having difficulty understanding non-literal expressions and concepts of time are having difficulties with which of the following areas? (Skill 6.8; Rigorous)

A. Syntax

B. Morphology

C. Semantics

D. Phonics

71. **Vocabulary of children assessed at age six has been shown to be a strong prediction of which future skill at age 16? (Skill 6.11; Rigorous)**

    A. Reading Accuracy

    B. Reading Comprehension

    C. SAT scores

    D. Analogy Completion

72. **Teaching students how to interpret _____ involves evaluating a text's headings, subheadings, bolded words, and side notes. (Skill 6.12; Rigorous)**

    A. graphic organizers

    B. text structure

    C. textual marking

    D. summaries

73. **In the _____ stage of writing, students write in scribbles and can assign meaning to the markings. (Skill 6.13; Rigorous)**

    A. role play writing

    B. experimental writing

    C. early writing

    D. conventional writing

74. **To enhance their students' effective listening skills, teachers can encourage which of the following strategies? (Skill 6.14; Average rigor)**

    A. Associate

    B. Visualize

    C. Repeat

    D. All of the above

75. **Third grade students are recording the length of the hallway. Which unit of measure would be used? (Skill 6.15; Average rigor)**

    A. Inches

    B. Feet

    C. Yards

    D. Miles

76. **A PreK student is distributing napkins for snack. He passes out 15 napkins which is not enough for the 18 students. After checking how many still need napkins, he determines that they need three more. Which math principles are demonstrated in this activity? (Skill 6.15; Rigorous)**

   A. Addition, rote counting

   B. Rote counting, one-to-one correspondence

   C. One-to-one correspondence, pre-subtraction skills

   D. Pre-subtraction skills, rote counting

77. **Which of the following is not one of the four main properties of maps? (Skill 6.16; Average rigor)**

   A. the size of the areas shown on the map

   B. Curved line directions

   C. The shapes of the areas

   D. Consistent scales

78. **An outline of a student's research project presentation should include: (Skill 6.16; Easy)**

   A. Objective

   B. Procedure

   C. Visuals

   D. All of the above

79. **When creating a model, what is the most important aspect of the possibilities listed below? (Skill 6.17; Rigorous)**

   A. population density simulation

   B. CAD model

   C. Seismogram

   D. All of the above

80. **Examples of technology-based tools commonly used by scientists include _____. (Skill 6.17; Easy)**

   A. computer-linked probes

   B. beakers

   C. graphing calculators

   D. both A and C

81. When children learn more complex motor patterns including running, climbing, jumping, they are said to be in the _____ stage of motor development. (Skill 6.18; Average rigor)

    A. first

    B. second

    C. third

    D. fourth

82. Which style of teaching physical skills involves the entire group of students taking part in the same task regardless of individual skill level? (Skill 6.19; Rigorous)

    A. command style

    B. practice style

    C. reciprocal style

    D. inclusion style

83. In which type of learning situation is learned helplessness likely to have the greatest impact on students? (Skill 6.19; Rigorous)

    A. one where students lack the motivation to succeed

    B. one where students have little control over how well they perform

    C. one where competition between students is encouraged

    D. one where rewards are in place to motivate students

84. What should be the first thing taught when introducing dance? (Skill 6.20; Easy)

    A. rhythm

    B. feelings

    C. empathy

    D. texture

85. When discussing color, the intensity of a color refers to the color's _____. (Skill 6.20; Average rigor)

    A. strength

    B. value

    C. lightness or darkness

    D. associated emotions

Diversity

86. **What are the most powerful factors influencing student's academic focus and success? (Skill 7.1; Average rigor)**

   A. teachers' knowledge and training

   B. teachers' preparation and planning

   C. students' attitudes and perceptions

   D. students' interests and goals

87. **The three areas of differentiated instruction are content, process, and _____. (Skill 7.1; Easy)**

   A. application

   B. product

   C. assessment

   D. structure

88. **Which strategy for adapting the curriculum would be most useful for the purpose of reducing the effect of a student's learning disability on completing an assessment task? (Skill 7.1; Rigorous)**

   A. differentiated instruction

   B. alternative assessments

   C. testing modifications

   D. Total Physical Response

89. **Which of the following characteristics are considerations when identifying children with diverse needs? (Skill 7.2; Easy)**

   A. ethnicity

   B. socioeconomic status

   C. physical disability

   D. all of the above

90. **What is it most important for a teacher to consider when planning homework assignments? (Skill 7.2; Average rigor)**

   A. access to technology

   B. ethnicity

   C. language difficulties

   D. gender

91. When dealing with a difficult family, what is it most important for a teacher to display? (Skill 7.3; Average rigor)

    A. strength

    B. excitement

    C. authority

    D. patience

92. In regards to dealing with parents, which term best describes the role that teachers should play in the education of children? (Skill 7.3; Average rigor)

    A. friends

    B. leaders

    C. partners

    D. managers

93. Which type of test is most likely to be a true indication of the content knowledge of ESOL students? (Skill 7.4; Average rigor)

    A. oral test

    B. written test

    C. timed test

    D. practical test

94. What is a student who has extreme trouble spelling most likely to be identified as? (Skill 7.5; Average rigor)

    A. dyslexic

    B. gifted

    C. autistic

    D. hyperactive

95. What should interventions for exceptional students be focused on? (Skill 7.6; Rigorous)

    A. caring

    B. curing

    C. academics

    D. both caring and curing

96. What type of problems are children who have been abandoned or neglected most likely to have? (Skill 7.7; Average rigor)

    A. behavioral problems

    B. medical problems

    C. social problems

    D. physical problems

97. If a school nurse is not available, who should assume responsibility for the administration of medication? (Skill 7.8; Average rigor)

   A. a qualified teacher

   B. the parent or guardian of the student

   C. the prescriber of the medication

   D. the principal of the school

Diagnosis, Assessment and Evaluation

98. What are tests, exams, and a science project all examples of? (Skill 8.1; Easy)

   A. observation

   B. informal assessment

   C. formal assessment

   D. norm-referenced assessment

99. Which of the following is the best method for a teacher to use to get to know the students initially? (Skill 8.1; Average rigor)

   A. running reading record

   B. entry survey

   C. norm-referenced test

   D. oral presentations

100. What type of assessment is a running reading record? (Skill 8.1; Average rigor)

   A. observation

   B. structured assessment

   C. informal assessment

   D. formal assessment

101. Which type of assessment would be used to determine if students are meeting national and state learning standards? (Skill 8.1; Rigorous)

   A. norm-referenced assessments

   B. criterion-referenced assessments

   C. performance-based assessments

   D. observation-based assessments

102. Which of the following tests would be administered by a teacher who wants to rank students into groups for the purpose of placing students into honors, regular, and remedial classes? (Skill 8.1; Rigorous)

A. No Child Left Behind

B. Adequate Yearly Progress

C. Florida Achievement Test

D. Washington Assessment of Student Learning

103. Which of the following best explains why teachers should consider carefully observations recorded by other teachers? (Skill 8.2; Average rigor)

A. Teachers may be manipulative

B. Teachers may be biased

C. Teachers may be dishonest

D. Teachers may be indifferent

104. Why are student records often a good indicator of student progress? (Skill 8.2; Easy)

A. They contain information from several people

B. They show changes over time

C. They contain information gathered over a period of time

D. all of the above

105. Which of the following statements would not be appropriate in an anecdotal record about a student? (Skill 8.2; Rigorous)

A. Jasmine completed only half of the homework assigned

B. Jasmine contributed only slightly to class discussions

C. Jasmine was not interested in learning the material

D. Jasmine did not volunteer to answer any questions

106. **Which type of assessment is most likely to be used to assess student interest and motivation? (Skill 8.3; Average rigor)**

    A. rating scales

    B. questioning

    C. portfolio assessment

    D. anecdotal records

107. **What does a student's portfolio typically contain? (Skill 8.3; Easy)**

    A. results of standardized Tests

    B. competed self-appraisal checklists

    C. samples of work

    D. results of all assessment activities completed to date

108. **What does portfolio assessment typically provide? (Skill 8.4; Average rigor)**

    A. opportunities for teachers to assess student's progress

    B. opportunities for students to reflect on their own progress

    C. opportunities for students to consider their approaches to problem-solving

    D. all of the above

109. **Which of the following is portfolio assessment most likely to encourage? (Skill 8.4; Average rigor)**

    A. self-esteem

    B. self-directed learning

    C. conflict management skills

    D. time management skills

110. **When addressing issues of concern in a parent-teacher conference, what is it best to focus on? (Skill 8.5; Easy)**

    A. likely explanations

    B. personal opinions

    C. statements from other students

    D. observable behaviors

111. **Which statement would it be most appropriate to make when speaking to parents about an issue of concern? (Skill 8.5; Rigorous)**

    A. Sandra is often distracted easily

    B. Sandra irritates other students

    C. Sandra is a frustrating student

    D. While completing the exam, Sandra started conversations with other students

112. **When sending a follow-up note to parents following a conferences, which of the following is it best to include? (Skill 8.5; Average rigor)**

    A. further details on the student's strengths and weaknesses

    B. a summary of the agreed plan of action

    C. a description of how the student has progressed since the conference

    D. praise for the parents on becoming involved in their child's education

113. **When is it appropriate for a teacher to talk to parents about another student's performance? (Skill 8.5; Rigorous)**

    A. when the parents of the student have been invited to participate

    B. when the student is having a negative impact on other students

    C. when the student is performing well and only positive information will be communicated

    D. when permission to discuss the student has been given by the principal

Guidance and Classroom Behavioral Management

114. **When should procedures that use social humiliation be used as behavior management techniques? (Skill 9.1; Average rigor)**

    A. never

    B. only in severe situations

    C. when the student is a danger to himself or others

    D. only when all other methods have been ineffective

115. Which of the following is not a recommended token for use in a token economy? (Skill 9.1; Easy)

    A. stamps

    B. stickers

    C. point cards

    D. poker chips

116. Which type of social skill assessment involves students ranking their classmates on set criteria? (Skill 9.2; Average rigor)

    A. direct observation

    B. paired-comparison

    C. peer nomination

    D. peer rating

117. A student is punished by taking five stars from their tally in the token economy. What type of punishment is this an example of? (Skill 9.2; Average rigor)

    A. time-out

    B. suspension

    C. overcorrection

    D. response cost

118. Consistency is important when managing the behavior of adolescents because it reduces _____. (Skill 9.3; Average rigor)

    A. emotional responses

    B. unpredictable reactions

    C. consequences

    D. power struggles

119. Which type of student is seclusion time-out least likely to be effective with? (Skill 9.3; Average rigor)

    A. outgoing

    B. intelligent

    C. shy

    D. aggressive

120. What is it important for students to have to develop problem-solving skills? (Skill 9.4; Easy)

    A. an understanding of the problem

    B. the information to solve the problem

    C. the responsibility to solve the problem

    D. all of the above

121. **Which conflict resolution principles focuses on finding a solution, rather than placing blame for what has happened? (Skill 9.4; Rigorous)**

    A. think before reacting

    B. find common ground

    C. accept responsibility

    D. focus on the future

122. **Which of the following is NOT a common character development trait? (Skill 9.5; Easy)**

    A. self-discipline

    B. respect

    C. patriotism

    D. decision-making

123. **Which classroom activity would be most useful for teaching character development? (Skill 9.5; Average rigor)**

    A. exam

    B. discussion

    C. project

    D. quiz

124. **Which of the following is a common sign that a student is experiencing stress? (Skill 9.6; Easy)**

    A. behavioral problems

    B. episodes of sadness

    C. aggressive behavior

    D. all of the above

125. **What should a teacher do first when they notice a student appears stressed? (Skill 9.6; Average rigor)**

    A. ask the student what the problem is

    B. praise the student

    C. hold a class discussion

    D. inform the parents

Post-Test Answer Key

1.	B	45.	A	89.	D
2.	B	46.	D	90.	A
3.	D	47.	B	91.	D
4.	D	48.	A	92.	C
5.	D	49.	B	93.	A
6.	A	50.	D	94.	A
7.	B	51.	D	95.	A
8.	B	52.	B	96.	B
9.	A	53.	A	97.	D
10.	B	54.	B	98.	C
11.	A	55.	B	99.	B
12.	A	56.	B	100.	B
13.	B	57.	C	101.	B
14.	D	58.	D	102.	C
15.	A	59.	A	103.	B
16.	B	60.	D	104.	D
17.	D	61.	A	105.	C
18.	A	62.	A	106.	A
19.	C	63.	D	107.	C
20.	C	64.	B	108.	D
21.	C	65.	D	109.	B
22.	A	66.	A	110.	D
23.	C	67.	D	111.	D
24.	B	68.	C	112.	B
25.	A	69.	B	113.	A
26.	C	70.	C	114.	A
27.	B	71.	B	115.	D
28.	C	72.	B	116.	D
29.	D	73.	A	117.	D
30.	B	74.	D	118.	D
31.	D	75.	C	119.	C
32.	B	76.	C	120.	D
33.	B	77.	B	121.	D
34.	D	78.	D	122.	D
35.	D	79.	A	123.	B
36.	A	80.	D	124.	D
37.	A	81.	B	125.	A
38.	D	82.	D		
39.	A	83.	B		
40.	B	84.	A		
41.	B	85.	A		
42.	D	86.	C		
43.	C	87.	B		
44.	A	88.	C		

Post-Test Rigor Table

	Easy %20	Average Rigor %40	Rigorous %40
Question #	1, 10, 13, 22, 34, 48, 50, 57, 59, 65, 66, 78, 80, 84, 87, 89, 98, 104, 107, 110, 115, 120, 122, 124	2, 3, 9, 11, 18, 20, 23, 26, 32, 35, 36, 37, 38, 43, 45, 46, 47, 51, 52, 56, 61, 64, 69, 74, 75, 77, 81, 85, 86, 90, 91, 92, 93, 94, 106, 108, 109, 112, 114, 116, 117, 118, 119, 123, 125	4, 5, 6, 7, 8, 12, 14, 15, 16, 17, 19, 21, 24, 25, 27, 28, 29, 30, 31, 33, 39, 40, 41, 42, 44, 49, 53, 54, 55, 58, 60, 62, 63, 67, 68, 70, 71, 72, 73, 76, 79, 82, 83, 88, 95, 101, 102, 105, 111, 113, 121

Post-Test Rationales with Sample Questions

Child Growth and Development

1. **Which of the following is NOT a sign of child abuse? (Skill 1.1; Easy)**

   A. Awkward social behavior around other children
   B. Participation in class discussions
   C. Awkward social behavior around adults
   D. Bruises

Answer B: Participation in class discussions

While the symptoms of abuse are usually thought to be physical (and therefore visible, like bruises), mental and emotional abuse is also possible. The impact of abuse on a child's development in other domains is often extensive. Abused children can be socially withdrawn, and typically, as one might suspect, their minds will not always be on their schoolwork.

2. **If child abuse is suspected what action should the teacher take? (Skill 1.1; Average rigor)**

   A. Wait to see if the child talks about it again
   B. Talk to your supervisor about your concerns
   C. Call the child's parent
   D. Talk to another teacher about your suspicions

Answer B: Talk to your supervisor about your concerns

The child who is undergoing the abuse is the one whose needs must be served first. A suspected case gone unreported may destroy a child's life, and their subsequent life as a functional adult. It is the duty of any citizen who suspects abuse and neglect to make a report, and it is especially important and required for State licensed and certified persons to make a report. If you contact the parent first and the parent is the abuser, then the child's life may be endangered.

3. **While children develop at different rates, which of the following can cause learning difficulties? (Skill 1.1; Average rigor)**

    A. Lack of sleep
    B. Poor nutrition
    C. Prenatal exposure to nicotine
    D. All of the above

Answer D: All of the above

Lack of sleep, poor nutrition and prenatal exposure to any drugs or alcohol (including nicotine) can cause learning difficulties.

4. **Which of the following is a true statement? (Skill 1.2; Rigorous)**

    A. Physical development does not influence social development.
    B. Social development does not influence physical development.
    C. Cognitive development does not influence social development.
    D. All domains of development (physical, social and cognitive) are integrated and influence other domains

Answer D: All domains of development (physical, social and cognitive) are integrated and influence other domains

The answer of this question explains its reasoning.

5. **Researchers and practitioners agree that the best method to teach young children to read and write is: (Skill 1.4; Rigorous)**

    A. Intense phonics instruction
    B. Exposure to numerous books
    C. Wait until child exhibits "readiness" and then the method won't matter
    D. Unknown

Answer D: Unknown

Best practices and strategies that teach young children how to read and write are controversial among educators and childhood development researchers. The formal approach to childhood literacy emergence includes intensive instruction and decoding skills that include phonics awareness of word pronunciation and reading contextual development. Other programs include direct immersion in literacy development for young readers. Childhood development researchers believe that reading readiness begins with physical and cognitive development. When children have reached a maturation point in development, researchers have shown that children are better able to develop and apply emergent literacy skills.

6. **A teacher notices that a student is quiet, and has several bruises on his head, arms and legs. When asked, the student tells the teacher that his dad hit him, but then begs her not to tell. The teacher should: (Skill 1.5; Rigorous)**

   A. Report suspected abuse to the school counselor
   B. Attempt to get more information from the student and agree not to tell anyone
   C. Consult a colleague and see what they would do
   D. Wait and see if other signs of abuse become evident

Answer A: Report suspected abuse to the school counselor.

The most important concern is for the safety and well being of the student. Teachers should not promise students that they won't tell because they are required by law to err on the side of caution and report suspected abuse. Failure or delay in reporting suspected abuse may be a cause for further abuse to the student. In some cases, a teacher's decision to overlook suspected abuse may result in revoking the teacher's license. Teachers are not required to investigate abuse for themselves or verify their suspicions.

7. **Bobby, a nine year-old, has been caught stealing frequently in the classroom. What might be a factor contributing to this behavior? (Skill 1.5; Rigorous)**

   A. Need for the items stolen
   B. Serious emotional disturbance
   C. Desire to experiment
   D. A normal stage of development

Answer B: Serious emotional disturbance.

Lying, stealing, and fighting are atypical behaviors that most children may exhibit occasionally, but if a child lies, steals, or fights regularly or blatantly, then these behaviors may be indicative of emotional distress. Emotional disturbances in childhood are not uncommon and take a variety of forms. Usually these problems show up in the form of uncharacteristic behaviors. Most of the time, children respond favorably to brief treatment programs of psychotherapy. At other times, disturbances may need more intensive therapy and are harder to resolve. All stressful behaviors need to be addressed, and any type of chronic antisocial behavior needs to be examined as a possible symptom of deep-seated emotional upset.

8. **Marcus is a first grade boy of good developmental attainment. His learning progress is good the first half of the year. He shows no indicators of emotional distress. After the holiday break, he returns much changed. He is quieter, sullen even, tending to play alone. He has moments of tearfulness, sometimes almost without cause. He avoids contact with adults as often as he can. Even play with his friends has become limited. He has episodes of wetting not seen before, and often wants to sleep in school. What approach is appropriate for this sudden change in behavior? (Skill 1.5; Rigorous)**

    A.   Give him some time to adjust. The holiday break was probably too much fun to come back to school from

    B.   Report this change immediately to administration. Do not call the parents until administration decides a course of action

    C.   Document his daily behavior carefully as soon as you notice such a change, report to administration the next month or so in a meeting

    D.   Make a courtesy call to the parents to let them know he is not acting like himself, being sure to tell them he is not making trouble for others

Answer B: Report this change immediately to administration. Do not call the parents until administration decides a course of action.

Anytime a child's disposition, attitude, or habits change significantly, teachers and parents need to seriously consider the existence of emotional difficulties. Emotional disturbances in childhood are not uncommon and take a variety of forms. Usually these problems show up in the form of uncharacteristic behaviors. Most of the time, children respond favorably to brief treatment programs of psychotherapy. At other times, disturbances may need more intensive therapy and are harder to resolve. All stressful behaviors need to be addressed, and any type of chronic antisocial behavior needs to be examined as a possible symptom of deep-seated emotional upset. In a case where the change is sudden and dramatic, administration needs to become involved.

9. **Learning activities for younger students (below age eight) should focus on short time frames because: (Skill 1.6; Average rigor)**

   A. Younger children tend to process information at a slower rate than older children (age eight and older).
   B. Young children have long attention spans.
   C. Young children can understand complex instructional activities.
   D. Young children need to sit quietly and listen to learn.

Answer A: Younger children tend to process information at a slower rate than older children (age eight and older)

Because of this, the learning activities selected for younger students (below age eight) should focus on short time frames in highly simplified form. The nature of the activity and the content in which the activity is presented affects the approach that the students will take in processing the information.

10. **Who developed the theory of multiple intelligences? (Skill 1.7; Easy)**

   A.   Bruner
   B.   Gardner
   C.   Kagan
   D.   Cooper

Answer B: Gardner

Howard Gardner's most famous work is probably *Frames of Mind*, which details seven dimensions of intelligence (Visual/Spatial Intelligence, Musical Intelligence, Verbal Intelligence, Logical/Mathematical Intelligence, Interpersonal Intelligence, Intrapersonal Intelligence, and Bodily/Kinesthetic Intelligence). Gardner's claim that pencil and paper IQ tests do not capture the full range of human intelligences has garnered much praise within the field of education but has also met criticism, largely from psychometricians. Since the publication of *Frames of Mind*, Gardner has additionally identified the 8th dimension of intelligence: Naturalist Intelligence, and is still considering a possible ninth—Existentialist Intelligence.

11. What is one way of effectively managing student conduct? (Skill 1.8; Average rigor)

 A. State expectations about behavior
 B. Let students discipline their peers
 C. Let minor infractions of the rules go unnoticed
 D. Increase disapproving remarks

Answer A: State expectations about behavior.

The effective teacher demonstrates awareness of what the entire class is doing and is in control of the behavior of all students even when the teacher is working with only a small group of the children. In an attempt to prevent student misbehaviors the teacher makes clear, concise statements about what is happening in the classroom directing attention to content and the students' accountability for their work rather than focusing the class on the misbehavior. It is also effective for the teacher to make a positive statement about the appropriate behavior that is observed. If deviant behavior does occur, the effective teacher will specify who the deviant is, what he or she is doing wrong, and why this is unacceptable conduct or what the proper conduct would be. This can be a difficult task to accomplish as the teacher must maintain academic focus and flow while addressing and desisting misbehavior. The teacher must make clear, brief statements about the expectations without raising his/her voice and without disrupting instruction.

12. **What was the result of studies done in low SES primary classrooms taught by effective teachers? (Skill 1.8; Rigorous)**

   A. More teacher-student interactions and less time in which a child is unoccupied
   B. No pauses between academic tasks
   C. More tasks chosen by the student
   D. More time spent in small group work

Answer A: More teacher-student interactions and less time in which a child is unoccupied.

Studies consistently find that variations in family circumstances, not variations in school quality, make the difference in children's educational achievement. This is hardly surprising: More than 90 percent of the waking hours of a child from birth to the age of 18 are spent outside school in an environment that is heavily conditioned, both directly and indirectly, by families. A wealth of literature exists documenting the strong ties between a family's socio-economic status (SES) and children's educational performance. It is an important predictor of cognitive development, school readiness, school achievement and school completion, as well as other measures of child and adolescent well-being. Three specific pathways have been identified through which the influence of SES is clearest: home environment, out-of-school time, and parental involvement. The home environment of high-SES families is more conducive to educational advancement. The strongest effects are through the parent-child interactions, such as the creation of "school-like" homes, stronger language and literacy relations, and less conflict within the home. High-SES families have better health and nutrition and follow a more structured daily routine.

High-SES families use out-of-school time (including summertime) in a more educative way. They enroll their children in preschooling and day-care centers, and they spend more time on reading. These differences are evident in the widening of educational performance over the summer period. Low-SES students have been found to fall further behind during the summer months. High-SES parents are more involved in their children's schooling. They are more likely to have exercised a direct school preference and to be involved in school-based activities. The school cannot supplement all of these advantages for low-SES children, but it can address some crucial ones. The teacher can make certain these children use every available minute to advantage by working to keep them occupied in enriching and meaningful activities. In addition, more one-on-one attention should be given to these children since they tend not to get much attention or input from adults at home.

13. **Research has shown that high teacher's expectations are likely to directly impact _____. (Skill 1.8; Easy)**

    A. co-worker morale
    B. student performance
    C. the district's overall rating
    D. student's enjoyment of school

Answer B: student performance

Considerable research has been done, over several decades, regarding student performance. Time and again, a direct correlation has been demonstrated between the teacher's expectations for a particular student and that student's academic performance. Obviously, if students are performing well, choices A, C, and D may also occur, but these are more indirect effects of the students' increased performance.

Foundations of Learning

14. **According to Piaget, when does the development of symbolic functioning and language take place? (Skill 2.1; Rigorous)**

    A. Concrete operations stage
    B. Formal operations stage
    C. Sensorimotor stage
    D. Preoperational stage

Answer D: Preoperational stage

Although there is no general theory of cognitive development, the most historically influential theory was developed by Jean Piaget, a Swiss psychologist (1896-1980). His theory provided many central concepts in the field of developmental psychology. His theory concerned the growth of intelligence, which for Piaget meant the ability to more accurately represent the world and perform logical operations on representations of concepts grounded in the world. His theory concerns the emergence and acquisition of schemata—schemes of how one perceives the world—in "developmental stages," times when children are acquiring new ways of mentally representing information. His theory is considered "constructivist," meaning that, unlike nativist theories (which describe cognitive development as the unfolding of innate knowledge and abilities) or empiricist theories (which describe cognitive development as the gradual acquisition of knowledge through experience), asserts that we construct our cognitive abilities through self-motivated action in the world. For his development of the theory, Piaget was awarded the Erasmus Prize.

15. According to Piaget, what is a child born with? (Skill 2.1; Rigorous)

    A. The tendency to actively relate pieces of information acquired
    B. The ability to adapt
    C. Primary emotions
    D. Desire

Answer A: The tendency to actively relate pieces of information acquired.

For information about Piaget's theories refer to the rationale for question #14.

16. Which of the following are widely known curriculum models for early childhood programming?   (Skill 2.2; Rigorous)

    A. Montessori, Highscope, DISTAR
    B. Montessori, Creative curriculum, High/Scope
    C. Montessori, DISTAR, Junior Great Books
    D. Montessori, High/Scope, Success for All

Answer B: Montessori, Creative curriculum, High/Scope

The philosophy and curriculum of the **Montessori method** is based on the work and writings of the Italian physician Maria Montessori. Her method appears to be the first curriculum model for children of preschool age that was widely disseminated and replicated. It is based on the idea that children teach themselves through their own experiences. Materials used proceed from the simple to the complex and from the concrete to the abstract and sixty-three percent of class time is spent in independent activity.

Creative Curriculum is used by Head Start, child care, preschool, prekindergarten and kindergarten programs. It focuses on ten interest areas or activities in the program environment: blocks, house corner, table toys, art, sand and water, library corner, music and movement, cooking, computers, and the outdoors.

The **High/Scope preschool approach** is used in both public and private half- and full-day preschools, nursery schools, Head Start programs, child care centers, home-based child care programs, and programs for children with special needs. It is based on the fundamental premise that children are active learners who learn best from activities that they plan, carry out, and reflect on.

17. **Which federal law directed states to construct curriculum models specific to the development of early childhood and elementary programs for academic enhancement? (Skill 2.2; Rigorous)**

    A. IDEA
    B. Head Start
    C. FERPA
    D. NCLB

Answer D: NCLB

The **NCLB (No Child Left Behind) Act** has directed the growth of both federal and state mandates in constructing curriculum models specific to the development of early childhood and elementary programs for academic enhancement. Our nation's special education law is the Individuals with Disabilities Education Act--commonly referred to as IDEA. The Family Educational Rights and Privacy Act (FERPA) (20 U.S.C. § 1232g; 34 CFR Part 99) is a Federal law that protects the privacy of student education records. Head Start is a national program that promotes school readiness by enhancing the social and cognitive development of children through the provision of educational, health, nutritional, social and other services to enrolled children and families.

18. **Head Start Programs were created in the early 60s to provide: (Skill 2.2; Average rigor)**

    A. A comprehensive curriculum model for preparation of low-income students for success in school communities.
    B. A national curriculum that ensures that "no child is left behind"
    C. A parent involvement program in every school
    D. Prekindergarten for every 4 year old

Answer A: A comprehensive curriculum model for preparation of low-income students for success in school communities.

The answer of this question explains its reasoning.

19. Which of the following is a true statement? (Skill 2.2; Rigorous)

    A. The quality of instruction doesn't matter if the correct curriculum is followed.
    B. The NCLB Act mandates which curriculum schools should use to guarantee student academic success.
    C. The quality of instruction is important for student academic success.
    D. The quality of instruction doesn't matter as long as parents are involved in their children's education.

Answer C: The quality of instruction is important for student academic success.

The NCLB (No Child Left Behind) Act requires states to develop curriculum models demonstrating excellent academic outcomes for all children, but a specific curriculum model is not mandated.
Researchers continue to show that most curriculum models produce effective academic outcomes when implemented as designed. However, there are limitations to how effectively the curriculum model is implemented in each classroom. Therefore, **the quality of instruction for students by experienced educators** will ultimately be what improves the academic outcomes for all students. Parent involvement alone will not guarantee the appropriate academic outcome desired for all students.

20. Effective curriculum models for early childhood programs should include which of the following: (Skill 2.2; Average rigor)

    A. Cognitive development
    B. Social development
    C. Both cognitive and social development
    D. None of the above

Answer C: Both cognitive and social development

Early childhood and elementary education programs must incorporate both the cognitive and social development of young learners in designing effective curriculum models. The most important premise of child development is that all domains of development (physical, social, and academic) are integrated. Development in each dimension is influenced by the other dimensions. (see Skill 1.2)

21. **What would be appropriate information to consider if a school was trying to determine if a child has a disability that may qualify the child for services under IDEA? (Skill 2.3; Rigorous)**

 A. The present levels of academic achievement and the child's current vision and hearing screening information
 B. A complete psychological evaluation
 C. Both A and B
 D. None of the above

Answer C: Both A (The present levels of academic achievement and the child's current vision and hearing screening information) **and B** (A complete psychological evaluation)

To begin the process of determining if a child has a disability the teacher will take information about the child's present levels of academic achievement to the appropriate school committee for discussion and consideration. The committee will recommend the next step to be taken. Often subsequent steps may include a complete psychological evaluation along with certain physical examinations such as vision and hearing screening and a complete medical examination by a doctor.

22. **Which school group meets to review information about children with exceptional learning needs? (Skill 2.3; Easy)**

 A. The Child Study team
 B. The Site Based decision-making committee
 C. The special education teachers
 D. None of the above

Answer A: The Child Study team

The first step in securing help is for the teacher to approach the school's administration for direction in attaining special services or resources for qualifying students. Many schools have a committee designated for addressing these needs such as a Child Study Team. These teams are made up of both regular and exceptional education teachers, school psychologists, guidance counselors, and administrators. The particular student's classroom teacher usually has to complete some initial paper work and will need to do some behavioral observations.

(NOTE: Schools may have a different name for the Child Study Team, but the purpose of the team is to review a child's progress and determine the next steps needed to assist the child in achieving the learning outcomes mandated by the NCLB law.)

23. It is important to make a report when abuse or neglect is suspected because: (Skill 2.3; Average rigor)

    A. Failure to do so could result in revocation of certification and license
    B. Failure to do so could result in a monetary fine
    C. Both A and B
    D. None of the above

Answer C: Both A (Failure to do so could result in revocation of certification and license) and B (Failure to do so could result in a monetary fine).

For state licensed personnel (teachers and school staff), failure to make a report when abuse or neglect is suspected is also punishable by the filing of criminal charges.

24. IDEA sets policies that provide for inclusion of students with disabilities. What does inclusion mean? (Skill 2.3; Rigorous)

    A. Inclusion is the name of the curriculum that must followed in special education classes.
    B. Inclusion is the right of students with disabilities to be placed in the regular classroom.
    C. Inclusion refers to the quality of instruction is important for student academic success.
    D. Inclusion means that students with disabilities should always be placed in classes for gifted and talented students.

Answer B: Inclusion is the right of students with disabilities to be placed in the regular classroom.

While Inclusion could mean that students with disabilities can be placed in classes for gifted and talented students (answer D), they would not always be placed here. Clarification on this policy also includes references to "least restrictive environment" and "mainstreaming." Least restrictive environment is the mandate that children be educated to the maximum extent appropriate with their non-disabled peers. If the GT class was the appropriate placement then it would be possible, but not probable. Mainstreaming is a policy where disabled students can be placed in the regular classroom, as long as such placement does not interfere with the student's educational plan. Until this law was passed, many students with disabilities were provided instruction in separate classrooms and separate programs and never had access to the curriculum in the regular classroom.

25. Under the IDEA, Congress provides safeguards for students against schools' actions, including the right to sue in court, and encourages states to develop hearing and mediation systems to resolve disputes. This is known as: (Skill 2.3; Rigorous)

    A. Due process
    B. Mediation
    C. Safe Schools Initiative
    D. Parent involvement

Answer A: Due process

States are required to develop hearing and mediation systems to resolve disputes. No student or their parents/guardians can be denied due process because of disability.

Research, standards and trends

26. Why should teachers view the websites of professional organizations like the IRA?   (Skill 3.1; Average rigor)

    A. To find new video games for teaching children
    B. To chat with other early childhood educators
    C. To find quality strategies to improve early childhood education for students
    D. To post student work for parent viewing

Answer C: To find quality strategies to improve early childhood education for students

It is important to stay current with the latest research and teaching strategies to meet the needs of all children. The best information can be found in a variety of books, websites, or journal articles provided by professional organizations devoted to the education of young children.

27. Which of the following organizations target improvement of education specifically for young children? (Skill 3.2; Rigorous)

A. SPCA, NCTM, and NAACP
B. NAEYC, SECA, and ACEI
C. NAACP, IRA, and NCTM
D. None of the above

Answer B: NAEYC, SECA, and ACEI

The focus of the National Association for the Education of Young Children (**NAEYC**) is on improving and developing programs and services for children from birth through the age of 8 years old. The Southern Early Childhood Association (**SECA**) is dedicated to improving the quality of life for the South's children and families. In order to assume that responsibility, this organization follows the progress of public policy debate and legislation, both nationally and in our 14 Southern states. The Association for Childhood Education International (**ACEI**) promotes and supports in the global community to optimize the education and development of children, from birth through early adolescence, and to influence the professional growth of educators and the efforts of others who are committed to the needs of children in a changing society.

28. You've received a job offer to teach pre-kindergarten, but you've never taught children this young. What professional organization might publish journal articles that would be useful to you? (Skill 3.2; Rigorous)

A. FCRR
B. IRA
C. NAEYC
D. AERA

Answer C: NAEYC

The focus of the National Association for the Education of Young Children (NAEYC) is on improving and developing programs and services for children from birth through the age of 8 years old. The other three organizations all focus on the improvement of reading instruction at the state, national and international level. While information from FCRR (Florida Center for Reading Research), IRA (International Reading Association,) and AERA (American Educational Research Association), would be valuable, only the NAEYC would have comprehensive information about teaching young children.

29. Teacher turnover is a problem in today's schools. What factors are contributing to this problem? (Skill 3.3; Rigorous)

    A. Violence in schools
    B. Increasing federal mandates
    C. Diversity of student needs
    D. All of the above

Answer D: All of the above

Violence in schools, increasing federal mandates, and diversity of student needs all are adding pressure to today's teachers causing many of them to leave their schools or the teaching profession.

30. Which current trend in education is creating conflicting issues which impact educational development and implementation of effective curriculum for young learners? (Skill 3.3; Rigorous)

    A. The NCLB law
    B. Innovations in technology
    C. The Whole Language movement
    D. Parent involvement

Answer B: Innovations in technology

Every student needs the ability to navigate through the 24/7 information flow that today connects the global community. For students to thrive in a world enabled by information technology, we must give them the skills to make sense of and use the information that engulfs them. They need to know how to learn new skills as quickly as technology creates new challenges. This is a challenge for teachers and administrators who did not grow up using technology applications.

31. When considering the comprehensive cost of educating students, what is a hidden cost that may not be often considered? (Skill 3.3; Rigorous)

    A. The increase in students speaking who do not speak English
    B. Federal mandates
    C. The cost of technology
    D. Teacher turnover rate

Answer D: Teacher turnover rate

While we are all familiar with unfunded federal mandates, the cost of technology, and the increase in students with limited English proficiency, there is a hidden cost not often considered. The cost of teacher turnover in school communities has been estimated to be in the range of 5-7 billion dollars which further impacts the legislature's ability to provide enough funding for all educational communities. When considering the comprehensive cost of educating students, more attention may need to be given to retaining current teachers through ongoing professional development training and support.

32. In traditional classrooms, what is the mode of learning for students seeking to understand new content? (Skill 3.3; Average rigor)

    A. Inquiry based learning
    B. Lecture
    C. Hands on learning
    D. None of the above

Answer B: Lecture

In traditional classrooms, the lecture becomes the mode of learning for students seeking to understand the context of mathematical application and real-life application of problem solving skills learned. The teacher "tells" while the students "listen." In an inquiry-based learning format, students are shown how to apply mathematical learning and are actively involved in real-life application of newly constructed knowledge. Involving students in the active processing of mathematical learning increases their ability to construct frameworks of understanding into useful applications of new knowledge. The teacher "asks" and the students "tell" while the teacher "listens" for their understanding.

33. What two things have contributed to a reduction in teaching and instructional time for young learners?   (Skill 3.3; Rigorous)

A. Increased expectations for learning coupled with increased teachers who are alternatively certified.
B. Increased early violence in communities coupled with classroom management issues
C. Increased expectations for learning coupled with a decrease in parent involvement
D. Increasing numbers of alternatively certified teachers coupled with a decrease in parent involvement

Answer B: Increased early violence in communities coupled with classroom management issues

Early violence in elementary school communities coupled with classroom management issues have contributed to a reduction in teaching and instructional time for young learners. Providing young learners with ethical and social strategies to improve cooperative learning and communication will go a long way in reducing the time spent on conflict and increase the time spent on learning acquisition.

Lack of parent involvement and increased learning expectations may influence young children's behavior, but if children are taught strategies for resiliency and self-management, then learning time can be increased. All teachers need continued training in strong classroom management skills to effectively teach today's learners, not just those who are trained through alternative certification programs.

34. Traditional assessment methods include the following: (Skill 3.3; Easy)

A. Multiple choice questions
B. Questions that require self-reflection
C. True/false questions
D. Both A and C

Answer D: Both A (Multiple choice questions) and C (True/false questions)

Traditional assessments are more inflexible with students choosing a prepared response from among a selection of responses, such as matching, multiple-choice or true/false. Alternative assessment is an assessment where students create an answer or a response to a question or task. Alternative assessment requires higher levels of thinking and may involve self-reflection about what was learned. It is also sometimes called "authentic assessment."

35. **Effective teachers use differentiated instruction to connect all students to the subject matter by using the following classroom management strategies: (Skill 3.3; Average rigor)**

   A. Peer teaching
   B. Flexible groups
   C. Whole class, teacher-led activities
   D. All of the above

Answer D: All of the above

Differentiated instruction encompasses classroom management techniques where instructional organization and delivery is maximized for the diverse student group. These techniques should include dynamic, flexible grouping activities, where instruction and learning occurs both as whole-class, teacher-led activities, as well peer learning and teaching (while teacher observes and coaches) within small groups or pairs.

Effective practices

36. **What is one component of the instructional planning model that must be given careful evaluation? (Skill 4.1; Average rigor)**

   A. Students' prior knowledge and skills
   B. The script the teacher will use in instruction
   C. Future lesson plans
   D. Parent participation

Answer A: Students' prior knowledge and skills.

The teacher will, of course, have certain expectations regarding where the students will be physically and intellectually when he/she plans for a new class. However, there will be wide variations in the actual classroom. If he/she doesn't make the extra effort to understand where there are deficiencies and where there are strengths in the individual students, the planning will probably miss the mark, at least for some members of the class. This can be obtained through a review of student records, by observation, and by testing.

37. When is utilization of instructional materials most effective? (Skill 4.1; Average rigor)

    A. When the activities are sequenced
    B. When the materials are prepared ahead of time
    C. When the students choose the pages to work on
    D. When the students create the instructional materials

Answer A: When the activities are sequenced.

Most assignments will require more than one educational principle. It is helpful to explain to students the proper order in which these principles must be applied to complete the assignment successfully. Subsequently, students should also be informed of the nature of the assignment (i.e., cooperative learning, group project, individual assignment, etc). This is often done at the start of the assignment.

38. What is evaluation of the instructional activity based on? (Skill 4.1; Average rigor)

    A. Student grades
    B. Teacher evaluation
    C. Student participation
    D. Specified criteria

Answer D: Specified criteria.

The ways that a teacher uses test data is a meaningful aspect of instruction and may increase the motivation level of the students especially, when this information takes the form of feedback to the students. However, In order for a test to be an accurate measurement of student progress, the teacher must know how to plan and construct tests. Perhaps the most important caveat in creating and using tests for classroom purposes is the old adage to test what you teach. Actually, it is better stated that you should teach what you plan to test. This second phrasing more clearly reflects the need for thorough planning of the entire-instructional program. Before you begin instruction, you should have the assessment planned and defined. One common method of matching the test to the instruction is to develop a table of specifications, a two-way grid in which the objectives of instruction are listed on one axis and the content that has been presented is listed on the other axis. Then the individual cells are assigned percentages that reflect the focus and extent of instruction in each area. The final step is to distribute the number of questions to be used on the test among the cells of the table in proportion to the identified percentages.

39. **What should a teacher do when students have not responded well to an instructional activity? (Skill 4.1; Rigorous)**

    A. Revaluate learner needs.
    B. Skill-building and analysis of outcomes
    C. Interaction with students and manipulation of subject matter
    D. Management techniques and levels of questioning

Answer A: Reevaluate learner needs.

The value of teacher observations cannot be underestimated. It is through the use of observations that the teacher is able to informally assess the needs of the students during instruction. These observations will drive the lesson and determine the direction that the lesson will take based on student activity and behavior. After a lesson is carefully planned, teacher observation is the single most important component of an instructional presentation. If the teacher observes that a particular student is not on-task, she will change the method of instruction accordingly. She may change from a teacher-directed approach to a more interactive approach. Questioning will increase in order to increase the participation of the students. If appropriate, the teacher will introduce manipulative materials to the lesson. In addition, teachers may switch to a cooperative group activity, thereby removing the responsibility of instruction from the teacher and putting it on the students.

40. **The teacher states, "We will work on the first page of vocabulary words. On the second page we will work on the structure and meaning of the words. We will go over these together and then you will write out the answers to the exercises on your own. I will be circulating to give help if needed." What is this an example of? (Skill 4.1; Rigorous)**

    A. Evaluation of instructional activity
    B. Analysis of instructional activity
    C. Identification of expected outcomes
    D. Pacing of instructional activity

Answer B: Analysis of instructional activity.

The successful teacher carefully plans all activities to foresee any difficulties in executing the plan. This also assures that the directions being given to students will be clear, avoiding any misunderstanding.

41. The teacher states that the lesson the students will be engaged in will consist of a review of the material from the previous day, a demonstration of the scientific aspects of an electronic circuit, and small group work on setting up an electronic circuit. What has the teacher demonstrated? (Skill 4.2; Rigorous)

    A. The importance of reviewing
    B. Giving the general framework for the lesson to facilitate learning
    C. Giving students the opportunity to leave if they are not interested in the lesson
    D. Providing momentum for the lesson

Answer B: Giving the general framework for the lesson to facilitate learning.

If children know where they're going, they're more likely to be engaged in getting there. It's important to give them a road map whenever possible for what is coming in their classes.

42. Which of the following words would be included on the classroom word wall? (Skill 4.4; Average rigor)

    A. High frequency words
    B. Words students encounter in their daily reading and writing
    C. Words that students misspell
    D. All of the above

Answer D: All of the above

A word wall is an organized collection of words displayed on a classroom wall to support students in correctly spelling high frequency words (A). The words should include the words students encounter in their daily reading and writing (B), and also words they frequently misspell (C).

43. As teachers select instructional materials it is important that teachers remember: (Skill 4.7; Average rigor)

    A. It is unlawful for students to study from textbooks or materials that are brought from home.

    B. It is unlawful for students to study from textbooks or materials that are more than 10 years old.

    C. It is unlawful to require students to study from textbooks or materials other than those approved by the state Department of Education

    D. None of the above

Answer C: It is unlawful to require students to study from textbooks or materials other than those approved by the state Department of Education

In considering suitable learning materials for the classroom, the teacher must have a thorough understanding of the state-mandated competency-based curriculum. According to state requirements, certain objectives must be met in each subject taught at every designated level of instruction. It is necessary that the teacher become well acquainted with the curriculum for which he/she is assigned. The teacher must also be aware that it is unlawful to require students to study from textbooks or materials other than those approved by the state Department of Education.

44. Prior experiences influence the individual's cognitive style, or method of accepting, processing, and retaining information. According to Marshall Rosenberg, students can be categorized as: (Skill 4.7; Rigorous)

    A. rigid-inhibited, undisciplined, acceptance-anxious, or creative

    B. hyperactive, well-behaved, disinterested or cognitively delayed

    C. Visual, auditory, kinesthetic or multi-modality learners

    D. None of the above

Answer A: rigid-inhibited, undisciplined, acceptance-anxious, or creative

In choosing materials, teachers should also keep in mind that not only do students learn at different rates, but they bring a variety of cognitive styles to the learning process. Prior experiences influence the individual's cognitive style, or method of accepting, processing, and retaining information.
According to Rosenberg, "The creative learner is an independent thinker, one who maximizes his/her abilities, can work by his/herself, enjoys learning, and is self-critical." This last category constitutes the ideal, but teachers should make every effort to use materials that will stimulate and hold the attention of learners of all types.

45. An early warning sign of emergent literacy difficulties is: (Skill 4.9; Average rigor)

A. Failure to identify the letters in their own name
B. Inability to count to 10
C. Trouble singing the ABC song correctly
D. Difficulty tying their shoes

Answer A: Failure to identify the letters in their own name

Parents and teachers should be aware of early warning signs of emergent literacy difficulties. These include:

- failure in identifying/recognizing letters in the child's own name
- lack of interest in singsong rhymes
- difficulty remembering/learning names and shapes of letters
- trouble comprehending simple instructions

46. Intervention and prevention of emergent literacy difficulties is most advantageous when it is diagnosed: (Skill 4.9; Average rigor)

A. Before the child finishes first grade
B. Before the child takes the first required state reading assessment
C. Early in the middle school years
D. Early in the preschool years

Answer D: Early in the preschool years

Intervention and prevention of emergent literacy difficulties is most advantageous when it is diagnosed early in the preschool period. If not caught early these difficulties are often persistent and influence the children's language and literacy learning throughout the following school years.

47. When teachers plan lessons around broad themes that students can identify with, such as "The Environment", this is known as: (Skill 4.10; Average rigor)

    A. Environmental curriculum
    B. Integrated curriculum
    C. Practical curriculum
    D. Child-centered curriculum

Answer B: Integrated curriculum

An integrated curriculum is a program of study that describes a movement toward integrated lessons that enables students to make connections across curricula. This curriculum links lessons among the humanities, art, natural sciences, mathematics, music, and social studies.

48. A child learns the following skills from playing: (Skill 4.11; Easy)

    A. Basic values and fine motor skills
    B. How to compete in today's world
    C. How to boss others around
    D. How to read and do math

Answer A: Basic values and fine motor skills

Play is an activity that helps teach basic values such as sharing and cooperation. Play helps to develop very important attributes in children. For example, children learn and develop personal interests and practice particular skills. The play that children engage in may even develop future professional interests. Finally, playing with objects helps to develop motor skills.

49. When a young child says "I'm bored," this may be a signal to do what? (Skill 4.12; Rigorous)

    A. Schedule an art class after school.
    B. Provide more unstructured play time.
    C. Increase the child's television watching time.
    D. Ask the teacher to test the child for gifted characteristics.

Answer B: Provide more unstructured play time.

Today's hurried lifestyles, changes in family structure and increased attention to academics, have reduced play time. It is important to remove barriers to children's opportunities to play. When children's lives are overscheduled with activities, sports and classes, they do not have time to themselves and time for unstructured play. When children watch too much television, their play often mimics what they see on TV (or the computer screen), and it robs them of valuable time when imagination and creativity take hold. When a child says "I'm bored," this may be a signal to add more unstructured time for play, not less.

50. The classroom should be like a little "community" where children get opportunities to: (Skill 4.12; Easy)

    A. Do whatever they want to do
    B. Be in charge of the class
    C. Earn income for work that is completed
    D. Help with chores and maintain responsibility for certain things as practice for citizenship skills

Answer D: Help with chores and maintain responsibility for certain things as practice for citizenship skills

Public education should be concerned with much more than academic standards. School is a place where children can learn skills of good citizenship, time management, goal setting, and decision-making. But teachers must be deliberate about teaching these skills. Like most good teaching, though, students will have much more success learning these things if they get the opportunity to practice them. That is why a classroom should be like a little "community" where children get opportunities to help with chores and maintain responsibility for certain things.

Family and Community Involvement

51. Assigning a student an adult mentor is an effective tool for addressing student achievement because: (Skill 5.1; Average rigor)

A. The mentor can reinforce learning through tutorial instruction
B. It provides the student with an appropriate adult role model.
C. The mentor can help the student with the practical application of the lesson.
D. All of the above

Answer D: All of the above

Mentoring has become an instrumental tool in addressing student achievement and access to learning. Adult mentors work individually with identified students on specific subject areas to reinforce the learning through tutorial instruction and application of knowledge. Providing students with adult role models to reinforce the learning has become a crucial instructional strategy for teachers seeking to maximize student learning beyond the classroom.

52. With state and federal educational funding becoming increasingly subject to legislative budget cuts, what can the school community provide to support the school? (Skill 5.1; Average rigor)

A. Money to supplement teacher salaries
B. Free notebooks, backpacks and student supplies for low income students who may have difficulty obtaining the basic supplies for school
C. Advice on how to save money when running a school
D. All of the above

Answer B: Free notebooks, backpacks and student supplies for low income students who may have difficulty obtaining the basic supplies for school

With state and federal educational funding becoming increasingly subject to legislative budget cuts, school communities welcome the financial support that community resources can provide in terms of discounted prices on high end supplies (e.g. computers, printers, and technology supplies), along with providing free notebooks, backpacks and student supplies for low income students who may have difficulty obtaining the basic supplies for school.

53. **Researchers have shown that school involvement and connections with community institutions yield greater retention rates of students graduating and seeking higher education experiences. What is a current barrier to community involvement? (Skill 5.1; Rigorous)**

    A. The current disconnect and autonomy that has become commonplace in today's society
    B. The amount of gang activity in many communities
    C. The tough economic times we are facing.
    D. None of the above

Answer A: The current disconnect and autonomy that has become commonplace in today's society

Daily life is more isolated than it used to be. With the ability to communicate easily and cheaply, families have scattered all over the globe, with few living in one community their whole life. Neighbors are isolated from neighbors, no longer sharing community activities. The general disconnectedness in our society is a barrier to school/community involvement.

54. **You've recently taken a job in a new school and you notice that there is a more diverse group of cultures represented in the student body. Since you've never taught in a similar school you ask your colleagues for advice. You learned that: (Skill 5.2; Rigorous)**

    A. You must treat all parents alike.
    B. Share personal things about each child so parents will feel more confident that their child will be "in the right hands."
    C. Establish that you are the expert and they are "just the parent."
    D. Criticize the parent for not being involved enough if the child is failing

Answer B: Share personal things about each child so parents will feel more confident that their child will be "in the right hands."

First, teachers must show respect to all parents and families. They need to set the tone that suggests that their mission is to develop students into the best people they can be. And then they need to realize that various cultures have different views of how children should be educated. Second, teachers will have better success when they talk personally about their children. Even though teachers may have many students, when they share personal things about each child, parents will feel more confident that their child will be "in the right hands." Third, it is very important that teachers act like they are partners in the children's education and development. Parents know their children best, and it is important to get feedback, information, and advice from them. Finally, teachers will need to be patient with difficult families, realizing that certain methods of criticism (including verbal attacks, etc.) are unacceptable.

55. A parent has left an angry message on the teacher's voicemail. The message relates to a concern about a student and is directed at the teacher. The teacher should: (Skill 5.2; Rigorous)

    A. Call back immediately and confront the parent
    B. Cool off, plan what to discuss with the parent, then call back
    C. Question the child to find out what set off the parent
    D. Ignore the message, since feelings of anger usually subside after a while

Answer B: Cool off, plan what to discuss with the parent, then call back.

It is professional for a teacher to keep her head in the face of emotion and respond to an angry parent in a calm and objective manner. The teacher should give herself time to cool off and plan the conversation with the parent with the purpose of understanding the concern and resolving it, rather than putting the parent in their place. Above all the teacher should remember that parent-teacher interactions should aim to benefit the student.

56. Which of the following should NOT be a purpose of a parent teacher conference? (Skill 5.2; Average rigor)

    A. To involve the parent in their child's education
    B. To establish a friendship with the child's parents
    C. To resolve a concern about the child's performance
    D. To inform parents of positive behaviors by the child

Answer B: To establish a friendship with the child's parents.

The purpose of a parent teacher conference is to involve parents in their child's education, address concerns about the child's performance and share positive aspects of the student's learning with the parents. It would be unprofessional to allow the conference to degenerate into a social visit to establish friendships.

57. Teachers and parents should be: (Skill 5.2; Easy)

    A. Enemies
    B. Friends
    C. Partners
    D. None of the above

Answer C: Partners

It is very important that teachers act like they are partners in the children's education and development. Parents know their children best, and it is important to get feedback, information, and advice from them.

58. Tommy is a student in your class, his parents are deaf. Tommy is struggling with math and you want to contact the parents to discuss the issues. How should you proceed? (Skill 5.2; Rigorous)

    A. Limit contact due to the parents inability to hear
    B. Use a TTY phone to communicate with the parents
    C. Talk to your administrator to find an appropriate interpreter to help you communicate with the parents personally
    D. Both B and C but not A

Answer D: Both B and C but not A

You should never avoid communicating with parents for any reason; instead you should find strategies to find an effective way to communicate in various methods, just as you would with any other student in your classroom.

59. Which of the following is a right of parents? (Skill 5.2; Easy)

    A. To be informed of the teacher's concerns about their child
    B. To require the teacher to use the teaching method that works for the child
    C. To administer discipline to their child in the classroom
    D. To attend all classes to support their child

Answer A: To be informed of the teacher's concerns about their child.

It is a parent's right to be involved in their child's education and to be informed of the teacher's reports on his/her progress as well as the teacher's concerns about their child's learning or behavior. Since parents are entrusting the child to the teacher's professional care, they are entitled to know what concerns the teacher about their child during their absence.

60. **Which of the following is NOT a true statement? (Skill 5.2; Rigorous)**

    A. Various cultures have different views of how children should be educated.

    B. Parent's views about how children should be educated are always correct.

    C. Various cultures share the same views of how children should be educated.

    D. Both B and C

Answer D: Both B and C

Teachers must show respect to all parents and families. They need to set the tone that suggests that their mission is to develop students into the best people they can be. And then they need to realize that various cultures have different views of how children should be educated (A, C). It is important that teachers act like they are partners in the children's education and development. Parents know their children best, and it is important to get feedback, information, and advice from them, but parent's views about education are not always correct (B).

Curriculum

61. **Which of the following is the most commonly practiced strategy to encourage literacy growth? (Skill 6.1; Average rigor)**

    A. Storybook reading
    B. Teaching phonics
    C. Teaching fluency
    D. Letter identification

Answer A: Storybook reading

Reading stories and reading aloud to children is the most common literacy growth strategy implemented in classrooms across the country.

62. **In the early childhood classroom, it is important to limit language that is considered teacher talk. This is because...(Skill 6.1; Rigorous)**

A. Typically it does not require a response
B. The vocabulary is too difficult for the children
C. Students need time to talk
D. It only creates gains in receptive language

Answer A: Typically it does not require a response

It is important in the early childhood classroom to limit teacher directive talk, which requires limited responses from the children in favor of more creative, expressive and conversational types of conversation. Doing this provides more increases in both expressive and receptive language skills than more traditional teacher interactions.

63. **Which of the following demonstrates the difference between phonemic awareness and phonological awareness? (Skill 6.3; Rigorous)**

A. Phonemic awareness is the understanding that words are made up of sounds while phonological awareness is the understanding that letters are the representation of sounds
B. Phonemic awareness is the ability to rhyme and identify beginning sounds while phonological awareness is the understanding that letters are the representation of sounds
C. Phonemic awareness is the understanding ability to distinguish sounds while phonological awareness is the understanding that letters are the representation of sounds
D. Phonemic awareness is the understanding that words are made up of sounds while phonological awareness is the ability to distinguish sounds

Answer D: Phonemic awareness is the understanding that words are made up of sounds while phonological awareness is the ability to distinguish sounds.

The concept of phonemic awareness and phonological awareness are often misunderstand and confused. It is important to understand clearly the difference and realize they cannot and should not be used interchangeably.

64. Michael keeps using phrases such as "She go to the store." Which of the following areas should Michael's teacher work with to improve Michael's skills? (Skill 6.4; Average rigor)

   A. Morphology
   B. Syntax
   C. Phonics
   D. Semantics

Answer B: Syntax

Syntax is the understanding of the rules of the English language to put words together in a grammatically appropriate manner. Michael is having difficulty with this concept and could benefit from some more instruction in this area.

65. Which of the following is NOT a type of common nonfiction? (Skill 6.5; Easy)

   A. Essay
   B. Biography
   C. Textbook
   D. Novel

Answer D: Novel

Nonfiction material is based on facts, while fiction is made up and mostly used for entertainment. Therefore, essays, biographies, and textbook material is considered nonfiction. Novels are categorized as fiction.

66. The smallest unit of sound is... (Skill 6.4; Easy)

   A. Phoneme
   B. Morpheme
   C. Syllable
   D. Letter

Answer A: Phoneme

A phoneme is the smallest unit of sound that has a different meaning. A morpheme is a word or word part that cannot be divided into any smaller parts of meaning.

67.   Research into students who are learning English as a second language has found that they have difficulty manipulating the sound system of English. This difficulty is in which area of reading development? (Skill 6.2; Rigorous)

        A. Comprehension
        B. Fluency
        C. Phonics
        D. Phonemic Awareness

Answer D: Phonemic Awareness

As is the case with many students who struggle with reading, it has also been found that students who are learning English as a second language often have difficulties with phonemic awareness skills.

68.   Which of the following is <u>not</u> a core part of phonics instruction? (Skill 6.3; Rigorous)

        A. Alphabetic principle
        B. Vowel Patterns
        C. Letter names
        D. Consonant Patterns

Answer C: Letter names

While it is consistent and regular instruction in the early childhood classrooms, the names in and of themselves are not direct phonics instruction. Tying the sound and symbol is phonics.

69.   Alex is in a small reading group with his teacher. She is teaching Alex about the word families –art and –at. Which of the following is Alex's teachers working on with his reading group? (Skill 6.4; Average rigor)

        A. Syntax
        B. Morphology
        C. Semantics
        D. Phonics

Answer B: Morphology

Morphology is the study of the inside parts of words. By working with word families and providing instruction into these parts of word, Alex's teacher is developing the morphology skills of the students.

70. **Children who are having difficulty understanding non-literal expressions and concepts of time are having difficulties with which of the following areas? (Skill 6.4; Rigorous)**

   A. Syntax
   B. Morphology
   C. Semantics
   D. Phonics

Answer C: Semantics

Listening and understanding the intentions of speakers (teacher/peers) involves semantics. Semantics is the understanding of words and language.

71. **Vocabulary of children assessed at age six has been shown to be a strong prediction of which future skill at age 16? (Skill 6.4; Rigorous)**

   A. Reading Accuracy
   B. Reading Comprehension
   C. SAT scores
   D. Analogy Completion

Answer B: Reading Comprehension

The correlation between vocabulary in young children and future reading comprehension skills provides further evidence of the importance of building vocabulary and oral language skills in the early childhood years.

72. **Teaching students how to interpret _____ involves evaluating a text's headings, subheadings, bolded words, and side notes. (Skill 6.12; Rigorous)**

   A. graphic organizers
   B. text structure
   C. textual marking
   D. summaries

Answer B: text structures

Studying text structures, including the table of contents, glossary, index, headings, etc., is an excellent way for students to increase comprehension of a text. Knowledge of these tools helps students to understand the organization and flow of their reading.

73.   In the _____ stage of writing, students write in scribbles and can assign meaning to the markings. (Skill 6.13; Rigorous)

    A. role play writing
    B. experimental writing
    C. early writing
    D. conventional writing

Answer A: role play writing

In the role playing stage, the child writes in scribbles and assigns a message to the symbols. Even though an adult would not be able to read the writing, the child can read what is written although it may not be the same each time the child reads it. In experimental writing, the student writes in the simplest form of recognizable writing. In the early writing stage, children start to use a small range of familiar text forms and sight words in their writing. Finally, in the conventional writing stage, students have a sense of audience and purpose for writing.

74.   To enhance their students' effective listening skills, teachers can encourage which of the following strategies? (Skill 6.14; Average rigor)

    A. Associate
    B. Visualize
    C. Repeat
    D. All of the above

Answer D: all of the above

Associating, visualizing, repeating and concentrating are four listed strategies to increase listening skills in students.

75.   Third grade students are recording the length of the hallway. Which unit of measure would be used? (Skill 6.15; Average rigor)

    A.   Inches
    B.   Feet
    C.   Yards
    D.   Miles

Answer C: Yards

The hallway could not be measured with miles (too large a measurement). It could be measured with inches or with feet, but these would not be the most efficient units of measure to use. *Yards* would be the best choice of measurement to use.

76. **A PreK student is distributing napkins for snack. He passes out 15 napkins which is not enough for the 18 students. After checking how many still need napkins, he determines that they need three more. Which math principles are demonstrated in this activity? (Skill 6.15; Rigorous)**

    A. Addition, rote counting
    B. Rote counting, one-to-one correspondence
    C. One-to-one correspondence, pre-subtraction skills
    D. Pre-subtraction skills, rote counting

Answer C: One-to-one correspondence, pre-subtraction skills

The student demonstrates one-to-one correspondence when giving each student a napkin. By determining the number of students left without napkins, he is demonstrating pre-subtraction skills. 18 students – 15 napkins = 3 additional napkins needed

77. **Which of the following is not one of the four main properties of maps? (Skill 6.16; Average rigor)**

    A. The size of the areas shown on the map
    B. Curved line directions
    C. The shapes of the areas
    D. Consistent scales

Answer B: Curved line directions.

Answers A, C and D are all properties as maps as cited in Skill 6.16. Straight line, not curved line, directions are the fourth property of maps.

78. **An outline of a student's research project presentation should include: (Skill 6.16; Easy)**

    A. Objective
    B. Procedure
    C. Visuals
    D. All of the above

Answer D: All of the above.

Quality social studies research project presentations should include purpose, objective, preparation, procedure, and visuals and artifacts.

79. **When creating a model, what is the most important aspect of the possibilities listed below? (Skill 6.17; Rigorous)**

    A. population density simulation
    B. CAD model
    C. Seismogram
    D. All of the above

Answer A: population density simulation

Graphical models combine probability theory and graph theory to provide a natural tool for dealing with uncertainty and complexity, two major issues in applied mathematics and science. A computer aided design (CAD) system can be used to generate graphical models of 2- or 3-dimensional objects. Simulations allow biologists to use data and information they collect in the field to make predictions and projections about the future of ecosystems and organisms. Because ecosystems are large and change very slowly, direct observation is not a suitable strategy for ecological studies. A seismogram would be used primarily in Earth science.

80. **Examples of technology-based tools commonly used by scientists include _____. (Skill 6.17; Easy)**

    A. computer-linked probes
    B. beakers
    C. graphing calculators
    D. both A and C

Answer D: Both A and C

Computer linked probes allow the gathering of continuous data without the continual presence of the researcher, as well as the ease of uploading that information. Graphing calculators have many applications. For example, biologists use algebraic functions to analyze growth and development, chemists must determine pH and balance concentration equations, and astronomers measure distance. Graphing calculators can manipulate algebraic data and create graphs for analysis and observation.

81. When children learn more complex motor patterns including running, climbing, jumping, they are said to be in the _____ stage of motor development. (Skill 6.18; Average rigor)

A. first
B. second
C. third
D. fourth

Answer B: second

Stage 1 includes basic reflexes and movements; stage 2 includes more complex patterns of movement such as running; stage 3 occurs later in childhood when the stage 2 movements become more fluid; finally in stage 4, adolescents develop specialized movements and practice, talent, and motivation affect their performance of these movements.

82. Which style of teaching physical skills involves the entire group of students taking part in the same task regardless of individual skill level? (Skill 6.19; Rigorous)

A. command style
B. practice style
C. reciprocal style
D. inclusion style

Answer D: inclusion style

Inclusion style involves all students taking part in the same task regardless of individual skill level. With this style, the students make decisions on how to practice and develop their skills, with the teacher exerting very little control over the activities.

83. **In which type of learning situation is learned helplessness likely to have the greatest impact on students? (Skill 6.19; Rigorous)**

    A. one where students lack the motivation to succeed
    B. one where students have little control over how well they perform
    C. one where competition between students is encouraged
    D. one where rewards are in place to motivate students

Answer B: one where students have little control over how well they perform

Learning helplessness occurs when a student's continued failure inhibits them from trying again. Learned helplessness most often occurs in situations where people experience events and feel they have little control over what happens to them.

84. **What should be the first thing taught when introducing dance? (Skill 6.20; Easy)**

    A. rhythm
    B. feelings
    C. empathy
    D. texture

Answer A: rhythm

Rhythm is the basis of dance. Teaching dance should begin by focusing on rhythm. This can be achieved through activities such as children clapping their hands or tapping their feet to express rhythm.

85. **When discussing color, the intensity of a color refers to the color's _____. (Skill 6.20; Average rigor)**

    A. strength
    B. value
    C. lightness or darkness
    D. associated emotions

Answer A: strength

Color is an important consideration when viewing art. Color can be considered in more depth by focusing on intensity, which is the strength of the color, and value, which is the lightness or darkness of the color.

Diversity

86. **What are the most powerful factors influencing student's academic focus and success? (Skill 7.1; Average rigor)**

    A. teachers' knowledge and training
    B. teachers' preparation and planning
    C. students' attitudes and perceptions
    D. students' interests and goals

Answer C: students' attitudes and perceptions

Students' attitudes and perceptions about learning are the most powerful factors influencing academic focus and success. The key is to ensure that objectives are focused on students' interests and are relevant to their lives. It is also important that students believe that they have the ability to perform tasks.

87. **The three areas of differentiated instruction are content, process, and _____. (Skill 7.1; Easy)**

    A. application
    B. product
    C. assessment
    D. structure

Answer B: product

Differentiated instruction includes the areas of content, process, and product. Content focuses on what is going to be taught. Process focuses on how the content is going to be taught. Product focuses on the expectations and requirements placed on students, where the product refers to the product expected of students.

88.	Which strategy for adapting the curriculum would be most useful for the purpose of reducing the effect of a student's learning disability on completing an assessment task? (Skill 7.1; Rigorous)

A. differentiated instruction
B. alternative assessments
C. testing modifications
D. Total Physical Response

Answer C: testing modifications

Testing modifications are changes made to assessments that allow students with disabilities equal opportunity to demonstrate their knowledge and ability on the task.

89.	Which of the following characteristics are considerations when identifying children with diverse needs? (Skill 7.2; Easy)

A. ethnicity
B. socioeconomic status
C. physical disability
D. all of the above

Answer D: all of the above

Diversity can be based on distinctive features such as race, ethnicity, and gender. Diversity can also be based on other differences such as physical or intellectual disability, and differences in socioeconomic status.

90.	What is it most important for a teacher to consider when planning homework assignments? (Skill 7.2; Average rigor)

A. access to technology
B. ethnicity
C. language difficulties
D. gender

Answer A: access to technology

When planning homework assignments, teachers must take into account students' access to technology. If socioeconomic status or other factors make it likely that some students do not have access to technology such as a computer or the Internet, assessments would not give these students equal opportunity to succeed in the task.

91. **When dealing with a difficult family, what is it most important for a teacher to display? (Skill 7.3; Average rigor)**

    A. strength
    B. excitement
    C. authority
    D. patience

Answer D: patience

When dealing with difficult families, teachers need to be patient. Teachers must also be aware that methods of criticism such as verbal attacks are not acceptable.

92. **In regards to dealing with parents, which term best describes the role that teachers should play in the education of children? (Skill 7.3; Average rigor)**

    A. friends
    B. leaders
    C. partners
    D. managers

Answer C: partners

It is important for teachers to act as partners in the education of children. This means accepting that parents know their children best and utilizing the feedback, information, and advice received from parents.

93. **Which type of test is most likely to be a true indication of the content knowledge of ESOL students? (Skill 7.4; Average rigor)**

    A. oral test
    B. written test
    C. timed test
    D. practical test

Answer A: oral test

In many cases, written tests may not provide teachers with any indication of an ESOL student's content knowledge. An oral test is much more likely to provide a true indication of content knowledge.

94.   **What is a student who has extreme trouble spelling most likely to be identified as? (Skill 7.5; Average rigor)**

   A. dyslexic
   B. gifted
   C. autistic
   D. hyperactive

Answer A: dyslexic

Dyslexia is a common learning disability that requires intervention strategies. Students with dyslexia often have difficulty reading and have extreme trouble spelling.

95.   **What should interventions for exceptional students be focused on? (Skill 7.6; Rigorous)**

   A. caring
   B. curing
   C. academics
   D. both caring and curing

Answer A: caring

Interventions for children with learning disabilities should be focused on caring for the children, rather than curing the children. This means accepting that children have unique needs and implementing interventions that aim to allow the child to have similar opportunities to the children that do not have learning disabilities.

96.   **What type of problems are children who have been abandoned or neglected most likely to have? (Skill 7.7; Average rigor)**

   A. behavioral problems
   B. medical problems
   C. social problems
   D. physical problems

Answer B: medical problems

Children who have been neglected or abandoned often have medical problems. They may also experience problems due to poor nutrition. These problems can be addressed by schools by providing healthy school lunches and medical attention.

97. **If a school nurse is not available, who should assume responsibility for the administration of medication? (Skill 7.8; Average rigor)**

    A. a qualified teacher
    B. the parent or guardian of the student
    C. the prescriber of the medication
    D. the principal of the school

Answer D: the principal of the school

If a school district has school nurses available on a daily basis, the school nurse should take responsibility for the administration of medication. If a school nurse is not available, the principal should take responsibility for the administration of medication.

Diagnosis, Assessment and Evaluation

98. **What are tests, exams, and a science project all examples of? (Skill 8.1; Easy)**

    A. observation
    B. informal assessment
    C. formal assessment
    D. norm-referenced assessment

Answer C: formal assessment

Formal assessments are highly structured methods of assessing student performance. Tests, exams, and science projects are all examples of formal assessments.

99. **Which of the following is the best method for a teacher to use to get to know the students initially? (Skill 8.1; Average rigor)**

    A. running reading record
    B. entry survey
    C. norm-referenced test
    D. oral presentations

Answer B: entry survey

An entry survey is a survey a teacher takes to get to know the students straight away. It typically focuses on finding out the students' backgrounds and experiences. Questions asked on an entry survey might ask about the student's interests, fears, and language spoken at home.

100. **What type of assessment is a running reading record? (Skill 8.1; Average rigor)**

    A. observation
    B. structured assessment
    C. informal assessment
    D. formal assessment

Answer B: structured assessment

A running reading record involves the teacher using a coding system to record what students do as they read aloud. The running reading records provides information on the students' strengths and weaknesses.

101. **Which type of assessment would be used to determine if students are meeting national and state learning standards? (Skill 8.1; Rigorous)**

    A. norm-referenced assessments
    B. criterion-referenced assessments
    C. performance-based assessments
    D. observation-based assessments

Answer B: criterion-referenced assessments

Criterion-referenced assessments are used to assess student learning goals as each student compares to a norm group of student learners. These are often used to determine if students and schools are meeting state and national standards.

102. **Which of the following tests would be administered by a teacher who wants to rank students into groups for the purpose of placing students into honors, regular, and remedial classes? (Skill 8.1; Rigorous)**

    A. No Child Left Behind
    B. Adequate Yearly Progress
    C. Florida Achievement Test
    D. Washington Assessment of Student Learning

Answer C: Florida Achievement Test

Teachers who want to rank students into honors, regular, and remedial classes would use a norm-referenced assessment. The Florida Achievement Test is an example of a norm-referenced assessment.

103. **Which of the following best explains why teachers should consider carefully observations recorded by other teachers? (Skill 8.2; Average rigor)**

    A. Teachers may be manipulative.
    B. Teachers may be biased.
    C. Teachers may be dishonest.
    D. Teachers may be indifferent.

Answer B: Teachers may be biased.

When reading another teacher's observations of a student, teachers must be aware that the teacher may be biased. This could result in either a more positive or a more negative assessment.

104. **Why are student records often a good indicator of student progress? (Skill 8.2; Easy)**

    A. They contain information from several people.
    B. They show changes over time.
    C. They contain information gathered over a period of time.
    D. all of the above

Answer D: all of the above

Student records are often a good indicator of student progress because they contain information from more than one person, because they contain information gather over a period of time, and because they show progress over time as well as results at the current time.

105. **Which of the following statements would not be appropriate in an anecdotal record about a student? (Skill 8.2; Rigorous)**

    A. Jasmine completed only half of the homework assigned.
    B. Jasmine contributed only slightly to class discussions.
    C. Jasmine was not interested in learning the material.
    D. Jasmine did not volunteer to answer any questions.

Answer: C: Jasmine was not interested in learning the material.

Anecdotal records of a student should include observable behaviors. Anecdotal records should not include assumptions or speculations about the student's motivation or interest. "Jasmine was not interested in learning the material" is not appropriate to include because it is speculation.

106. Which type of assessment is most likely to be used to assess student interest and motivation? (Skill 8.3; Average rigor)

A. rating scales
B. questioning
C. portfolio assessment
D. anecdotal records

Answer A: rating scales

Rating scales are often used to assess behavior and effective areas. They can be used to assess interest and motivation, whereas most other assessment types are not appropriate for this purpose.

107. What does a student's portfolio typically contain? (Skill 8.3; Easy)

A. results of standardized tests
B. competed self-appraisal checklists
C. samples of work
D. results of all assessment activities completed to date

Answer C: samples of work

A student's portfolio typically contains samples of work created throughout the year. These can be selected by the teacher, the student, or can be samples linked to learning objectives.

108. What does portfolio assessment typically provide? (Skill 8.4; Average rigor)

A. opportunities for teachers to assess student's progress
B. opportunities for students to reflect on their own progress
C. opportunities for students to consider their approaches to problem-solving
D. all of the above

Answer D: all of the above

Portfolio assessment has a number of useful purposes. It provides opportunities for teachers to assess student's progress, opportunities for students to reflect on their own progress, and opportunities for students to consider their approaches to problem-solving.

109. **Which of the following is portfolio assessment most likely to encourage? (Skill 8.4; Average rigor)**

    A. self-esteem
    B. self-directed learning
    C. conflict management skills
    D. time management skills

Answer B: self-directed learning

One of the main advantages of portfolio assessment for students is that it provides them with the opportunity to assess and reflect on their own work. This also encourages self-directed learning.

110. **When addressing issues of concern in a parent-teacher conference, what is it best to focus on? (Skill 8.5; Easy)**

    A. likely explanations
    B. personal opinions
    C. statements from other students
    D. observable behaviors

Answer D: observable behaviors

When addressing issues of concern in a parent-teacher conference, teachers should focus on observable behaviors and on providing concrete examples.

111. **Which statement would it be most appropriate to make when speaking to parents about an issue of concern? (Skill 8.5; Rigorous)**

    A. Sandra is often distracted easily.
    B. Sandra irritates other students.
    C. Sandra is a frustrating student.
    D. While completing the exam, Sandra started conversations with other students.

Answer D: While completing the exam, Sandra started conversations with other students.

When addressing issues of concern in a parent-teacher conference, teachers should focus on providing concrete examples, while avoiding making judgments. "While completing the exam, Sandra started conversations with other students" is the most appropriate statement to make because it provides concrete information and avoids judging Sandra.

112. **When sending a follow-up note to parents following a conferences, which of the following is it best to include? (Skill 8.5; Average rigor)**

   A. further details on the student's strengths and weaknesses
   B. a summary of the agreed plan of action
   C. a description of how the student has progressed since the conference
   D. praise for the parents on becoming involved in their child's education

Answer B: a summary of the agreed plan of action

A follow-up note to parents should follow around two days after the conference. It should briefly summarize the plan, while ensuring that the note is professional and not chatty.

113. **When is it appropriate for a teacher to talk to parents about another student's performance? (Skill 8.5; Rigorous)**

   A. when the parents of the student have been invited to participate
   B. when the student is having a negative impact on other students
   C. when the student is performing well and only positive information will be communicated
   D. when permission to discuss the student has been given by the principal

Answer A: when the parents of the student have been invited to participate

Information about a student's school performance is confidential and comes under the Privacy Act. Information can be given only to the student's parents or guardians. If another student must be spoken about, that student's parents or guardians must be invited to participate.

Guidance and Classroom Behavioral Management

114. **When should procedures that use social humiliation be used as behavior management techniques? (Skill 9.1; Average rigor)**

   A. never
   B. only in severe situations
   C. when the student is a danger to himself or others
   D. only when all other methods have been ineffective

Answer A: never

Procedures that use social humiliation should never be used as behavior management techniques. Procedures that involve withholding of basic needs, pain, or extreme discomfort should also never be used.

115. **Which of the following is not a recommended token for use in a token economy? (Skill 9.1; Easy)**

A. stamps
B. stickers
C. point cards
D. poker chips

Answer D: poker chips

A token economy should use tokens such as stamps, stickers, stars, or point cards. Poker chips should not be used as they increase the likelihood of theft and loss.

116. **Which type of social skill assessment involves students ranking their classmates on set criteria? (Skill 9.2; Average rigor)**

A. direct observation
B. paired-comparison
C. peer nomination
D. peer rating

Answer D: peer rating

There are many ways to assess student's social skills. Peer rating is a method where students rate their peers on set criteria.

117. **A student is punished by taking five stars from their tally in the token economy. What type of punishment is this an example of? (Skill 9.2; Average rigor)**

A. time-out
B. suspension
C. overcorrection
D. response cost

Answer D: response cost

Response cost is a type of punishment where there is a cost to the student by having something taken away. When a token economy is in place, this involves the student having points taken away.

118. Consistency is important when managing the behavior of adolescents because it reduces _____. (Skill 9.3; Average rigor)

    A. emotional responses
    B. unpredictable reactions
    C. consequences
    D. power struggles

Answer D: power struggles

Consistency is especially important when managing the behavior of adolescents. It reduces the likelihood of power struggles. It also teaches them that predictable consequences will follow their actions.

119. Which type of student is seclusion time-out least likely to be effective with? (Skill 9.3; Average rigor)

    A. outgoing
    B. intelligent
    C. shy
    D. aggressive

Answer C: shy

Seclusion time-out is often not effective with students who consider the seclusion a reward rather than a punishment. Shy, solitary, or withdrawn children may consider seclusion a reward and prefer it to being in the classroom.

120. What is it important for students to have to develop problem-solving skills? (Skill 9.4; Easy)

    A. an understanding of the problem
    B. the information to solve the problem
    C. the responsibility to solve the problem
    D. all of the above

Answer D: all of the above

For students to develop problem-solving skills, there are three key elements necessary. The first is an understanding of the problem to be solved. The second is the information needed to solve the problem. The third is the opportunity to assume responsibility for solving the problem.

121. **Which conflict resolution principles focuses on finding a solution, rather than placing blame for what has happened? (Skill 9.4; Rigorous)**

    .   A. think before reacting
        B. find common ground
        C. accept responsibility
        D. focus on the future

Answer D: focus on the future

One conflict resolution principle is "focus on the future." This means focusing on finding a solution to avoid conflict on the future, rather than assigning blame for past conflicts.

122. **Which of the following is NOT a common character development trait? (Skill 9.5; Easy)**

        A. self-discipline
        B. respect
        C. patriotism
        D. decision-making

Answer D: decision-making

There are various common character development traits that are developed in children. These include responsibility, caring, self-discipline, citizenship, honesty, respect, and patriotism.

123. **Which classroom activity would be most useful for teaching character development? (Skill 9.5; Average rigor)**

        A. exam
        B. discussion
        C. project
        D. quiz

Answer B: discussion

Teaching character development has been found to be most effective when students take part in discussions focused on the moral implications of their everyday life.

124. **Which of the following is a common sign that a student is experiencing stress? (Skill 9.6; Easy)**

    A. behavioral problems
    B. episodes of sadness
    C. aggressive behavior
    D. all of the above

Answer D: all of the above

There are various stress factors that are indications that a student may be experiencing stress. These include: behavioral problems; a drop in grades; episodes of sadness; nightmares; aggressive behavior; and an increase in physical complaints.

125. **What should a teacher do first when they notice a student appears stressed? (Skill 9.6; Average rigor)**

    A. ask the student what the problem is
    B. praise the student
    C. hold a class discussion
    D. inform the parents

Answer A: ask the student what the problem is

The first thing a teacher should do when they notice a student appears stressed is ask the student what the problem is. This simple step can reduce the student's stress.

XAMonline, INC. 21 Orient Ave. Melrose, MA 02176

Toll Free number 800-509-4128

TO ORDER Fax 781-662-9268 OR www.XAMonline.com

FLORIDA TEACHER CERTIFICATION EXAMINATIONS   - FTCE - 2008

PO#   Store/School:

Bill to Address 1   Ship to address

City, State Zip

Credit card number_____-_____-_____-_____   expiration_____

EMAIL _____

PHONE   FAX

13# ISBN 2007	TITLE	Qty	Retail	Total
978-1-58197-900-8	Art Sample Test K-12			
978-1-58197-801-8	Biology 6-12			
978-1-58197-099-9	Chemistry 6-12			
978-1-58197-572-7	Earth/Space Science 6-12			
978-1-58197-921-3	Educational Media Specialist PK-12			
978-1-58197-347-1	Elementary Education K-6			
978-1-58197-292-4	English 6-12			
978-1-58197-274-0	Exceptional Student Ed. K-12			
978-1-58197-294-8	FELE Florida Ed. Leadership			
978-1-58197-919-0	French Sample Test 6-12			
978-1-58197-615-1	General Knowledge			
978-1-58197-916-9	Guidance and Counseling PK-12			
978-1-58197-089-0	Humanities K-12			
978-1-58197-640-3	Mathematics 6-12			
978-1-58197-911-4	Middle Grades English 5-9			
978-1-58197-912-1	Middle Grades General Science 5-9			
978-1-58197-286-3	Middle Grades Integrated Curriculum			
978-1-58197-284-9	Middle Grades Math 5-9			
978-1-58197-913-8	Middle Grades Social Science 5-9			
978-1-58197-616-8	Physical Education K-12			
978-1-58197-818-6	Physics 6-12			
978-1-58197-657-1	Prekindergarten/Primary PK-3			
978-1-58197-903-9	Professional Educator			
978-1-58197-659-5	Reading K-12			
978-1-58197-270-2	Social Science 6-12			
978-1-58197-918-3	Spanish K-12			
			SUBTOTAL	
ndling $8.25 one title, $11.00 two titles, $15.00 three or more titles				
			TOTAL	

CPSIA information can be obtained at www.ICGtesting.com
Printed in the USA
LVOW031953080612

285309LV00004B/29/P